Facing
Messy Stuff
in the
Church

Facing Messy Stuff in the Church

Case Studies for Pastors and Congregations

Kenneth L. Swetland

Kregel
Academic & Professional

Facing Messy Stuff in the Church: Case Studies for Pastors and Congregations

© 2005 by Kenneth L. Swetland

Published by Kregel Publications, a division of Kregel, Inc., 2540 Oak Industrial Dr. NE, Grand Rapids, MI 49505.

The presentation of differing theological viewpoints, ministry practices, or controversial issues in this book is a part of the case study format and does not represent an endorsement of any such issue by the author or the publisher.

Library of Congress Cataloging-in-Publication Data
Swetland, Kenneth L.
    Facing messy stuff in the church: case studies for pastors and congregations / by Kenneth L. Swetland.
        p.   cm.
Includes bibliographical references.
    1. Pastoral theology. 2. Pastoral counseling. I. Title.
BV4011.3.S95   2004
253—dc22   2004019276

ISBN 978-0-8254-3696-3

Printed in the United States of America

8 9 10 / 18

To
Brock and Reid,
sons who make their
father proud

CONTENTS

PREFACE

Pastors are on the front line, facing an array of human problems. One pastor I know refers to his daily ministry as "facing messy stuff." This book contains case studies that reflect a variety of the "messy stuff" that churches and pastors face in the normal course of being the church in the world.

The reader may think the problems addressed in the book are far-fetched. The likelihood that a church will encounter murder, for example, is remote, but the scenarios described in these chapters are not that uncommon. Church leaders see such things happening in their congregations on an all-too-regular basis. Churches are, after all, made up of sinners whose lives are broken—sometimes because of their own choices, sometimes because of experiencing wrongs outside of their control. Pastors and church leaders often encounter the effects of such sins, and resolutions are not always easy to come by.

Some churches are blessed; the lives of the people in their congregations involve very little messy stuff. But other churches face such problems seemingly nonstop. Healthy, spiritual churches take sin seriously—not ignoring the problems people face—but they also come alongside hurting people to minister the redeeming and healing grace of God. Yet even then the effects of sins and wrongs often persist and won't be resolved completely until the heavenly kingdom arrives—a day we long for. Meanwhile, we need God's help and grace to deal with the messy stuff we encounter daily.

This case book is a result of my interviewing fifteen pastors and church leaders to talk about the issues they face in the normal course of their Christian lives. The churches represent a variety of denominations in various parts of the country, and the pastors are graduates of several different seminaries.

The messy stuff these pastors encounter is enough to sober the most seasoned of pastors. Think, then, of the new pastor who hasn't lived long enough or had the privilege of dealing with many of life's messes on behalf of the God of mercy and grace. The messy stuff can seem daunting or even overwhelming. It makes one realize all the more that God, and God alone, must call and equip men and women to serve Him in this world.

By definition, case studies do not end in resolution. It's up to the readers to reflect on the issues involved and determine what they would do if ministering under similar circumstances. Case studies ask for a response, without the answers or "end of the story" being clear.

Sometimes God may lead one person to deal with a messy situation one way and another person to deal with it in a different way. Remember, it is God who works through His people to extend mercy and grace to those in need (cf. how in 1 Kings 18, Elijah and Obadiah were used by God in very different ways in the same situation). In some cases, therefore, a course of action might be clear; in other cases, the reader might consider several courses of action. Nor do Christians always agree on the best way to resolve a case.

Case studies thus are an educational tool. As stated, they describe and raise issues, leaving the reader to determine how to resolve the situation. Thus, case studies are best used in a group-discussion format in which individuals can voice their concerns and offer suggestions for how to resolve a given situation. Often, a wisdom emerges in groups that goes beyond anything an individual could devise, reflecting the guiding work of the Holy Spirit as He directs His people.

This book may be used in a classroom by students in Bible colleges and seminaries, for instance, as they prepare for service in the church. Ministerial fellowships may also use the book for regular discussion in a kind of continuing-education seminar. Lay leaders will also find the book useful in determining how to approach certain situations they face in the church. Individuals in the groups who've experienced problems themselves will be more sensitive to the issues raised in the cases than are people who've led relatively problem-free lives. The apostle Paul recognized as much in writing to the Christians at Corinth:

> Praise be to the God and Father of our Lord Jesus Christ, the Father of compassion and the God of all comfort, who comforts us in all our troubles, so that we can comfort those in any trouble with the comfort we ourselves have received from God. For just as the sufferings of Christ flow over into our lives, so also through Christ our comfort overflows. (2 Corinthians 1:3–5)

The church, then, fulfills what Paul envisioned—a fellowship of people who come together to worship God, serve Him in the world, and be agents of healing in the lives of the broken people who make up the church. Some churches do a better job of this task than others. Case studies such as those found in this book make concrete the problems people face, and a discussion of the issues involved might help pastors and church leaders become better healers and comforters to those in their own churches.

The main purpose of these case studies is not to assess how well the church or pastor involved dealt with a specific matter, but rather to help leaders evaluate how they might handle a given situation and thus be better prepared if a similar one arises in their ministry.

In several of the case studies in this book, pastors and leaders are not prepared to face the messy problem that arises, and in some cases the churches seem to avoid dealing with an obvious problem. Reflecting on the cases in dialogue with other Christian leaders can thus lead to formulating a plan of action for dealing with similar situations.

Although the core information in the case studies is true, certain identifying information has been disguised to protect the privacy of those involved. Individual names, places, names of churches, and areas of the country have all been changed. In a few cases, the denomination has also been changed, but only to a compatible group so that the issues make sense in a given context. Such disguising of information is a common, recommended practice in case writing.

The central individuals in the stories have given permission for the case studies to be told in this format. Their desire was for other people to learn from their experiences. For many of the pastors, telling the story contributed to their ongoing reflection on how they handled the situation. In some cases the situation is now resolved, most of the time with a happy ending; but not always. In some of the cases, the situation is still evolving.

The discussion questions at the end of each chapter are to aid the reader in thinking through the issues and to guide group discussion. Additional questions are often included in the body of the case itself and should be incorporated into the discussion format.

An appendix on how to use case studies is included at the end of the book. Experienced case teachers will want to develop their own teaching plan, but the suggestions in the appendix may help in getting started. A bibliography on each particular issue is also attached at the end of the book. These resources will help the reader in continuing to work on the issues described.

Pastors and church leaders know about sin—their own and that of others. Our desire is to be effective and productive as ministers of the gospel, especially in the knowledge of our Lord Jesus Christ and the sufficiency of His grace to minister to hurting people. Often, there are no easy answers, but that doesn't mean we shouldn't respond to the crises in people's lives in a caring and helpful way. Knowing ourselves as sinners, being forever redeemed by Christ, and addressing the issues as they come up can contribute to becoming a healthy, spiritually vibrant church that is faithful to the only true God who has called His people to be salt and light in the world. To this end, the case studies in this book are offered.

ACKNOWLEDGMENTS

I'm grateful to the students in my pastoral counseling class at Gordon-Conwell Theological Seminary who used selected cases from this book in class, thereby giving me helpful information on how the cases could be improved. A special word of thanks is due to Jason McConnell, my student assistant, for the invaluable work he did in helping to compile the bibliography and looking at the discussion questions from a student's perspective.

Appreciation is also expressed to Christopher Wilkins, Coordinator of the Faculty Grant Program for the Association of Theological Schools, and to the Grants Committee, for the financial aid I received to help cover expenses in connection with the trips I took to churches to conduct the interviews for the case studies. This help was invaluable.

Finally, I express gratitude to my wife, Anne, who was able to accompany me on several of the trips for interviews (although she did not participate in the interviews). I appreciated her presence and support, especially during the time we were in Cambridge, England, on sabbatical, when I wrote the case studies.

1

DEPRESSION
The Many Faces of Melancholy

Ron, pastor of Faith Baptist Church, listened carefully to Hugh's voice. He was speaking to Elaine, the church secretary, in the outer office. But Ron didn't need to strain to hear what Hugh was saying.

"I'm God," Hugh's voice boomed.

Ron then heard Elaine giggle and say lightheartedly, "Well, I'm pleased to meet you, 'God'; I talked to you this morning in prayer."

But then Hugh responded rather angrily, "You did not! I didn't hear you!"

Elaine quickly said, "I'm sorry," with concern in her voice.

At that point, Ron scribbled something on a piece of paper and walked out of his study. He handed the piece of paper to Elaine as he greeted Hugh. "Good morning, Hugh," Ron said and extended his hand. "Come into my office and let's talk." Hugh followed him into the study and Ron closed the door.

Elaine read Ron's scrawled note: "Call the police" was all it said. She hastily dialed 911 and, hoping the shakiness in her voice wasn't too obvious, told the operator what had happened. Although Elaine realized she was scared, she still had the presence of mind to request that the police not come with their siren wailing. The day school was in full swing at the church that morning with about twenty children and staff present, and other people were also in the building. She didn't want too much attention focused on the church offices, but she did ask the police to come quickly. The operator responded that help was on the way and that no siren would be used.

In less than five minutes, two police officers walked into Elaine's office. Not knowing what else to do, Elaine buzzed Ron on the intercom and said that the people he'd requested were waiting. Seconds later, Ron opened his study door and asked the police to enter. As they came into the study, Ron turned to Hugh and said that the officers were there to take him to the hospital.

Hugh erupted, "You can't do that! I'm God."

Ron quickly responded, "No, Hugh, you're not, but I know at this moment you think you are. These men are here to help you. And the best place for you to be right now is the hospital where your doctor can monitor your medication."

At that point, Hugh muttered, "Okay," but when one of the officers took his elbow to escort him to the police car, Hugh jerked his arm back and said, "Don't touch me!"

Ron spoke quietly to one of the policemen. "Hugh is under psychiatric care for a bipolar condition. I'll call Hugh's doctor right away. The psychiatric unit of the hospital will know what to do with Hugh when you arrive." The policeman nodded and left with Hugh.

When they left, Ron said to Elaine, "I'll be a few minutes calling Hugh's doctor and the hospital, but when I'm off the phone, we'll talk." Ron made the phone calls, then, feeling a bit shaken himself, he asked Elaine to come into his study so that he could brief her on the situation. "I think I need a nice cup of tea to settle my nerves," was the first thing he said. "How about you?" he asked Elaine.

"Oh, yes, please," she nodded.

After getting the hot tea from the staff pantry next to his study, Ron sat down and said, "Whew! That was scary, wasn't it?"

"Yes," Elaine responded. "At first, I thought he was joking, so I responded in kind. But when he got angry, I wasn't sure what was going on. I'm so glad you were here."

"I realize now," Ron said, "that I should have told you about Hugh in case he ever came to the office and spoke to you. But I wanted to protect his privacy and I thought that he really was doing okay. But with such a severe bipolar case, you never know."

Over the next thirty minutes or so, Ron outlined Hugh's case. At one time, Hugh had been married, but his persistent bouts of depression had contributed to the breakup of his marriage. At that point, a year or so ago, Hugh came to Faith Baptist Church and sought counsel from Ron. In the course of their discussion over four or five intense sessions, Ron learned that Hugh had struggled with depression for years, but recently had been experiencing some "highs" along with the "lows." Hugh was under the care of a psychiatrist and was on medication to treat his bipolar condition.

"What exactly," said Elaine, "does *bipolar* mean?"

"That's a fairly recent term. The medical community uses *bipolar* for what used to be called 'manic-depressive' condition."

Elaine nodded. "I've heard of manic-depression."

"I hadn't been familiar with the word *bipolar* either," said Ron, "until I met Hugh and talked with his doctor." He shook his head. "Obviously, today Hugh was in an extremely manic phase, actually thinking that he was God.

"During the course of our counseling sessions," Ron continued, "Hugh became a Christian. Before that, he hadn't thought too much about church, but when he did think about it, he saw it as, in his words, a 'place for wimps.' When he told me this, Hugh had sighed and said, 'I guess I'm a wimp myself and need God or something. Life is pretty bad at this point.'"

When Ron first met Hugh, he was lamenting the breakup of his marriage, but at the same time he could understand how his persistent depression had a debilitating effect on his wife and the nature of their relationship. So he didn't really blame his wife for leaving him, but the divorce made him feel even more depressed. He felt like a total failure, and he missed seeing his child.

That was when Hugh made two good, life-changing decisions: he sought help from a psychiatrist, and he visited Faith Baptist Church one Sunday. He'd driven past the church building many times and noticed there was a lot of activity going on, and not just on Sunday mornings. He noted from the church's ad in the newspaper the time of the service and decided to arrive not a minute too early and sit near the back in case he decided to leave.

When he visited the church that first Sunday, Hugh found to his surprise that he appreciated the structure of the worship service even though it was a new experience for him. He observed that the people were serious about worship and they seemed like normal people to him, not like the fanatics he was afraid they might be. He was especially touched by Ron's sermon. Ron struck him as a good communicator and a caring person. Hugh liked Ron's down-to-earth style of preaching and felt his own heart drawn to something mysterious and unknown, but at the same time something he needed and wanted. The message seemed to touch a longing that he couldn't identify.

Just before the benediction, Ron invited anyone who wanted prayer for any reason to come to the front of the sanctuary, where elders would be present to pray with him or her. Hugh had never heard of such a thing and almost went forward after the benediction but decided instead to meet the pastor first to talk about what was going on in his life. Wondering how he could meet the pastor for a conversation, Hugh decided that he'd phone the church the next day. The phone number was on the church bulletin.

As Hugh left church that morning, however, Ron was greeting people at the door. Hugh took that as another sign that the pastor was approachable, so he asked him if he could talk to him soon. Ron responded cheerfully that Hugh should call the office and set up a time to meet that week. Ron then gave Hugh his business card, which showed both his home phone number and that of the church.

"Oh, yes," said Elaine, drawing them both back to the present. "After all these months I'd forgotten—I set up that first meeting between you and Hugh."

Ron, too, had set up appointments with Hugh that Elaine didn't always know about; they were usually in the evenings when Hugh could come after work, and Ron always made evening appointments himself. So, until today, Elaine had not seen Hugh since the initial appointment, although she recalled seeing him occasionally in church on Sunday mornings.

Ron told Elaine he'd had the privilege of leading Hugh to Christ during their next-to-last formal counseling session. Earlier discussions had touched on the need for Christ as the only means of reconciling with God, but Ron was also careful not to promise Hugh that everything would be all right after he became a Christian. Ron, in fact, pointed out that, through Christ, the presence of God's Spirit would be with Hugh for comfort and strength, but that the depression with which Hugh struggled might continue. Hugh respected and appreciated the honest counsel that Ron gave, and he said that he was ready to become a Christian. For Ron, it was one of the highlights of his ministry—leading to Christ someone whom God had brought to Ron. "God plopped Hugh in my lap," was how he explained it to Elaine.

In his early sessions with Hugh, Ron quickly realized that Hugh was facing a deep depression, and he was relieved to hear that Hugh had started seeing a psychiatrist. During one of his conversations with Hugh, Ron asked if Hugh would give permission for him to talk to Hugh's psychiatrist. Ron explained to Hugh that he wanted the doctor to know that he was Hugh's pastor and, if it was appropriate, would like to be "kept in the loop" in extending pastoral care to Hugh. By that time, Hugh was grateful for Ron's caring and honest help, and he gladly signed the consent form that granted Ron permission to talk with Hugh's doctor.

To Ron's delight but not surprise, the psychiatrist welcomed Ron's inquiry. From Ron's own experience in visiting church people at the hospitals in town, he knew that in recent years a substantive shift had occurred in how the medical community viewed pastoral caregivers. Not many years ago, psychiatrists were skeptical of ministers, and some of them even viewed ministers as part of the problem. But now the vast majority saw ministers as part of the healing team and would sometimes, albeit rarely, even call a minister to initiate a conversation about how pastoral care might help a patient.

The doctor explained to Ron that he thought Hugh was definitely bipolar and that medication had been prescribed to help Hugh become more stable. "People with bipolar condition, however," said the doctor, "tend not to take their medication consistently. And if they begin to slip into the manic phase of the illness, they often avoid the medication intentionally, which only makes the manic phase worse." The doctor said that one way Ron could help Hugh was to encourage him to take his medication. Hugh's condition was biological in origin, stemming from an imbalance of chemicals and enzymes in the brain. The doctor emphasized that medication was absolutely necessary for Hugh if he was to maintain any kind of emotional stability.

In talking with Hugh's doctor, Ron learned further that many types of depression have been diagnosed, including something called *dysthymia*, major depression, and bipolar illness. As Ron listened to the doctor, he took notes and resolved to study more about the "many faces of melancholy," as he had heard one of his seminary professors describe depression. After several years as a pastor, Ron was aware that depression affected a number of people in the congregation, although Hugh was one of the worst cases he'd seen.

The psychiatrist explained to Ron that bipolar illness strikes more men than women and that it's not unusual for the manifestation of the manic phase to develop in adulthood, following a long period of depression. That clearly seemed to be the case with Hugh. Ron and the doctor agreed to keep in touch and that either would call the other if they noticed anything about Hugh that needed attention.

"It's likely," said the doctor, "that Hugh will be on medication for the rest of his life." Being a middle-aged man, Hugh would probably need to change medication over the course of time as his body built up tolerance, that is, the dosage that worked at one time might not continue working in the long run. Or Hugh might need to take the medication in stronger doses for it to be effective over time. In such an eventuality, the drugs could become addictive. "New medications are being constantly developed, though," the doctor added. Thus, a better drug might soon be available for treating people with bipolar illness.

"I wonder," Ron now said to Elaine, "if Hugh needs a different kind of medication. Or perhaps Hugh stopped taking his pills, and that's why he was as high as a kite today." Ron said that he'd left word at the doctor's office about sending Hugh to the hospital and explained what Hugh had been doing. "The doctor's receptionist said their office would contact the hospital, too, and would ask the triage staff to admit Hugh to the psychiatric unit."

"Well . . . thanks for taking the time to tell me about this," Elaine said. "I knew depression was fairly common. In fact, I've known some people in the church who have battled depression—I've even been down at times myself—but I've never seen anyone who was bipolar, at least not to the extent that I saw today."

As Elaine got up to return to her office, Ron said, "I'll talk with the elders about developing a plan on how to handle bizarre or scary situations. That way the staff will know what to do if anything strange or disastrous happens in the future."

The elders were, in fact, already developing a crisis management plan in light of the September 11, 2001, terrorist attacks in the United States. Faith Baptist Church was near the downtown center of a moderate-sized city. City officials had requested churches and civic groups to develop emergency evacuation and response plans. Ron would add the incident with Hugh to the list of possible events that might need a carefully planned response.

Elaine stuck her head back in the door quickly and asked, "What did you talk about with Hugh while we were waiting for the police?"

"Oh," Ron replied, "I just engaged him in small talk—sports, the weather, whether he wanted some coffee, that kind of thing. I was beginning to run out of things to talk about, though, so I'm glad the police arrived as quickly as they did. Mostly I just tried to stay calm and deliberately went into low gear, which I hoped would help him quiet down. That seemed to work."

A few minutes later, it dawned on Ron that Hugh's car was probably in the church's parking lot. He looked, and sure enough, there it was. Ron walked out and peeked inside, hoping that the car keys might be there. If so, someone could drive the car to Hugh's house, but it was locked. Ron chuckled to himself, *Phooey. I hoped 'god' would have left the keys in the car.* Then he added in a lighter mood, *I guess God wouldn't need keys anyway, but I do!* While looking in the car, he noticed that the back seat was full of packages of merchandise bought from area stores. *Oh, no!* he thought. *Hugh must have gone on a buying spree before he came here.* In his study of bipolar illness, Ron had learned that excessive spending sometimes accompanies the manic phase, and this seemed to be the case with Hugh.

When Ron returned to his study, he suddenly thought about Hugh's job and wondered if he should call Evan, Hugh's boss, to tell him what had transpired. He'd talked to Evan once before when Hugh was hospitalized, and found out that Hugh had disclosed to Evan that he was bipolar. The company where Hugh worked had a policy that people with chronic illnesses would be allowed to keep their jobs if the illness didn't severely interfere in their keeping up with the work load. So far, that hadn't been a problem for Hugh, and Ron hoped that the current episode wouldn't jeopardize Hugh's position. He decided to call Evan because it was now late morning, and he'd likely be wondering where Hugh was.

Speaking with Evan, Ron learned that there'd be no problem, assuming that Hugh could return to work in due course if the doctor released him for continuing work. "Some of us here," said Evan, "noticed recently that Hugh had been getting 'hyper,' and we wondered if he was entering a new phase of the depressive illness."

Ron and Evan briefly discussed whether the situation was serious enough that Hugh might be put on long-term disability (LTD). But they quickly concluded that the doctor would have to make that recommendation and initiate the process for LTD compensation. Evan had explained that the company maintained, as one of its benefits, an LTD policy on all employees.

As the conversation was ending, Evan said, "You're the only pastor who's ever called me about one of my employees. Of course," he quickly added, "Hugh's situation is a bit different, but I'm impressed with your concern for him and I want you to know that I've even been thinking of visiting your church with my family. What time is your service on Sunday?"

Ron gave him the information and hung up the phone, thanking God. Even something like the problem Hugh was facing might result in other people coming to know Christ. He breathed a prayer for God to be glorified in every detail of what was going on. Ron prayed, too, for God to give Hugh peace and to work in the lives of Evan and his family.

As Ron sat in his study, reflecting on the morning's events, he wondered if he should call Hugh's ex-wife. Hugh had given Ron her new married name and the city where she now lived. When Hugh and she were married, they had had one child, a boy, who would now be around ten years of age. Hugh didn't have visitation rights, and the ex-wife lived some distance away. Hugh hadn't even seen his son since the divorce. As Ron thought about it, knowing that bipolar illness is often passed along to progeny in the genetic code, he wondered if Hugh's ex-wife was aware of the depth of his illness.

In thinking about whether Hugh's ex-wife might interpret a phone call as intrusive, Ron's mind wandered over the last few years of ministry in the church, and the pervasiveness of depression among the congregation. Some questions formed in his mind, questions which he'd thought about before, but now they pressed for attention. *Are people who suffer from depression responsible for the feeling? In other words, can they "pull themselves up*

by the bootstraps" and conquer depression by human effort? Can Christians
expect that God will deliver them from depression, that if they pray and believe
enough, God will give victory, or is it enough to know that God is present even
in the midst of suffering, and in the heavenly kingdom to come all suffering
will be done away with? And where does medication figure in the equation—as
a benefit from the grace of God or a man-made dependence?

Ron was aware that some people in the church thought that good Christians do not get depressed, that emotional illness was not the same as physical illness. Therefore, they thought that Christians should deal with their emotional problems by sheer willpower and trust in God, not by counseling or medication. He didn't hold that view, however, nor did he think that most Christians did. Still, it was a perspective that had to be faced on occasion.

As he mused on those questions, he recalled the occasion when he preached on 1 Kings 18. He'd pointed out that the two main godly characters in the story—Elijah and Obadiah—had very different ways of facing the evil they encountered under the rule of Ahab and Jezebel. Elijah thundered judgment from God and God used him to demonstrate His glory by igniting the water-soaked wood and rocks. But Obadiah worked inside the court of evil Ahab and Jezebel, trying valiantly to uphold God's truth, and even protected the prophets of God, hiding them in a cave when the rulers desired to kill them. Thus, when individuals face the same situation, God sometimes leads them in very different ways; only God can use different responses to accomplish His purposes.

A few people who heard the sermon were not pleased with Ron's emphasis. They couldn't see how God would lead Elijah and Obadiah in different ways. To them, Elijah was the hero, not Obadiah (whose very name, Ron explained, means "servant of Jehovah"). Ron then preached the following Sunday on 1 Kings 19 and Elijah's time of despair and depression—when he was longing even for death and thinking that he was all alone. Ron talked about depression in general and how a stunning victory—such as Elijah had seen—was often followed by a "down" period when one could feel spiritually alone.

Many of the people in the church responded with appreciation to the sermon and commented on how it helped them trust the sovereignty of God at times when they couldn't figure out what was going on. But a handful of people had expressed their displeasure, questioning the sermon's emphasis on depression and how God could use that to help a person grow. To those people, depression was not the same thing as a physical illness.

The doubters were good people, people who eagerly desired to follow Christ and be obedient to the teaching of God's Word. As Ron thought about it, he couldn't, in fact, think of one person in the church who was blatantly self-righteous. Most of the congregation had been Christians for a long time and were mature in their faith. But that didn't mean that they fully understood emotional illnesses such as depression. *No wonder depressed people tend to hide their illness,* Ron mused. *They're probably afraid someone in the church will think that they're not good Christians.*

Faith Baptist Church was a congregation of two hundred people, having a wide spectrum of ages. Because of its location near the heart of the city with only a few residences in the immediate area, most of the members lived in the outlying suburbs. But the commute was not difficult, and people happily drove to the church building for the various ministries of the church. A small parking lot adjacent to the church accommodated people for most of the weekly activities, and on Sundays a nearby parking garage was available at reduced prices to church people. The church was stable and mature, and had modest numerical growth. Its range of ministries met the needs of the congregation and served the surrounding community through its day-care program, food-and-clothes pantry, and weekly free meal for the elderly.

Ron had been at Faith Baptist Church for five years, and was happy to be their pastor, having served as an associate pastor at another church in the preceding five years. He liked being a pastor, enjoying the various tasks that fall to a minister—preaching; equipping the church to be the people of God in the world; working with leaders in support of their ministry in the church and the world; and visiting people in their homes, hospitals, or nursing homes to pray and minister the Word of God. He even enjoyed the administrative tasks of the church and saw this work as necessary to make the whole enterprise efficient.

Counseling was the area where he felt least prepared to minister to people. He took the required course in pastoral counseling in the M.Div. program at seminary, and he thought that he'd be a helpful and caring pastor for people in need. But he didn't see himself as having a call to make pastoral counseling a primary emphasis in his ministry. And, truth be known, when he was in seminary, he didn't think that he'd encounter much need for intensive counseling in the church. When it might be needed, he'd refer people to professionals, but it wasn't something about which he'd given much thought.

That was ten years ago, and numerous times since then he'd chuckled at how naïve he'd been to think that Christians in the church wouldn't face serious problems. He did observe that Christians might not face the extent of problems that non-Christians did, and that Christians could rely upon the presence of a sovereign God—in the person of the Holy Spirit— to come alongside them for guidance and comfort. Still, he wasn't fully prepared to address the issues about which people came to talk—issues related to marriage, sex, business, children getting involved with drugs or not following the Lord. The list could go on and on.

In seminary, Ron had read a helpful book by Eugene Peterson entitled *The Contemplative Pastor.* In it, Peterson discussed "Sundays being easy" and "the sanctuary being clean" on Sundays in worship, but between Sundays, Peterson observed, "an unaccountably unruly people track mud through the holy places, leaving a mess" (61). Most ministry takes place on the six days between Sundays, Peterson wrote, and in regard to the problems people experience, "attention must be given" by the pastor by "practicing the art of prayer in the middle of the traffic" (62).

Ron certainly did pray for people who came to him with problems—as their pastor he was privileged to do so. But he also felt the need to bolster his skills in pastoral counseling, so he'd attended a number of seminars on various topics pertaining to emotional health, and had read a great deal about the issues he faced with people in his church. Issues related to marriage and divorce were the two most common. The third most common was issues related to depression.

As he thought about the various problems faced by people in the church, Ron realized that Christians often had a different perspective on emotional issues. Such problems as marriage difficulties, divorce, wayward children, or aging and senile parents elicited responses of support and caring from fellow believers. But many didn't view with the same care and understanding such problems as depression, anger, anxiety, and low self-esteem that might debilitate normal functioning. They viewed the former problems as things over which a person might not have a great deal of control and, thus, may not be completely responsible. But they viewed the latter as things a Christian ought to be able to conquer on his or her own or within the family. Of all of the emotional problems people had, Ron observed, depression was the one that Christians—especially people who were blessed with a happy disposition to begin with—had the most difficulty understanding.

Another book Ron had read while in seminary was the classic work by Williams James, *Varieties of Christian Experience.* In his book, James described the "twice-happy person" as one who was born happy, and becoming a Christian only made the person happier. On the other hand, the "sin-sick soul" was the person who, even though he or she might be a Christian, was born unhappy, and grace from God in the knowledge of salvation didn't make a great deal of difference in the person's outlook on life.

The more Ron studied the phenomenon of depression, the more he saw why counselors call it "the common cold of emotional problems," meaning that it's pervasive and universal. He was astounded to learn that, worldwide, millions of people are afflicted with the more serious forms of clinical depression. One study indicated that in the U.S. population, 5 percent of people between the ages of twenty and twenty-five struggle with depression, whereas 9 percent of those between the ages of twenty-five and forty-four had depression. Older people, with around 1–4 percent having depression, don't face the illness in quite the numbers as do younger people. Depression in children was hard to diagnose but, in recent years, clinical workers reported seeing an increase in depression among children.

Another study indicated that 15 percent of the total U. S. population, and as much as 25 percent of the female population, suffered from depression. College students have a depression rate of around 25 percent, and 33 percent of college dropouts suffer depression at the time they leave college. With these figures in mind, Ron concluded that as many as thirty people in his church might at any one time be suffering from depression.

Ron also learned from a study conducted in 1991 by the Centers for Disease Control that 3.6 million students that year thought about suicide, and one million actually attempted it. He also learned that 15 percent of all people who took their own lives had told someone that they were thinking of doing so. Ron knew that the link between suicide and depression is strong, and he wondered, *How many people in the church have thought about taking their own lives? How many have even attempted suicide?*

Ron learned, too, that depression cannot always be diagnosed easily. Depression is sometimes a symptom of something else, such as a serious physical disease or even a side-effect of something as common as the flu. Sometimes depression is caused by medication that's being taken for some other health problem. In such cases, clinicians may refer to the depression as a "mood disorder." Further, depression sometimes is a reaction to some traumatic life event such as the death of a loved one, the loss of a job, an incapacitating surgery, or witnessing a catastrophic event. Clinicians call this form of depression "reactive depression," and it's usually easily identified with the object or person lost and normally is of short duration.

How long people struggle with depression and how deep the depression goes into their psyche has many variables. Sometimes depression is low-grade, moderate, or high. Even low-grade depression can be persistent and difficult to diagnose; over the long haul, it can have a debilitating effect on the sufferer. Studies show that close relatives of people with a "major depressive disorder" (another one of the types of depression) have a two to three times higher likelihood of being depressed than the rest of the population.

The so-called "endogenous depressions" (i.e., "from inside the person") involve a complicated mix of brain circuits and chemicals. The neurochemical and endocrine balances in the brain play key roles in depression. In his research, Ron discovered some of the diagnostic factors that clinicians use in differentiating one kind of depression from another. A "major depressive episode" is when a person has a cluster of at least five symptoms—such as depressed mood, diminished interest in sex or other pleasurable activities, hypersomnia or insomnia, decreased ability to think straight, weight gain or loss, or extreme fatigue—experience them almost daily for a period of two weeks, and which constitute a change from usual patterns.

A major depressive episode is differentiated from "dysthymia" in that dysthymia indicates a chronically depressed condition for a period of at least two years. Ron also learned a bit about bipolar depression, wherein the person has periods of being depressed alternating with periods of being "high"—usually irrationally so—such as what he'd witnessed with Hugh. Further, something called "unipolar" depression is a subcategory of bipolar in which the depressive cycle is predominant.

Yet another bipolar condition called "hypomanic" is a less severe form of bipolar condition. In the manic phase, bipolar depressives are characterized by grandiose views of themselves, engaging in aggressive and risky behavior. They are also easily angered and often experience a significant reduction in sleep. The depressive side of the bipolar condition parallels the usual depression of the dysthymic disorder. Bipolar depression is biochemical and is treated with a combination of medication and psychotherapy.

Caregivers, especially close friends and family, who work with moderately or severely depressed people often need help to deal with their own depression. Such is the case with 40 percent of caregivers. Knowing this, Ron wondered how the church could support people who lived with and cared for depressed people.

Having all of this information, Ron concluded that he'd learned enough to help him extend pastoral care to people in the church who experienced depression. He also recognized that he was not called to specialize in counseling or to become an expert in helping depressed people. He did, however, contact several psychologists and social workers who specialized in counseling, as well as the psychiatrist who treated Hugh, and discussed with them their specialization. In so doing, he compiled a resource file of names and specialties that he now used in referring church people to professionals for counseling. In every case, he was careful to assure those people that he would continue to be their pastor and would follow their progress with prayer and concern in the days ahead.

Now, after the strange incident with Hugh in the morning, Ron reviewed other cases in which people in the church had experienced some type of depression. Tammy, for instance, a woman in her late twenties, had postpartum depression for almost a year following the birth of her second child. She hadn't experienced anything like that with the first child and, had it not been for her understanding and patient husband, Joel, Ron feared that the marriage might not have made it. A few people in the church had begun to lose patience with Tammy and wondered openly why she couldn't just get over the depression. They hadn't experienced it in giving birth to their children, so they didn't understand what it was like for Tammy. Medication and counseling had helped her pull through, and Joel's going the extra mile and picking up much of the household chores aided her recovery and lessened the strain on the marriage. Ron saw Joel as a model of Christian grace and understanding.

Alexandra's marriage, however, had not fared so well. She experienced intense depression accompanied by irrational thinking and behavior a week before her menstrual period each month. Her husband, Glenn, found it hard to tolerate her outbursts or excessive crying and often responded with anger. They often threw objects at each other, causing bumps and bruises when an object hit its mark. At such times, one of them usually would storm out of the house and spend a night or two with a friend until things calmed down.

They had come to talk to Ron about the strain on their marriage. In those sessions, Ron talked about how premenstrual syndrome (PMS) is sometimes very difficult for a number of women. He urged understanding on Glenn's part, coaching both of them in how to communicate differently when the stress was high. He talked about the biblical graces of patience, love, understanding, and forgiveness, and he even begged Alexandra to see her primary care physician or a psychiatrist to get medication to help with PMS. She refused, however, and never saw her behavior as being as bad as Glenn viewed it.

In the end, Glenn decided he'd had enough. During one of their fights when she was premenstrual, he walked out on Alexandra and never came back. It took almost two years for her to get over the hurt of Glenn's leaving, and eventually she left the church herself. As he thought about her leaving the church, Ron wondered, *Was it out of shame, or because of disappointment in how the church handled it?* When he tried to contact her to talk about what had happened, she said that she preferred that he not visit her, a request he respected but found disappointing and frustrating.

Ron was thankful that, in the midst of the chaos between Alexandra and Glenn, no children were involved. *At least there were no children to suffer any ill effects,* he thought. The church's response to the situation with Alexandra and Glenn was silence, although the situation was common knowledge. Even the elders appeared uncomfortable when Ron talked with them about how the church could help the couple. The elders' comments indicated that they thought the situation was irredeemable; the best thing to do was pray for the couple but not get more deeply involved.

Another difficult situation involved Sam. He had attempted suicide but a quick intervention saved his life. Single, in his late twenties, and despondent for many years, Sam had taken an overdose of painkillers, which had been prescribed for a sports injury. But he'd called Ron when he took the pills. Prior to the attempt, Ron conducted short-term counseling with Sam before referring him to a professional. Sam made a "suicide contract" in which he agreed to call Ron if he were tempted to take his own life. So, when he did call Ron, he said, "It's too late, I've taken the pills, but I wanted you to know what I'd done since I promised you I'd call." With that he hung up before Ron could respond.

Ron immediately called the police and told them what had happened, asking them to get Sam to the hospital as soon as possible. Next, he called the Poison Control Center hotline for his region and told the receptionist what he knew. The receptionist asked the standard questions about type of medication, Sam's age and weight, and how many pills he'd taken. Ron didn't know the answer to the last question, but the receptionist had enough information to say that Sam's life was in danger and that his stomach would have to be pumped. Next, Ron called the hospital where Sam was heading in the police ambulance and told them what he knew. They were ready to treat Sam when he arrived.

As Ron drove to the hospital, he reflected on the incident. He was surprised that Sam had taken pills, because men usually choose a more violent method to commit suicide. They are thus more successful in taking their lives than are women, who usually overdose on pills.

By the time Ron arrived at the hospital, Sam's stomach had been emptied and he was being sedated. Someone from the triage staff was also there and said that he would get in touch with Sam's psychologist. Ron visited Sam briefly and said, "I hope you'll thank me some day for rescuing you. I love you and so does God, and He doesn't want His children taking their lives into their own hands. When you get out of the hospital, we'll talk more." With that he prayed for Sam and left.

In the subsequent weeks, Ron met with Sam several times and, to the delight of his heart, Sam was indeed appreciative of the rescue that Ron had precipitated. They talked about the peace and comfort that God gives when we're down, and the need to trust God in every circumstance. And with a change in medication, Sam's depression lifted to the point that he was no longer suicidal.

But the whole incident with Sam left Ron with an uneasy feeling. *Whew!* he thought shortly after the suicide attempt. *When I was in seminary, I never thought I'd have to face something like this or get involved in calling the Poison Control Center, and the police, and the hospital.* He was thankful for the continuing education seminars he'd attended, where he learned about this kind of pastoral response to people in need.

Ron thought, too, about how many people in the church had responded with love and concern toward Sam. Some were a little skittish around him but, for the most part, people seemed to understand suicide and responded with concern and love. This care had a noticeable effect on Sam, and he began to feel less lonely.

The one incident of depression that many people in the church could not understand involved Kristen. A woman in her late thirties, she was diagnosed with Seasonal Affective Disorder (SAD), a condition in which the brain chemicals, especially serotonin, contribute to a depressed mood. This phenomenon happens particularly among people who live in northern regions that have less sunlight during the winter months. For people affected with SAD, common characteristics are depressed mood, excessive sleep, and weight gain. SAD is sometimes called the "hibernation effect" and usually goes away during the spring and summer months.

In Kristen's case, as in most cases of SAD, the treatment that helped was simple. Sitting for two or three hours a day under a special light that displayed the whole light spectrum elevated her mood. Or, if the weather wasn't bad, she could take long walks or sit in the sun during the day, and then she wouldn't be depressed.

Five percent of the population, especially women, who live in northern climates, suffer with SAD. The condition has been clinically diagnosed and proven by the scientific community, yet some people in the church had little patience with Kristen. "It's all in her head," or "It's just a figment of her imagination," was the attitude of many people.

On more than one occasion, Ron wondered, *Why is it that Christians have so little patience with and understanding for people who struggle with depression? Are they fearful of something happening to them as though it were contagious? Or do they honestly think that it's all a figment of one's imagination? Or do we not really think of psychological or emotional problems the same way we think of physical problems? And how can the church be more responsive to and caring for people who are depressed? What can I do as a pastor to bring this subject to a higher level of discussion so that the church can really be helpful to people and aid them in their Christian walk?*

As Ron reflected on these past events in the church and thought further about the questions in his mind, he mused about the Scripture passages that reflected depression among God's people. He read again Psalms 42, 69, 88, and 102, in which the despondency of the writers is clear. He remembered the times when biblical characters—Job, Moses, Elijah, Jonah, and perhaps Peter—were down. Some of his pastoral friends even saw Jesus as being depressed in the Garden of Gethsemane before He went to the cross.

Then, too, some outstanding leaders in the history of the church struggled with depression. The reformer Martin Luther struggled with depression, as did the hymn writer William Cowper and the renowned preacher Charles Haddon Spurgeon. In American history, such luminaries as Abraham Lincoln and John Quincy Adams also experienced depression, as did Winston Churchill in England. Clearly, depression is no respecter of persons.

Suddenly, Ron's phone rang. Elaine told him that Hugh's psychiatrist was on the phone. Quickly, Ron picked up the receiver and said, "Hello, doctor. Thanks for calling back. What can I do to help?"

Discussion Questions

1. Do Christians consider psychological or emotional problems as an illness the same as they do physical problems? If not, why not?
2. If the statistics about depression are true, every church will likely have people present on Sundays who struggle with some form of depression. How can preaching help such people? Are programs or activities available that might be helpful?
3. Can you name biblical figures, other than those mentioned in the

preceding case, who might have struggled with depression? Does the biblical narrative include clues about how they responded to it?

4. How might pastors work effectively with clinical and professional counselors, even if the professional is not a Christian?

5. What are some of the community resources that pastors might use in caring for people with psychological or emotional problems?

2

Sexual Harassment
The Philandering Elder

"How do you think we should handle this?" said Gary. He and Dan sat in Dan's office, talking about Frank, one of the elders of their church. Dan was the experienced senior pastor of First Presbyterian Church (PCUSA), Gary the associate pastor and in his first pastoral position out of seminary. Together, they wondered how best to respond to the situation facing them.

A few days earlier, Luci, a woman in the church, had come to Gary and reported that Frank had embraced her and kissed her when he visited her house recently. At first, it wasn't clear what Luci wanted, but in a subsequent phone conversation with Gary, she had said stridently, "Frank is known as a 'womanizer' and now I know what people mean." She added, "I think he ought to leave the church."

First Presbyterian had more than four hundred members, and the congregation had been divided into small groups of twelve to fifteen people. An elder was assigned to each group to extend pastoral care and help in discipling the people in the group. Luci was one of the people in Frank's care group.

Luci was in her twenties and had come from a troubled background. Her childhood had been chaotic. She was from a broken home and it was suspected that as a young girl she'd been sexually abused by one of her mother's boyfriends. She'd hinted as much to a few people in the church, but details were lacking and no one knew for sure. When Luci was a teenager, she ran away from home, and no one heard from her or knew anything about her for five years.

She'd returned to her hometown, though, two or three years ago when she was pregnant and desperate for help. The father of the child didn't come with her, and where she'd been and what she'd done since running away from home were mysteries.

Upon returning home, Luci had turned to First Presbyterian Church for help because the church was near where she grew up, and she'd walked past it many times as a child. The church quickly and willingly took her in and, in a real sense, the church became her family and supported her both emotionally and financially through her pregnancy. They celebrated with her the birth of her healthy baby, gave her additional help during the early months of her new motherhood until she could find a job and day care for her infant. Luci was maturing as a new Christian and was grateful for the help of the church. She eagerly accepted Gary's recommendation that she join one of the care groups.

During the first couple of group meetings, Luci was drawn to Frank. She viewed him as a stable, godly, and caring husband and father. In some ways, she saw him as the good father she'd never known. In his mid-forties, Frank was married and had a teenage son. The whole family—Frank, Barbara, and Frank Jr.—was active in church.

Luci had watched them as a family and longed to be in such a family. So she was delighted when Frank suggested that he come to her house. That way he could get to know her better and ascertain how the church could continue to provide support for her. It was not, after all, uncommon for elders to visit care group members in their homes. *Besides,* Luci thought, *I can learn a lot from him about my new faith in Christ and how to be a Christian parent.* So she looked forward eagerly to his first visit and had even composed a mental list of questions to ask him.

During that first home visit Luci was flattered when Frank paid her some compliments about how well she was doing as a new mother and how nice she looked. She wasn't used to men giving such compliments, and she welcomed the attention. She was especially touched by his prayer for her at the end of their conversation and happily agreed to another home visit set for the next week.

This began a series of weekly meetings when Frank would visit Luci in her home to talk about Christian matters and help her gain confidence as a new mother. Luci sensed that Frank was occasionally a bit flirtatious, but she was flattered by his attention and was also being somewhat flirtatious herself. Although she wondered at times if the flirting was appropriate, she kept thinking, *This is harmless fun. He likes me, and I like him. He's helping me. And, besides, he's one of the elders of the church and is a fine husband and father.*

In one of the home visits, Frank said to Luci, "I'm growing very fond of you."

She replied lightly, "And I'm fond of you, too."

He laughed and said, "I think we may be using *fond* in different ways." She was puzzled by this comment but said nothing. Her puzzlement deepened, however, after he prayed for her and then gave her a big hug as he was leaving. *That hug felt like there was something more,* she mused after he left.

Luci was flattered by the attention and time that Frank was giving to her, but the more she thought about it, she decided to confide in Joan. Joan was one of her new female friends at the church who was in one of the other care groups. Luci and Joan often sat together in church, participated in social events together as single mothers, and talked on the phone frequently about life and motherhood.

In a face-to-face conversation with Joan, Luci casually mentioned some of the details of Frank's visits. Joan listened carefully, and Luci observed that she appeared increasingly concerned as Luci talked about the situation. "You'd better be careful," Joan said. "Frank has a reputation around the church of being a womanizer. He's looked at me in ways that made me wonder what he was thinking. Then one time he made an inappropriate remark to me about how I looked. I told him I didn't appreciate his comment. He just grinned. I've heard other women say to watch out for him. You'd better trust your instincts."

Although Luci didn't say anything to Joan at the time, she wondered if she was at least partly responsible for Frank's compliments and flirtatious behavior. On the one hand, she was flattered by his attention and longed to have a good Christian male role model who was old enough to be her father. On the other hand, she wondered if she'd led him on by her eager and grateful responses to his reaching out. She'd grown aware that in the past she'd used her physical attractiveness to seduce men, and she wondered, *Did I do something to send the wrong signal to Frank?* She alternated between being scared of how Frank was behaving and being mad at herself for flirting with him.

At the next visit from Frank, Luci was quieter than usual, subdued almost, wondering if she should say anything to Frank about her concerns. Frank asked, "Is something wrong?" and Luci, unsure of what to say at the moment, responded, "Oh, I'm not feeling well."

Upon hearing that, he stepped over to where she was sitting and said, "What you need is a man to love you." Then he drew her up by her arms, embraced her, turned her face toward his, and kissed her on the lips.

Luci was stunned and, after a few seconds, pushed him away gently. "Please leave," she said in almost a whisper.

Immediately she was afraid that he would hit her or force himself on her, as men had done in the past, but he just smiled and said, "Hmm, I thought you would enjoy that." He left without praying.

Unnerved, Luci shook for several minutes after he left. After drinking a cup of tea to help calm herself, she called Joan. Upon hearing what had happened, Joan insisted that Luci tell one of the pastors. "If you don't, I will," she said to Luci. Joan insisted that Frank had "crossed the line" and was abusing his authority as an elder of the church. The more they talked, the more Luci was willing to admit that Frank was coming on to her. Somewhere in the recesses of her mind she'd known it, but hadn't wanted to acknowledge it. It reminded her of earlier abuse she'd experienced as both a child and a preadolescent.

After the conversation with Joan, Luci sat in her kitchen and reflected on what had happened. In doing so, she was aware of conflicted and confused feelings—gratefulness for Frank's attention, worry over whether she'd led him on, and fear of what would happen if she told one of the pastors. The more she thought about it, the more she wondered, *Have I really grown much from my earlier experiences?* Unsettling and fearful flashbacks flitted through her mind. *Do I invite this kind of attention from men?* she wondered. Other thoughts raced through her mind as well: *Is it my fault? If I tell anyone, I'll probably get blamed. Either that or Frank will probably be in trouble. I don't want him to visit me again, but he's been helpful in many ways. What am I going to do?*

After a restless day thinking about it, Luci decided to take Joan's advice and talk with Gary. As associate pastor, he had responsibility for the care groups, having recommended to Luci that she join a group when she talked with him about church membership. With some misgiving, she phoned the church and asked to speak with Gary. "I need to talk with you about something personal," she said. "May I come to see you?"

"I'd be happy to talk with you," Gary said. "When would you like to come by?"

On the day of the appointment, Luci arrived at Gary's office in the church at the scheduled time. Sitting in the lobby, she sipped the cup of coffee the secretary had given her while she waited for Gary to get out of a staff meeting. Then Gary came from the meeting and stood in the lobby with Dan and three directors of ministries at the church. Luci felt awkward. They glanced at her, said, "Hi" in friendly ways, and went on their way. But Luci felt as though they saw right through her or at least were wondering why she was there. Fighting back the impulse to jump up and run away, but she meekly followed Gary when he said, "Let's step into my office."

He smiled and motioned for her to sit in one of the comfortable chairs in a conversational area. "Would you like a refill on coffee?" he asked.

"No," she replied. She already felt hyper and anxious and didn't need the additional caffeine.

"Mind if I get a refill for myself?" he asked.

"No, of course not, help yourself." Her voice sounded a bit high to her and she told herself, *Get a grip.*

Gary was back quickly, sat in a chair opposite her, and said, "Well, Luci, it's good to see you. What did you want to talk about?" She was silent for a few seconds, then Gary went on. "I recall you said something about your care group. Is that it?"

"Yes," she replied, "but I'm not sure what to say."

Gary nodded and said thoughtfully, "Sometimes it's hard to know where to start. Why don't you just jump in somewhere, and we'll go from there?"

His gentle, sincere manner was disarming to Luci, and she said, almost in a whisper, "The church has been so helpful to me; I don't know what I would've done if FPC hadn't been here."

"I'm glad," Gary said and then waited for her to continue.

After a long pause, Luci said, "I've never talked to a minister before like this; I'm not sure how this works."

"It may seem intimidating to talk to a minister," Gary responded, "but I'm here to help in any way I can."

With some hesitation, Luci asked, "Is what we say here confidential? I mean . . . I wouldn't want to get anyone in trouble."

A little alarm went off in Gary's mind, and he hoped that his face didn't show his concern. Quickly, he replied, "Yes, what we talk about will be kept in confidence." Immediately he wished that he hadn't been so definite without even knowing what was troubling her. "Is there something about your care group that's bothering you?" he continued.

After another pause, Luci said, "I guess so." She then slowly and with hesitation related to Gary the details of Frank's visits to her home outside of the group meetings. While Gary listened, he made a mental note: *in the next leaders' training class, include a discussion on protocol for home visits to care group members, such as not going alone to see a group member of the opposite sex.*

As Luci talked, Gary sensed that something bad had happened between her and Frank, but Luci clearly had difficulty getting it out. Her ambivalence was evident. Between sentences, she would mutter something like, "It's probably my fault." Gary had begun to suspect the worst, that Frank had seduced her.

While Luci talked, Gary recalled a recent conversation with Dan in which he revealed his concern for Frank and Barbara's marriage. Dan had said that Barbara had come to him for counsel, and during the course of their conversation, she revealed that she'd had an abortion a few years ago, done out of concern for family finances and because of marriage troubles. Since she was unsure if Frank really loved her and whether the marriage would survive, she hadn't wanted another child to complicate matters.

In talking with Dan, Barbara had commented with a note of sadness, "Frank is always paying attention to younger women; he has this flirtatious streak and comes on to women. He was always a little like this, but it's gotten more pronounced since the abortion." She and Frank felt extremely guilty about the abortion and it seemed to drive a wedge between them. "He's been somewhat distant from me since then," she told Dan.

As these thoughts flitted through Gary's mind while Luci talked, he wondered if Frank had had an affair with Luci. When Luci finally said that Frank had hugged and kissed her during his last visit, Gary almost felt relieved.

"Did anything else happen?" he asked, apprehensive of what she would say.

When Luci replied, "No," Gary breathed again. "Except," said Luci, "that I asked him to leave, and he said, 'I thought you might enjoy that.' He usually prayed for me, but he didn't that time." Again she muttered, "It's probably my fault."

Luci explained that she'd talked to Joan about what had happened, and Joan insisted that she tell one of the pastors. "I seem to have this effect on men. Do you think it's my fault?"

"You may have contributed to what happened," Gary responded, "but Frank was clearly out of bounds."

He noted that she seemed relieved, but he also saw her ambivalence when she quickly added, "I don't want to get him in trouble or cause problems. This church has been so good to me."

"Let me talk to Dan about the situation," said Gary. "After that, I'll meet with you again." He was about to say something about his promise of confidentiality when Luci broke in.

"I thought you said this would be kept in confidence!" Her voice was sharp, and an expression of disappointment crossed her face. "Why do you have to talk with Dan about it?"

Gary responded gently but firmly, "I shouldn't have agreed to confidentiality without knowing what you were going to say. I'll take responsibility for that, but now that I know what happened, I have to talk to the senior pastor. I assure you that he and I will be discreet and that we take very seriously what Frank did with you. Dan and I will talk about it, and then we'll include you in deciding what should be done."

Luci seemed satisfied with that, and they set another appointment for the following week.

After Luci left, Gary went immediately to Dan, who was still in his office and alone. Gary reported the details of his conversation with Luci, including the part about confidentiality. Dan picked up on the confidentiality part. "I've done that myself," said Dan. "Now, though, when someone asks if what they share will be kept in confidence, I tell them I don't know. I need to hear what they're going to share, then I'll use discernment in revealing information, and keep them informed of what I do. I've never had anyone *not* want to go on after I've said that."

Gary appreciated the friendly and easy relationship he enjoyed with Dan. Although Dan was the senior minister, he treated Gary with respect and never put him down or demeaned him.

"The next thing we've got to do is talk with Frank," Dan said after Gary conveyed the details of his conversation with Luci. Dan picked up the phone and called Frank, asking if he could stop by the office after work.

With a hint of concern in his voice, Frank asked, "Is everything okay?"

Dan replied in as upbeat a manner as he could, "We need to talk about how things are going in your care group." Frank agreed to come immediately.

When Frank arrived at Dan's office, he noted that Frank seemed nervous and overly friendly. Dan buzzed Gary on the phone and asked him to join the conversation. Without any small talk, Gary reported on his conversation with Luci. Both Dan and Gary observed that Frank's shoulders sagged when Gary mentioned the hugging and kissing incident and that Frank looked away at that point.

When Gary finished, Frank looked at them with tears in his eyes and said, "I know I shouldn't have done it, but she's as much to blame as I am. She was really coming on to me, and . . . well . . . you know, things haven't been that good between Barbara and me . . . so I guess I was weak. But Luci has to accept some of the responsibility, too. She really came on to me."

Gary said, his voice calm and reasonable, "Even if she did come on to you, Frank, you're the leader and need to observe proper boundaries with people."

They talked about how vulnerable Luci was and how Frank had taken advantage of her to meet his own needs. They also said that a new segment would be added to the training sessions for care group leaders, outlining protocol for private home visits by leaders to group members. Toward the end of the meeting, Frank admitted again that what he'd done was wrong, but he insisted that he wasn't entirely at fault, that Luci had to accept some responsibility for what had happened.

Before Frank left, they talked about the next steps. Frank had already indicated that he didn't want to step down as a care group leader, "But," he said, "if you think I should, I will." Dan and Gary both indicated that they thought he should resign.

"But . . . what reason will I give?" Frank asked.

"No reason has to be given," Dan replied. "People come and go from leadership positions, and reasons aren't always given."

Gary then stated that Frank should tell his wife about what had happened and make a commitment to work on his marriage. Frank blurted, "No! Barbara must never know about this. It would destroy her. Besides, nothing really bad happened between Luci and me."

Dan and Gary were silent for a few seconds, then Dan said, "We think what happened is bad enough. Perhaps God is warning you to deal with this aspect of your life before something more serious happens."

Frank made no visible or verbal response, but Dan and Gary thought that he was on the verge of either breaking down in tears or saying something in anger. Finally, Dan suggested they take a day or two to reflect further about the matter and meet again, just the three of them. Frank agreed and left the room in silence.

The next day, Luci phoned Gary and said that she'd talked again with Joan, and the more she talked and thought about it, the angrier she got. Luci was adamant in saying, "Joan says that Frank came on to her, too, and she told him where to go. He's known as a womanizer, and now I know what people mean. I think he ought to leave the church. He's dangerous. Something has to be done about him. Don't you think something needs to be done?"

Gary assured her that he and Dan were dealing firmly with the matter and had already met once with Frank and would soon meet with him again. "When you and I meet next week, Luci," he said, "I'll have more information for you."

Two days later, at the follow-up meeting with Frank, Dan and Gary told him that Luci had requested he leave the church. They asked him what he thought needed to be done. Frank said, "I've been thinking about it nonstop since our first meeting." He paused then and squared his shoulders. "I'm ready to step down as care group leader; I'll just tell everyone that my schedule is too busy." He reiterated, though, that under no circumstance must Barbara know what had happened. He reminded them that he'd been ordained as an elder for life, so he didn't think he needed to resign as an elder. He also indicated that he didn't want to leave the lay pastor training program. "In fact," he went on, "I've enjoyed the lay pastor training program so much, I've been thinking of leaving the business world and going to seminary to train for pastoral ministry. Both Barbara and Frank Jr. are supportive of it." In comparing notes afterward, Dan and Gary thought that Frank wore a triumphant smile as he said that.

While still meeting with Frank, though, Dan and Gary were silent a moment, then Dan said with feeling, "Frank, we don't think you're taking what happened with Luci seriously. You're already doing lay ministry now, and this isn't the time to think about vocational ministry. As a lay minister, you made a serious mistake with a young woman, and you don't seem to be dealing with it. Gary and I are even wondering if you should resign as an elder and drop out of the lay pastor training program until your marriage is stable and you've dealt with troubling personal issues. We have a counselor to recommend, and we want you to know that we'll still be your pastors and will support you any way we can. But right now you seem to be ignoring some pretty crucial issues in your life."

The tears flowed as Frank stated, "I've asked the Lord's forgiveness for what I did, and I know He's forgiven me. You were right; what happened with Luci was a warning from God, but I've learned my lesson. I won't do that again. God has forgiven me. Why can't you? I thought you'd be happy that I'm willing to go into vocational ministry."

After this meeting, Dan and Gary talked privately about what should be done. Should the board of elders be told about what happened? It would be a good learning experience for the board, and the board's maturity as Christian leaders suggested that they could handle the confidential nature of Frank's situation. Also, both Dan and Gary were convinced that Barbara needed to know about it, but because Frank refused to tell her and didn't want them to do so, they wondered how to handle the matter with her. They were also concerned about Luci's growth as a Christian and her maturing process as a person and mother. They didn't want to jeopardize her well-being further, nor did they know what she might do if Frank didn't resign and leave the church. They discussed bringing Joan into the conversation because she evidently was giving Luci strong suggestions about what needed to be done. Furthermore, they wondered what to tell the presbytery if Frank persisted in pursuing a vocation in ministry that would necessitate presbytery support. Finally, Dan said to Gary, "Okay, partner, we've got some decisions to make."

Discussion Questions

1. Where is the line drawn between friendliness and sexual harassment?
2. Should pastors or elders ever visit parishioners of the opposite sex if they go alone?
3. How can pastors protect themselves from making premature promises of confidentiality?
4. Should the board of elders in this case be informed about Frank's philandering? What about informing the presbytery and the seminary where Frank might apply to be a student?
5. Should Frank be asked to resign his lay ministry position, eldership, or church membership?
6. How much information should the church body be given about what happened?
7. How can churches be educated about sexual harassment?

3

GAMBLING, PORNOGRAPHY, AND DIVORCE
Where Is the Church?

Rachel was afraid to answer the phone. It might be another bill collector or even her ex-husband, Derek. Usually she waited until the answering machine started recording the message, and if the person calling was someone she wanted to talk to, she'd snatch up the phone. But she got very few calls from people she really wanted to talk to. "How do I get out of this mess?" she said aloud to no one.

As a divorced mother of three children, her life was difficult at best. It was made all the more so by the continuing shenanigans of Derek. He was a compulsive gambler, which had put the family deeply into debt, and he was addicted to pornography too, engaging in serial affairs. As if that weren't enough, Derek also had an explosive temper. He'd never hit anyone, but his angry outbursts resulted in frequent verbal abuse to almost anyone he met or had dealings with. The past twenty years had been a nightmare for Rachel. And it wasn't over yet.

Rachel and Derek had met at church. He was a seminary student at the time, and she worked as a secretary for a large company. Derek was attracted to Rachel almost from the moment he met her. At first, she declined his invitations to dinner or a movie; something about Derek made her uncomfortable. He was superconfident, almost cocky, and opinionated about everything. As he saw it, no one could do anything right except him. He was a bundle of energy and loved all kinds of sports, especially golf. And he was a risk-taker.

Rachel knew little of this Derek when she first met him. As a seminary student, he was doing field education as part of his M.Div. program at the church where Rachel was a member. He was always on the go, always hyper about everything. People in the church would laugh at his antics, but a few people wondered about his suitability for pastoral ministry. Some of Rachel's friends warned her to be cautious when it became clear to everyone that Derek was interested in Rachel. But when he set his mind to something, he didn't stop until he got it.

In due course, Rachel finally accepted Derek's dinner invitation, primarily to settle him down about her. She wanted to "get him off my back" as she expressed it to a friend. She was also curious about what he was really like. What she learned made her think that she'd never go out with him again.

During dinner, he did nothing but criticize the quality of the food, how it was prepared, and the bad service. Rachel actually enjoyed the meal and thought that both the food and service were excellent. On the drive back home, Derek drove so fast and recklessly that Rachel feared for her life. She'd never been so frightened. And, although it was uncharacteristic of her to demand anything of anyone or to speak sharply, at one point she cried out, "Please slow down." Derek laughed and slowed down a little. Rachel vowed never to go out with him again.

Derek's risk-taking and aggressive behavior, however, continued unabated. Shortly after Rachel's first date with him, the risk-taking got him into trouble. He was in a major accident with a tractor-trailer truck. The law held that the truck driver, by not having his truck under control at all times, was technically at fault. But the accident was actually Derek's fault for cutting in front of the truck, causing the driver to lose control.

It almost cost Derek his life. His body was mangled so badly that the surgical staff in the hospital emergency room didn't think he'd live. In addition to multiple broken bones, he had massive internal injuries. But Derek proved them wrong. His fighting spirit was evident to all of the medical personnel who were involved with him. Gradually, his condition was upgraded from grave to critical, then to stable and, after weeks in the hospital, to good.

During Derek's long hospital stay, friends from seminary and the church prayed fervently for him. Derek believed that God used those prayers to heal his broken body. He was finally discharged from the hospital, but had to spend the next several weeks in a rehabilitation hospital as an inpatient. He had to learn to walk again and use his arms, but he was determined to gain full use of his body. His determination paid off, and eventually he proved wrong the physical therapists who'd said that he'd have only limited use of his arms and legs. He not only regained complete use of his limbs but also recovered sufficiently to get involved again in the love of his life—sports.

It took almost two years for Derek to recover fully, and it seemed to many people, including Rachel, that during this time Derek had softened noticeably. He wasn't as critical as he'd been, was more patient with everything, and seldom got angry. And his need to control everything was not as evident. But, as Rachel was to learn later, these aspects of his personality had simply gone underground for a time.

When Derek first had the accident, Rachel wasn't among those who visited him in the hospital. She was angry at him for driving so recklessly but at the same time somewhat ashamed that she wanted nothing further to do with him. She was also thankful that they hadn't had an accident the one time she rode with him.

Derek kept asking his hospital visitors to tell Rachel that he wanted to see her. After numerous such requests, she did visit him. He seemed changed to her, more subdued and gentle. When others confirmed similar observations over the months of his recovery, Rachel began to feel drawn to him. Although she remained concerned about some of his "rough edges," as she called them, she grew to love him. He said that he'd never stopped loving her from the first day he met her.

After Derek had generally recovered from the accident, he resumed his seminary studies. Shortly after he graduated with the M.Div. degree, he and Rachel were married. They moved to a new location where Derek was called to be an associate pastor at a Baptist church. Derek began his work at the church and Rachel started training to be a registered nurse. As the associate pastor, Derek was responsible for the church's overall education program and for family and youth ministry.

Very quickly problems arose. Derek began to be critical of everything—how the church was structured, inept lay people, inadequate programs, the senior minister's preaching. According to Derek, nothing was right.

He saw himself as more capable than anyone else in the church, and he talked often about how things would be better if he were in charge.

Most afternoons he went to play golf. While golfing one day, he was paired with three other people who were also golfing alone. Two of the others were women, and by the end of playing eighteen holes, he'd invited one of them to go with him on a young people's skiing retreat.

When Rachel found out about it, she was aghast and told him how it would look to other people. "Don't be stupid," he said. "Why should anyone think I did something wrong? This girl needs a friend, and this will expose her to good Christian young people."

The church, however, took a dim view of what he did, just as Rachel had predicted. And because he wasn't fulfilling his pastoral duties except in the most minimal way, the elders, upon recommendation of the senior minister, voted to terminate Derek's employment at the church. The severance package included three month's salary, which was generous given that Derek had been there for only one year.

Although Rachel didn't know it, Derek had been circulating his résumé to churches while at the first church, and very quickly he was called to be the pastor of a small church in a farming community in another state. He and Rachel were to move to the new church in a couple of weeks. Derek congratulated himself on his cleverness in finding another place of service while he was still receiving pay from the first church, thereby giving them extra money.

Rachel herself had grown up on a farm, and understood farmers and the farming lifestyle. They were good, decent, hard-working people who appreciated the hard work of others. She liked their independent spirit and self-reliant approach to life. These characteristics also were built into the fabric of her own being.

Derek, on the other hand, had grown up in the city and often had made disparaging remarks about rural Americans. He saw them as uneducated and unable to do anything better with their lives. So Rachel was dumbfounded when Derek told her where they'd be moving. She fretted that it wouldn't be a good placement for Derek, but her words fell on deaf ears.

As it turned out, Rachel was right. Derek didn't fit the church or the community at all. He wanted to play all the time, and the hard-working farmers didn't appreciate his playing golf several afternoons a week. They also learned that Derek had asked the course manager if he could play free as a courtesy to clergy. The manager agreed, but he didn't know at the time that Derek would be there so often. Derek enjoyed it, though, because he had the course pretty much to himself, and thus could play to his heart's content. The men of the church, however, were appalled that Derek would spend so much time playing golf and that he'd asked to do it for free. They couldn't imagine anyone making that kind of request.

In their early months at the church, Rachel's grandmother became seriously ill, and the family asked if Rachel could come to help. Rachel was only too glad to a grandmother whom she loved. It also gave her opportunity for hands-on practice in the nursing field; she'd continued to study at the regional hospital in the community where the church was.

When Rachel was preparing to go to her grandmother's aid, Derek informed her that he'd arranged for a woman to stay at the parsonage while Rachel was gone. He'd met this woman while golfing, and she would do the housework, including cooking and laundry chores for him. Rachel was stunned and had a hard time convincing Derek that it wasn't the thing to do, that it would look bad. Derek defended his plan, saying that the woman needed a job and that he didn't care what it looked like to other people. In the end, however, he went along with Rachel because she was so upset. It was one of the few times that he actually did what Rachel requested.

Two weeks later, Rachel came home because her grandmother was improving. Upon her return, she learned that in her absence the church had asked Derek to leave. The leaders had informed him that the church as a whole was dissatisfied with his pastoral work, especially his not working at the job very diligently. Hard work was of high value to them, whereas Derek saw his role as convincing other people to do the work. Kindly, the leaders informed him that they thought he was not suited for pastoral work. They encouraged him to consider another kind of vocation.

Having nowhere else to go, they rented a house in the community, and Rachel continued her work and study at the hospital. She was close to completing her RN program, and Derek enrolled at a state school about an hour away to earn credentials to teach mathematics on the secondary school level.

Although Rachel worked full time and was also considered a full-time student, she also did all of the household chores. Her typical week involved seventy hours outside the home. Derek did nothing but take college courses on a part-time schedule, but he'd complain loudly and at length if he didn't have the clothes he wanted on a given day. Rachel was working night and day, either at the hospital or at home, and got little sleep, whereas Derek spent half of every day playing golf.

One of the long-range effects of Derek's car accident was that he was unable to achieve a penile erection. He could experience orgasm but without an erection. Surgery for a penile implant helped, and Rachel and he worked on how they could satisfy each other sexually. Sex was not as frequent as either of them desired, but with Rachel tired all of the time, it was all she could do to keep up with the demands of daily living, let alone attend to Derek's sexual desires.

When Rachel was unable to conceive a child, they made plans for adoption. Rachel had some misgivings about it in light of the stress she felt in the marriage. On the other hand, she wanted a baby, and she continued to think that the marriage would survive. She thought that perhaps having a baby would, in fact, help Derek spend more time at home.

Living in rural America complicated the adoption process because most adoption agencies and resources were located in urban areas. Still, such agencies valued rural placements and did not often receive requests from couples who lived in rural communities. Adopting was a slow process, however, and took almost five years from the date of filing the application until news came that an infant girl was available to them. The adoption was completed at about the time both of them finished their studies.

About this time, the claim for Derek's accident was settled with the insurance company, resulting in Derek's receiving almost a quarter of a million dollars beyond medical expenses. Rachel was surprised that the amount was that large; only later did she learn that Derek also received his lawyer's share of the money because he'd threatened to sue the lawyer for not handling the case well. To appease Derek and stop the lawsuit, the lawyer gave Derek his own share of the settlement.

With their financial worries behind them, they sought genetic counseling, which resulted in fertility treatment for Rachel. Thirteen months later, when their adopted daughter was eighteen months old, Rachel gave birth to twins. She had remained at work up until two weeks before the twins were born but then took a leave of absence to care for the two infant children and a toddler. With three small children, Rachel had her hands full day and night.

In the fall, following the twins' birth in the spring, Derek finally got a job at the local high school where he could complete the practical requirement for state certification to be a teacher. The woman who was his supervisor was every bit as controlling as he, and their battles were known far and wide. She won the war, though. She told Derek that he wouldn't make a good teacher because of his critical attitude and impatience. More convincing, though, she showed him the salary he'd make and how little time he'd have to play golf. Derek aborted his student teaching in mid-semester and never looked back.

With the money from the accident settlement, Derek bought a low-cost but new van to make it easier for Rachel to transport three children. It was one thing that Rachel really appreciated. She didn't know, however, that Derek was making risky investments in the stock market. In a little more than a year, he lost almost all of the settlement money, and that was in the mid-1990s, when the stock market was booming. But, despite the huge losses, Derek still prided himself on knowing how to invest money.

What money he didn't lose in the stock market he gambled away on sporting events. Again, Derek prided himself on being able to pick winners. But for every dollar he won, he lost five. Soon, the money was gone entirely, although Rachel was unaware of it. She'd counted on being able to live off the money and not having to work during the early years of the children's lives.

To continue the gambling habits he'd developed, Derek got cash advances on their credit cards, and they were not small. By the time Rachel discovered what was going on, the debts were huge and, with neither Derek nor her working, they had no way to pay them off.

For once Rachel put her foot down and insisted that Derek get a job. Even with him not working, all of the household duties were entirely hers. She knew that Derek would never care for the children if she went to work, so she let Derek know that he'd better find something to do. Derek, for once, started looking for work. Much to Rachel's surprise, he said that he wanted to try being a pastor again, but she had little time or energy to argue. She was just pleased that he became serious about finding employment.

A few months later, a Baptist church in a small, rural community called Derek to be their pastor. It was about three hundred miles away, though, so once again, Rachel and Derek pulled up stakes and moved.

In many ways, Rachel was glad to move. When the earlier church had released Derek they remained in the community, but he'd stopped going to church altogether. Rachel, however, joined another evangelical church in town, but had made only a few friends there. No one even offered to help when the twins were born; but then, Rachel never asked for help. At one point, she mustered her courage and told the pastor of that church about some of the difficulties she and Derek were having. The pastor said that he didn't know what to say but that he'd pray for her. After that, it seemed that the pastor went out of his way to avoid contact with her.

So she hoped that a new church might be a new and better beginning. They arrived in the new community in the dead of winter. Although the salary was low, the church took pride in the parsonage they owned, having gone to considerable trouble to redecorate for their new pastor and his family. From the moment they arrived, however, Derek did nothing but complain about the house. As he saw it, nothing in it was adequate—and he didn't care who heard him talk about it.

In his first sermon at the church, Derek, referring to "the workman being worthy of his hire," told the people in no uncertain terms that his salary was wholly inadequate. The congregation was understandably confused because Derek had agreed to come at the salary offered, and now on the first Sunday he said that it was insufficient. They were hurt, too, that he apparently didn't appreciate the parsonage, which they'd taken great pains to redecorate.

But, after this rocky start, things soon settled down at the church—at least on the surface. That was not the case at home, however. One day Rachel found a copy of *Playboy* magazine on the living room coffee table. When she asked Derek about it, he said that he'd picked it up "in a weak moment" but wouldn't do it again. The next month, however, a new issue of *Playboy* was on the coffee table. Rachel found it on a Sunday morning and was so upset that she couldn't go to church that morning. Derek, too, was upset—not because she'd found the magazine, but because she wouldn't go to church.

Rachel was particularly upset because of what had happened the night before. She thought that Derek was in a romantic mood, and she'd snuggled up to him, hoping that they might enjoy sex together. But he pushed her away and gruffly stated that he needed to conserve his strength for Sunday morning's sermon. Rachel was hurt by his rebuff, but then finding the magazine the next morning made her just plain angry. When Derek came home from church, she exclaimed, "You won't have sex with me, but you'll look at those disgusting pictures and apparently have some kind of sex with them!" Derek said nothing but looked at her with a scornful expression.

The following week, Derek discovered that the church secretary had been embezzling money from the church. Derek was proud that his math skills helped him uncover her crime, and he was furious at the loss of money. It amounted to several thousand dollars, and contributed to the reason for his low salary; the congregation didn't think that they had as much money as they really did.

At this point, Derek insisted that the church give him a raise. They did so, but grudgingly. Derek also wanted to see the secretary prosecuted and put in jail, but the church would have nothing to do with that course of action. She was one of their own and had repented of her deed, agreeing to pay back every penny. That arrangement satisfied the people of the church.

Rachel was mystified that Derek had no patience for anyone else's sins but was oblivious to his own. To him, no one else could do anything right, but he could do no wrong.

The church, however, grew tired of Derek's litany and at one congregational meeting summarily dismissed him. Derek was there when the motion was made to fire him. Rachel had stayed home with the children, not knowing that anything was afoot. The woman who made the motion pointed her finger at Derek and said, "You are the most untrustworthy person I have ever met. You should not be a pastor." The motion carried unanimously, although a few people abstained from voting. The dismissal was effective immediately, with no severance pay. He was given two weeks to vacate the parsonage.

Rachel never felt more lonely in her life. No one from the church called her. No one sent a note. Nothing. What the church did to Derek affected her well-being enormously, but no one said anything to her. And she had only Derek's word that they'd need to move in two weeks. Derek seemed not to care about anything and asked Rachel to arrange for them to move somewhere. "With what?" she asked, astounded, adding, "We have no money and no place to go."

He replied, "You'll figure something out."

Rachel searched the Internet and found a hospital in another state that was offering a good salary for qualified nurses. She applied online and, a few days later, was offered a job. She called the hospital and explained to the director of nursing services that she'd need financial help with moving. A cash advance on her salary was arranged, and the family moved a thousand miles away. Derek was right. She had figured something out.

Rachel worked the night shift at the hospital from 11 P.M. to 7 A.M. This shift paid a higher salary and it allowed Derek to be at home with the children when they were sleeping at night. When she got home at 7:30 in the morning, he'd practically run out the door. Where to or what to, she didn't know. Bone weary, she would get the oldest daughter off to kindergarten, but they couldn't afford day care for the twins, so Rachel would care for them throughout the day, taking a nap here or there when she could.

Derek usually came home for supper, so Rachel insisted that he watch the children while she slept for a few hours before leaving for work at 10:30. Derek resented this arrangement and sometimes didn't show up at supper time at all, but he'd come home in time for her to leave for work on time. More than once Rachel didn't get any sleep, other than naps, for more than twenty-four hours.

During their vacation the following summer, Derek, Rachel, and the three children attended a family reunion on Derek's side of the family. Many children were rough-housing with each other, and at one point Derek lost his temper and yelled at the kids. A relative chuckled and said to Rachel, "He's just like his father." When Rachel asked what she meant, she said that Derek's father was a very proud man who was opinionated and intolerant. Rachel started to ask, "Was he also irresponsible, lazy, and self-centered?" But she said nothing.

Shortly thereafter, when Rachel returned from work one morning, she found Derek at the computer. He quickly turned it off when Rachel came into the room and left the house a few minutes later. Suspicious, Rachel turned on the computer, and it booted up to a pornography Web site. Usually Rachel didn't have time to spend at the computer, but this morning she allowed the children to sleep late while she explored what Derek had been up to.

She could hardly believe her eyes. She read e-mail messages that Derek had saved from various women, many of them commenting on how much fun they'd had with Derek in sexual activities. Some of it was so graphic and disgusting that Rachel almost threw up. She couldn't imagine people doing the things being described, but that the women would write about it was even more appalling. She was incredulous, too, that Derek had saved the messages where she could easily find them, although she seldom ever did anything at their home computer because of her busy schedule.

When Derek came home that day, Rachel had taken the children to a babysitter and was waiting for him. "You've never listened to me before, but you're going to listen to me now," she said as he walked through the door. "Sit down, and for once in your life tell me what's going on with you."

Derek looked surprised, but he did sit down. Rachel told him what she'd found on the computer and demanded that he explain what he was doing. He just shrugged and replied that what he did was no business of hers.

"Oh, yes it is my business," she responded with ice in her voice. "I'm your wife, and it is, indeed, my business." But Derek refused to say anything. Rachel then informed him that he'd need to stay home the next day to watch the children, saying that she was going to see her doctor for a test. She added that the doctor's office had called to say that her recent Pap smear had shown an "abnormality." Derek looked at her in silence for several seconds, then said, "Okay."

Derek did stay with the children the next day, and when Rachel came home she informed him that she had a sexually transmitted disease (STD). Derek then accused her of sleeping around, but she spoke sharply and told him in no uncertain terms that she got it from him. She was angry at not only Derek, who obviously gave her the STD, but at the doctor, who suggested that she had contracted the disease through her own promiscuous behavior. Derek then replied that she wouldn't have to put up with him much longer, and the way he said it made her think that he planned to commit suicide.

At work that night, Rachel kept wondering if she'd come home to find Derek dead. But when she came home in the morning, he met her at the door and handed her a letter indicating that he was initiating a divorce. She knew she shouldn't have been surprised, but she was.

When Derek was a pastor, he preached on three dominant themes: (1) abortion was wrong; (2) divorce was wrong; (3) Christians must tithe. She knew that he never tithed, and now he was initiating a divorce. She wondered if he'd ever fathered a child that had been aborted. She soon learned the answer.

A woman named Val phoned Rachel and introduced herself as Derek's girlfriend. Rachel recognized the name from the e-mail exchanges. Val said that she was pregnant with Derek's baby but that Derek was insisting she get an abortion. "What do you think I should do?" Val asked Rachel.

Rachel calmly told the woman that she thought it would be a tragic mistake to get an abortion. "I think it's a sin," she said, "and you'll regret it for the rest of your life." Rachel was amazed at how calm she felt. It was almost surreal, as though it was happening to someone else.

Val then asked Rachel if she could talk more about Derek. To her own surprise, Rachel heard herself say, "Go ahead." Val then described some of Derek's controlling behavior, self-centered actions, and temper tantrums. "Welcome to the club," Rachel replied. After talking further, Val indicated that she thought she'd carry the baby to term and that she hoped she and Derek would get married before the baby was born. She even said to Rachel as the conversation ended, "I hope you and I can be friends."

"Perhaps," was all Rachel could say.

Derek moved out of the house and spent several weeks visiting his relatives. Rachel explained to the children, who were too young to understand divorce, that he was on a business trip and would be gone a long time. Then the divorce papers came in the mail. Rachel signed them and made copies for herself. It was a no-contest divorce, and she saw no need to consult a lawyer.

But Rachel refused to sign loan papers that the bank had sent to her. Derek had applied for a loan using the house as collateral, and Rachel's signature was required because the house was in both of their names. She knew that Derek was a poor risk, and she didn't want to lose the house. Derek was enraged at her refusal to sign for the loan, and Rachel felt a little guilty about it, but held her ground. Too much was at stake to do otherwise, but she had to steel herself against signing, especially when Derek yelled at her.

Rachel's venereal disease necessitated surgery on an out-patient basis. Derek was back in town, staying with Val, on the day the surgery was scheduled. Rachel asked him to keep the children for a few days while she recovered from surgery, because bed rest for two or three days was recommended. Derek said he'd do it but never showed up, so Rachel was forced to get out of bed when she least felt like it to care for the children. She got through the ordeal, however, as she always did.

The divorce came through with no problems. Derek was to cover the children's expenses and pay half the bills, including the mortgage. He was also to have the children with him two weekends a month and longer periods during the summer. The papers were drawn up by Derek's lawyer, but Rachel thought the conditions were fair.

As it turned out, Derek never paid a penny for anything. And he continued to spend money like it grew on trees. He'd listed Rachel's name on accounts and given her address as his own, so unpaid bills and overdue notices flooded into the house, even after the divorce.

When it came time for Val to deliver the baby, she called Derek on his cell phone while he was playing golf. She told him that she'd started labor, and in his rush to get to the hospital, he was stopped for speeding. The policeman who stopped him did a routine check and discovered that Derek was behind on alimony payments and child support and, in fact, had never paid anything. The officer then arrested Derek on the spot and had his car impounded.

Derek called Rachel from jail and explained what was happening. He then asked if she could post bail for him. For reasons that Rachel herself did not fully understand, she agreed. She immediately went to her bank's ATM and got a cash advance on the only credit card she had in her name, and posted bail for him. He then rushed off to the hospital to be with Val and his newborn son, without even saying "thank you" to Rachel.

In the midst of all of these events, Rachel began to experience some depression. She felt that life had been so hard for her, and she couldn't shake off the feeling that it was all her fault. Only after several other women called her to talk about their relationship with Derek did Rachel allow herself to think that something was terribly wrong with Derek. At that point, she decided to see a counselor.

In the first session with the counselor, he advised her to cancel all credit cards that had both her and Derek's names on them. She agreed to do that. The counselor then gave her the name of a financial counselor who would help sort out her finances and help her gain some stability in that area. He also recommended that she see a lawyer to address the terms of the divorce.

Early on, the counselor asked about Rachel's Christian faith. He wanted to hear more about how the church had responded to Rachel's situation through the years. She said that many people in the churches she'd attended, including the three that had dismissed Derek, didn't know many details surrounding the events in Rachel's and Derek's lives. She'd never talked about it with anyone and, in fact, had very few friends. Further, people who did know some of the details—or at least probably knew something was wrong—seemed not to care. At least they did nothing about it. On the other hand, Rachel explained that twins and a toddler were overwhelming to many people so she understood the reluctance of some to help her or to get involved in her life. Rachel found it curious that all the counselor would say to this was, "Oh, really?"

At the end of that session, the counselor said, "I'd like you to think about two matters that we'll discuss next time." One matter was what the church, as a community of believers, could do for members in need. "I want to hear you talk about your theology of the church," he said.

"What do you mean 'theology of the church'?" she asked.

The counselor responded, "I mean what you think the church is, what God would have His people be for each other."

Rachel said she'd think about it but wasn't sure she could say much. She stated that she alone was responsible for her life, that she should not burden others with her problems.

The second matter the counselor mentioned stumped her even more. "Have you heard the term *codependence*?" he asked.

"Yes," she replied, "but I'm not sure what it means. You don't think I'm codependent do you?"

"We'll talk about it next time," he replied.

Rachel left the session wondering if she would return. *I'm not sure this is going to be of much help,* she thought. But she also wondered what to do next.

Discussion Questions

1. How do the various complex issues interrelate in this case? What do you see as the dominant issue, and how does this affect the other elements portrayed?
2. How significant in the life of the church are the issues portrayed in the case?
3. At what points (if any) in the case might intervention or different responses by churches or Rachel have changed the outcome? What might have been done differently to effect a better resolution?
4. Is divorce justified in this case? If so, why?
5. What is "codependence," and how might an understanding of this dynamic have an affect upon events along the way?
6. What advice would you give to Rachel at various points along the way and at the end of the case?
7. What would you like to say to Derek?

SUICIDE

Is It Unforgivable?

The alarm clock went off, but Jack lay in bed. He pondered with a measure of dismay the day's activities ahead of him. The church where he was pastor, an independent evangelical church in the Baptist tradition, was in the midst of a conflict that could split the church. A power struggle was going on between him and Rod, a man who exerted strong influence in the church. Rod had a significant group of followers who were opposed to Jack's preaching and leadership style. Attendance at worship on Sundays had already dropped from two hundred to one hundred because of the conflict, and Jack wondered if he should resign to spare the church any more loss. At the same time, however, he was concerned for the doctrinal purity of the church if the opposing group gained control; he saw their beliefs as aberrant to biblical teaching.

As Jack thought about these matters—things that occupied almost every waking moment for him these days—the phone rang. He glanced at the clock—6:00 A.M. *Uh-oh*, he thought, *this can't be good news.* Hoping that it was a wrong number, but fearing a new and bad development in the church conflict, he answered the phone with a cheery, "Good morning!"

"Pastor, I have some bad news." Jack recognized the voice of Tim, a member and leader of the church and one of Jack's friends and supporters. "Sharon . . . our daughter-in-law . . . was found dead in her car during the night. She took her own life."

"Oh, no," Jack responded, "what happened?"

"She was found by two hunters," Tim explained, "early this morning;

she shot herself in the head. There was a suicide note on the seat next to her."

"I'm so sorry," Jack said sincerely, and quickly added, "What can I do?"

"Could you come over now?" Tim asked.

"Of course," Jack replied. "I'll be there as soon as I can."

Jack's wife, Debbie, was listening to his end of the conversation as they lay in bed. She knew that something bad had happened. Listening to Jack, she prayed for God to give him wisdom and strength for whatever he was facing. When Jack hung up the phone, he hurriedly told her the news, and they had a brief word of prayer together before he showered, shaved, and dressed. Debbie made some toast and coffee, and after a quick bite Jack left for Tim and Helen's house.

He noted that it had been only thirty minutes since the phone rang, and in that brief time his mind had been jumping from one thing to another. His thoughts raced from the conflict in the church, to the pain that Tim and Helen were experiencing, to what had caused Sharon to take her own life. How, too, would her suicide affect her husband, Scott, and son, Stan? He knew that Scott and Sharon were struggling in their marriage and that they were among those who'd left the church because they were sick and tired of the conflict. Jack wondered if Sharon's suicide was at all connected to that conflict and if some people in the church would use this tragedy to reinforce their position for or against the pastor. He prayed, *Lord, please help me and somehow use this tragedy for your purpose in the church.*

Jack kept thinking about how much he hated early morning phone calls. *I don't think I've ever had good news in a middle-of-the-night or early morning phone call.* The coming days would without a doubt be stress filled. *I already have enough stress with the church conflict,* he thought, and then he asked for the hundredth time, "Heavenly Father, what are You up to?"

Jack was thinking as well about how his sermon preparation, as well as his administrative and pastoral duties for the week, would be radically changed by Sharon's death. And he wondered if he should change his sermon for Sunday in light of what had happened. But, in spite of these jumbled thoughts racing through his mind, he also thought, *What a privilege it is to come alongside people at their most difficult times and minister God's grace.* He prayed, *Lord, help me to serve You and these dear families and this church well today and in the coming days.*

Tim saw Jack pull up in front of the house and opened the door to greet him. The two men embraced and cried freely. Then Jack and Helen also hugged, the tears flowing for both. After the three of them had regained their composure, Jack said, "Tell me again what happened."

They sat down, and Tim and Helen told him what they knew. Their son Scott had called them at five that morning, saying that the police had come to his house in the middle of the night. They told him that a car registered to him and Sharon had been found in the woods by two hunters, and that there was a woman inside who was shot in the head. A pistol was on the car floor, and a suicide note was on the seat. Two or three vodka bottles were also on the floor of the car. The police asked if Scott could come with them to identify the body. Scott told the police that Sharon had not come home that night and that one of their cars was missing. He didn't tell them that these days Sharon often had not come home at night.

Scott called a neighbor who came immediately to baby-sit Scott and Sharon's nine-year-old son, Stan, while Scott went with the police to the hospital morgue. The officer in charge warned Scott that what he was about to see wasn't going to be pleasant. Scott's worst fear proved true when he identified the body as that of Sharon. The police allowed him to read the suicide note but needed to keep it for evidence, along with the pistol, which would be fingerprinted as further confirmation that Sharon's death was suicide, not murder. Scott recognized the writing as Sharon's and requested a copy of the note. The police readily made a copy for him. He gathered her purse and other miscellaneous items that had been taken from the car and left with an officer who would take him home.

The police were gentle and professional in their dealings with Scott, which he very much appreciated. Several times in their talking about the details of what they'd found, they said to Scott how sorry they were. And when Scott identified Sharon's body, one of the officers had his arm on Scott's shoulder. The drive in the police car back to Scott's house was quiet.

On the ride home, Scott was surprised that no tears had come. In some ways, he wasn't surprised that Sharon had committed suicide; on the other hand, the violence of shooting herself in the head shook him. He felt numb all over, mixed with intense anger that had no focus. As the squad car pulled up in front of Scott's house, the policeman said, "I'm so sorry." Scott thanked him and walked into his house. There, he told the neighbor what had happened. The neighbor looked shocked, spoke a brief word of condolence, and went home. Scott sat in his favorite chair and thought first about how he'd break the news to Stan. That's what he dreaded most.

At 5:00 A.M., he called his parents, Tim and Helen, and gave them the information, which they now repeated to Jack. They explained further that Scott had waited until 5:00 A.M. because he wanted to gather his thoughts a bit and not disrupt their sleep too much. They indicated that as soon as Jack left they planned to go to Scott's house, about a fifteen minute drive away. They wanted, of course, to be with him and Stan, whom Scott would keep home from school that day.

Tim and Helen weren't sure if Jack would be asked to oversee the funeral. But they thought Scott would want him to be involved and for the funeral to take place at the church.

After reading Psalm 23, Jack prayed for Tim and Helen, and especially for Scott and Stan, in this time of grief. Tim and Helen indicated that they'd call Jack as soon as they had more information and thanked him for coming so quickly and offering pastoral support.

On the drive back to his house, Jack glanced at his watch and saw that he'd been with Tim and Helen for almost an hour. In this initial visit, nothing was said about the conflict that was tearing the church apart. The focus had been entirely on the grief that Tim and Helen were experiencing and learning details of Sharon's suicide. Jack was relieved to sense that the church conflict was not an obvious factor in Sharon's action, but he also knew that some church members and former members might make a connection that could mean more trouble. He knew, too, that some church folk were former Roman Catholics who viewed suicide as an unforgivable sin. In their perception, suicide preempted the role of God and took upon oneself the authority to take life. He knew how he could answer any such concerns, but he hoped it wouldn't be a problem. Enough doctrinal uncertainty was swirling around the church without adding this issue to the mix.

Still, his primary concern was how to minister to Tim and Helen and Scott and Stan in this time of intense shock and grief. Although Scott and Sharon had left the church, Jack wanted to be their pastor, especially since they hadn't yet settled in another church home. He wondered if he should call Scott or wait for Scott to call him. He felt like kicking himself for not discussing the matter with Tim and Helen. Not wanting to alienate Scott further, he was unsure of what to do, but he finally decided to take a risk and call Scott.

"Scott," Jack began, "I just came from Tim and Helen's, and they told me about Sharon." Jack indicated that he was more than willing to offer any pastoral help that Scott wanted. He also emphasized that he was praying for Scott and Stan in a special way.

Scott seemed pleased to hear from Jack, although Scott was a man of few words. Scott indicated that he'd welcome a visit from Jack. "I still see you as my pastor," he said.

"Call me," said Jack, "as soon as you feel it's convenient, and I'll come to the house. And Scott . . . may I inform the prayer chain at the church?"

"Yes," said Scott. "Please do."

"What do you want me to say about Sharon's death?"

"Inform people that she took her own life," Scott replied. "There's no need for secrecy. The police told me the story would be in the evening papers, so we might as well be up front about it. The hunters who found . . . the car have already been interviewed by the media. The reporters heard the news on their scanners." Scott paused and sighed. "We can't keep it quiet. Besides, her friends knew she was depressed, so they'd probably wonder about it anyway."

After talking with Scott, Jack called the head deaconess, who was responsible for hospitality when church people experienced a death in the family. She assured him that church people would be happy to take meals to Scott's house for several days even though he was no longer part of the church family. "It's something we would want to do," she said, and added, "as much for Tim and Helen as for Scott and Stan."

Next, Jack called the church secretary, who was already at the office and was wondering where Jack was. He was usually in his study by the time she arrived. He told her the news so that she'd be familiar with events if anyone called, and they reviewed his schedule for the day. It was a fairly light day of appointments, and the secretary said that she could easily reschedule them so that Jack could devote himself to the needs of the grieving family.

Jack then called the person who headed the prayer chain ministry and reported to her what had happened. He knew that within an hour most church families would be apprised of Sharon's death and the details of how it had happened. He then sat down with Debbie for a cup of coffee and more breakfast and told her the details of the last two hours.

"Wow. You never know what a day will bring, do you?" she said. "Since the phone call, I've been praying for God to give you strength and wisdom and for the Lord to draw Tim and Helen and Scott and Stan close to Him at this time." She laid a hand on his arm. "I love you, and I'm with you in this. I know you'll do a good job. And I know God is here with us and with the church family."

Once again, as had happened so often in his pastorates, Jack was thankful for the gift of his wife, who was consistently tender and gracious, but at times like this she was especially supportive. He told her how much she meant to him, and actually choked up as he said it. Clearly, he was feeling fragile himself, and it didn't take much to bring on the tears. They talked further about the schedule for the rest of the day and the days to come, and noted the inevitable stress that would accompany Jack's doing pastoral care. After Jack and Debbie prayed together again, he left for his office at church.

When he arrived at the church, the secretary told him that several people had already called and expressed their concern and support for Jack. Word had spread quickly, and these early callers wanted Jack to know that they were praying for him. Callers also expressed concern for Tim and Helen, who were "pillars" of the church, Tim as the head elder and Helen as a teacher and musician. People also wanted to know how they could help Scott and Stan, even though they were no longer part of the church.

Upon hearing these things, Jack said to the secretary, "This is how it should be—Christians stop bickering among themselves and instead reach out to minister to each other, especially when a Christian brother and sister are hurting."

In the quietness of his study, Jack thought about what to preach on Sunday. He'd already decided that he must directly address Sharon's suicide and offer the comfort and hope that the gospel gives to people of faith. Although Scott hadn't yet asked Jack to conduct the funeral, he nonetheless thought about what he'd preach if he were asked. From the brief phone conversation that he 'd had with Scott, Jack thought that Scott would likely ask him to conduct the funeral service. Sunday's sermon and the funeral service could be close together, and Jack made notes about what he'd say at each service.

As he thought about the sermons, Jack was convinced that he'd have to address the issue of suicide; everyone there would know the circumstances surrounding Sharon's death. His conviction was that a pastor's words about a situation needed to be public to the same degree as people's knowledge of the situation. But he also wanted his remarks to be appropriate to the occasion, not something macabre or containing unnecessary and graphic details. He thought, too, about how to address the concern that suicide was the unforgivable sin. In the midst of making his notes, Jack also considered what to say to Scott and what passage of Scripture to read when they met together.

An hour or so later, the secretary buzzed Jack to say that Scott was on the phone. The conversation was brief, with Jack stating again how sorry he was for what had happened. He told Scott that he'd been praying for him, that the peace and comfort that only Christ could give would sustain Scott and Stan at this time.

"Thank you, Jack," Scott responded, "I'm grateful for your help and your prayers." Scott then asked if Jack could come to the house.

"I'll be there in fifteen minutes," said Jack.

Dropping everything, Jack left immediately for Scott's house. Scott met him at the door, and they sat down to talk. Several of Scott and Sharon's friends were there, but they vacated the living room when Jack arrived so that he and Scott could talk privately. Jack indicated that Tim and Helen had given him some of the details about Sharon's death, and he invited Scott to share what he wanted. Scott replied that there wasn't much more to be said.

"But, I do have one question," Scott said. "You know that Sharon was a Christian, even though she struggled with the effects of her childhood. But still she loved Christ. Do you think she's in heaven now, or . . . " He hesitated for several seconds before finally saying, ". . . or . . . not?"

As a pastor, Jack had heard this question in some form from almost every grieving person he'd met. He'd given much thought to the matter of suicide, so he was prepared with his answer. He explained gently that

God's grace, not human works, kept believers in fellowship with Him, and that salvation was eternal, not something that could come and go. He quoted Jesus' words from John 10, Jesus telling His disciples that as the Good Shepherd He would keep His sheep secure. He quoted 1 Corinthians 1:9, where Paul talked about the faithfulness of God in holding people in His fellowship. He also summarized Paul's teaching in Ephesians 2:8–10 about the saving grace of Christ, not human efforts, that redeems a person eternally. Finally, he quoted Philippians 1:6, where Paul assured the Philippian believers that God, "who began a good work in you will carry it on to completion until the day of Jesus Christ."

"So, yes," concluded Jack, "I think Sharon is now in the presence of God. I think that is the good news of the gospel."

By this time, Scott's friends had drifted back into the room and were listening intently to what Jack was saying. "But . . . why then," Scott responded, "do some Christians say that suicide is the unforgivable sin?"

Jack was acutely aware of the stillness that had fallen over the room. He responded gently that the only unforgivable sin mentioned by Jesus in the gospel records was in regard to the ultimate rejection of what God was doing in Christ. "Ascribing God's work of redemption to the Devil is the unforgivable sin," said Jack, "not taking one's life." He quickly added that suicide was not advised or the best way to handle problems, and that it was an act of desperation. "But suicide is forgivable. It's not the unforgivable sin," Jack stated again, softly but with conviction.

Then he pointed out that of the few instances of suicide in the Bible, no word of condemnation was offered, but only description. "Still," he concluded, "it's not the way we ought to handle things because it is taking matters into our own hands instead of trusting God and seeking help from His people. But suicide is not the unforgivable sin," Jack repeated for the third time. "Rejecting Christ is. And Sharon did not reject Christ." It was a message that he was to repeat many times in the coming days.

After Jack had finished addressing the matter of suicide and redemption, he sensed general relief from the listeners and even saw a few smiles. The friends drifted away. A few seconds of silence ended with Scott saying simply, "Thanks." Scott then asked if Jack would do the funeral, to which Jack responded that he would be happy to officiate. They discussed the details of the service—when it would occur, setting an evening time when working friends of Scott and Sharon could attend. It was noted that throughout the visiting hours at the funeral home the casket would not be open because of the circumstances of Sharon's death.

Jack shared with Scott the gist of what he'd like to say at the funeral, indicating that his statements about suicide not being the unforgivable sin would be repeated in his sermon. He added that he'd refer to Sharon's depressed state of mind and would urge people who were depressed not to consider suicide as an option but—if tempted to take their own lives—to seek help from God and from Christians. "I don't want to give people permission to take their own lives," he said, "but offer them hope that God cares for them and that Christ died and rose to redeem them."

"I think that will be fine," Scott replied. "It's what I believe, too."

After finishing the preliminary plans for the funeral, Jack indicated that he'd like to pray for Scott and Stan, as well as for the friends who were there, and he asked if Scott thought it appropriate to include Stan in the prayer circle. Scott called for the friends to return, then went to get Stan. When Stan came into the room, holding his father's hand, Jack could see that the boy's eyes were red from crying. He put his hand on Stan's shoulder and said softly, "I know this is a terrible time for you; I'm praying for God to give you peace." Then Jack offered a brief prayer, thanking God on behalf of Scott and Stan and their friends and asking God to give all of them His comfort and peace.

As Jack was leaving, Scott said that his parents could give Jack some background information on Sharon. Hearing it might help Jack understand what Sharon was feeling. "Right now it's hard for me to talk about it," he said, "but I've told them what had been going on. When they asked if they could share it with you, I said yes."

Jack thanked him and said that he'd follow up on it. During his conversation with Scott, Jack was once again aware that Scott was a man of few words—something that Jack had observed when Scott and Sharon were in the church. But Scott didn't seem hostile, and nothing was said about the family's having left the church. Jack thought, *We'll save a discussion about that for another day.*

When Jack met with Tim and Helen later in the day, they talked specifically and in detail about Scott and Sharon. It wasn't a pretty picture. Although Jack was aware of some tension in Scott and Sharon's marriage and knew a little of Sharon's background, he wasn't aware of the details. Tim and Helen told the story.

Sharon had grown up in a tough neighborhood of a working-class community. Her home atmosphere was extremely negative, her mother being especially critical of everything that Sharon did. That was bad enough, but there was an added horror. Sharon had been sexually abused as a child by several family members and friends of the family. By the time Sharon was in her teens, she was heavily into drugs and alcohol. She was depressed and angry most of the time and acted out in high-risk behaviors with sex, drugs, and motorcycles. Although her family was Roman Catholic in name, none of them attended church or believed much of anything.

Scott and Sharon met in high school and began dating seriously in their senior year. Scott had grown up in a Bible-believing, faith-practicing family, and had himself genuinely professed faith in Christ. He knew his parents wanted him to date Christians, but he was attracted to Sharon for her good looks and wild lifestyle. It appealed to his desire for adventure. After two years of dating, they were married. Stan was born two years later.

In the first few years of their marriage, everything seemed to be going well. They attended church with Tim and Helen and, through the influence of Scott and his parents, Sharon had accepted Christ as her Savior. In many ways, Tim and Helen were the good parents that Sharon never had. Both Tim and Helen were very fond of Sharon, and she knew it, basking in their love. Helen and Sharon were especially close, taking long walks together and discussing Christian matters and basic questions of life and parenthood.

Out of financial need, Scott and Sharon both worked full time and put Stan in day care several months after he was born. Scott worked in business, and Sharon found a job as a secretary at a Christian organization. The other Christians who worked there were, as Sharon saw it, divided into two distinct groups. One group thought that because God's grace covered any sin, a person could "live it up" in any way he or she desired and still be "saved." This group went to bars for cocktails after work, experimented with drugs, and were promiscuous in their sexual behavior. This reflected a lifestyle with which Sharon was familiar, and that group sought to involve Sharon in their after-work activities. But she was trying hard to forget her old ways in her new life as a Christian.

The other major group of Christians at Sharon's work place took another view of the Christian life. They believed essentially that the Holy Spirit of God would give believers victory over any sin or problem if a person had enough faith. Thus, for them, problems were a reflection of a lack of faith. Although Sharon was "clean" at the time, she was constantly tempted to return to her former lifestyle, and the mere fact of this temptation, which she freely admitted, caused this group to shun her. Sharon felt their rejection and condemnation for not having "victory" over her temptations even though she was not acting out. Their lack of acceptance was a factor in Sharon's drifting in the direction of the "libertines," as the "victory" group called them.

As Sharon began to follow the libertine group, she quickly reverted to behavior typical of her teen years, including drug and alcohol abuse. She was soon back with the motorcycle crowd she knew in high school and was eventually involved in serial sexual affairs. Her marriage was seriously affected by this behavior. The more Scott tried to intervene and help Sharon deal with problems in more constructive ways, however, the worse Sharon behaved. She not only ignored her husband and son but also became increasingly more depressed, convinced that she was no good and doomed to failure.

In their walks and talks, Sharon shared with Helen only a little of what she was doing or how she felt about herself. But Helen sensed that there was more to the story. Scott also was mum with his parents about what was going on, partly out of embarrassment and partly out of a desire to protect Sharon's image in the eyes of his parents. Only after Sharon took her life did Scott reveal the full story to his parents. In a conversation with them earlier that day he explained the extent of her destructive behavior and their deteriorating marriage. He revealed further that Sharon had tried twice before to take her own life by overdosing on pills but that he'd caught her in time and had gotten her to the hospital for emergency treatment. Again, he hadn't shared these events with his parents or anyone else at the time they happened.

Finally, after eleven years of marriage, Scott acknowledged within his own soul that his marriage was lost and that he could do nothing more. He concluded that either she would leave him for someone else or her destructive behavior would end up destroying her. But never in his wildest thoughts did he imagine that she would shoot herself. He told Tim and Helen that he'd already grieved the loss of his marriage; he mourned now, though, that Sharon wouldn't be a part of his or Stan's life. He also expressed deep regret over the violent end that she'd chosen.

When Scott related all of this to his parents in the hours following Sharon's death, he showed them the copy of Sharon's suicide note. They read it together in silence, their faces portraying the sadness they felt as they read her note of anguish and despair. In the note, Sharon talked about her growing despair that she'd ever be free of difficulty. She admitted that she was not a good wife or mother and asked for forgiveness from Scott and Stan. The note answered the question that both the police and the family had about where she got the gun; she'd stolen it from the man with whom she was living. She also disclosed that she'd taken several bottles of vodka from him as well. Her writing was less legible as the note went on, reflecting the effects of the alcohol on her motor skills. In the note, she stated that she was drinking to get up the courage to pull the trigger. Although it was hard to read, the last sentence said, "May God forgive me."

Tim and Helen showed the note to Jack. As he read it, he could hardly keep from crying. "What torment she was in," he said as he finished reading it. "And, yes, I think God has answered her prayer. Indeed, He does forgive our sins."

By this time, friends from work and church were phoning Tim and Helen to tell them they were thinking of them. Some dropped by the house with food. Hugs and tears abounded. Jack was thankful for the response of church people to their friends in need. Tim and Helen were loved in the church, and Jack saw that others were surrounding them with love and prayer.

Tim and Helen had decided to be open about the details of Sharon's suicide. Their openness to talk and share what they were feeling—grief, shock, anger, guilt—allowed others around them to talk freely about it as well. But Jack worried about how Scott would fare. Scott's being quiet and reserved made it harder for people to talk freely with him or even to find out what he was feeling

Sunday would approach quickly, and Jack hadn't yet settled in his mind what he'd say in the pastoral prayer and sermon. The funeral was set for Monday, and he wondered how to craft both a worship service and a funeral scheduled so closely together. His constant prayer was for guidance.

To his knowledge, this was the first time that the church had experienced a suicide, and he knew that people were confused about it. The phone calls and conversations he had with individuals in the hours following Sharon's death revealed prejudice, confusion, and fear about suicide. The conflict rolling through the church was set aside at the moment because of the crisis and the grief of Tim and Helen, but Jack knew that it wouldn't take much to get it started again. He feared that those who opposed his leadership would use Scott and Sharon's having left the church and Sharon's taking her own life as evidence that he was not a good pastor.

Added to Jack's concerns was whether he had, in fact, let Scott and Sharon down when they left the church. He wondered, *Should I have been more proactive in meeting with them and trying to retain them in the church family?* Further, although he had a vague sense that their marriage was not good, he'd never taken the initiative to talk with them about it. *Could I have helped strengthen their marriage and perhaps even have prevented Sharon's suicide?* It was time for him to talk with his wife about what to do for the long haul, and to prepare his heart and mind for Sunday and Monday.

Discussion Questions

1. What does the Bible say about suicide? How is the issue of suicide and salvation addressed in Scripture? How does biblical teaching affect your understanding of salvation for a Christian who commits suicide?
2. In the case of suicide, how should a pastor respond to people's prejudices, confusion, and fears?
3. What resources in the community might help a church respond to the suicide of one of its members?
4. What can a pastor and church do to reduce the potential for suicide among parishioners?
5. How would you craft a worship service and a funeral scheduled so closely together?
6. Did the conflict in this church have any bearing on the suicide and the outcome?
7. Were the questions in Jack's mind fair for him to be asking at this time? Why or why not?

AIDS

A Question of Who Should Know

Al sat at the desk in his study and thought about Steve. A decade ago at his previous church, Al had ministered to Steve, who was in the last stages of AIDS. Al wondered, *Now I'm in a different church and facing another situation involving AIDS. Should I handle it differently than before?*

At that time, Joyce, the wife of Frank, one of the church's elders, came to him and asked if he'd make a pastoral call on Frank's brother Steve. She informed Al that Steve had AIDS and that his condition was serious. She also reported that neither Steve nor his wife, Linda, were Christians, but they were both open to the gospel, especially at this vulnerable time. Al quickly agreed to visit Steve and Linda and made an appointment for the next day.

When Al arrived at Steve and Linda's house, Linda greeted him at the door and escorted him to the back porch, where Steve was sitting. It was a warm summer day, but Steve was wrapped in a blanket and, as Al would say later, "Steve looked like death warmed over." As a pastor, Al had often ministered to hurting people, but this was the first time he'd encountered face to face someone with AIDS. He hoped that his countenance did not reflect the shudder he felt in his soul as he looked at Steve.

Al explained that Joyce had asked him to come and that she'd told him about Steve's situation. "Is there anything I can do for you as a minister?" Al asked.

"I'm dying," Steve responded, "and there's not much that can be done now."

In talking with people who weren't Christians, Al's usual approach was to build a relationship and allow the gospel message of salvation through Christ to flow naturally from the relationship. With Steve, however, he decided to move quickly to "the heart of the gospel," as he put it. Al explained to Steve how he could have the gift of eternal life through faith in Christ, laying before Steve God's grace and forgiveness through the death of Christ. Al then asked Steve if he desired to accept Christ as his Savior. Steve called Linda to join the conversation and asked Al to tell her, too, about how they both could have eternal life in Christ. Both Steve and Linda immediately said that they desired to be Christians. In that moment, Al relished one of the joys of being a pastor, praying with them as they put their faith in Christ and accepted Him as their Savior.

During the conversation, the discussion was interrupted several times by deep coughing spasms by Steve. The coughing was so deep and prolonged that Al was afraid that Steve was about to die on the spot. But each time the coughing subsided, and Steve was able to continue listening to Al and talking about his situation.

When they talked in that first meeting, Al learned that Steve likely contracted the AIDS virus when he was a nurse in a hospital. Apparently, according to Steve, he accidentally stuck himself with an infected needle. Having heard that HIV was sometimes acquired this way, Al thought no more about it. But in the weeks following their conversation, Al learned more about Steve's lifestyle before he met Linda. Although they never talked about it, Al wondered if the actual cause of Steve's infection was his promiscuous sexual experiences, not an accident with an infected needle in a hospital.

After they'd prayed together, Linda introduced their two children to Al. The older of the two was a girl, age six. The boy was two years old. Both children were cute and well-behaved, and Al was immediately drawn to them. Al introduced himself as the pastor of the church where their uncle Frank was an elder, and he invited the whole family to come to church together the following Sunday. They readily agreed to do so.

As Linda walked with Al to the door to see him out, he observed that she was a bit shy but pleasant. She seemed pleased that Al had come and warmly thanked him for his concern for her family. Al said that he was happy to be of help, and almost as an afterthought, he told Linda that it might be best not to tell anyone at church that Steve had AIDS.

"We think not saying anything is best," said Linda. "We've had several unpleasant remarks and responses from people on the street or in stores. They look at Steve and suspect that he has AIDS."

Later that day, Al called Frank and Joyce to report what had happened. They were thrilled to hear about Steve and Linda's commitment to Christ. "This is something we've been praying about for a long time," Frank stated, "but until now Steve saw no need for Christ. He said it was okay for me and Joyce, but it just wasn't something that meant much to him."

"Many people respond to the gospel that way at first," said Al.

"Other times when I've talked to Steve about the Christian faith," said Frank, "he said that he had done some 'terrible things in the past' and needed to try to be a better person before God would have anything to do with him. No matter how much I talked about grace and forgiveness, it never seemed to reach him."

As they talked about it, Al emphasized to Frank that he'd obviously laid the groundwork. "You planted, I watered, and God brought it into flower," Al said.

"Yeah," Frank replied, "I guess there's nothing like facing imminent death to bring one to a point of realizing the need for God." He paused, then said, "Thank you for seeing Steve and Linda," and Al could tell that Frank was choking back the tears as he said it.

While on the phone, Al asked Frank if he knew whether Steve and Linda's children were aware of their father's critical condition. "No," said Frank, "Steve and Linda think that the children are too young to understand what's going on, and they want to protect them from any taunts or snide remarks from others." Frank indicated that, as far as he knew, other than Steve's doctors and Steve and Linda themselves, only he and Joyce—and now Al—knew for sure that Steve was dying of AIDS.

"I asked Steve and Linda if it was all right for me to tell my wife," Al explained, "so that she could be available to help if needed. They agreed." So, as far as Frank and Al could determine, only six people beyond the doctor's staff knew the whole story, and they agreed that it would be best to keep it that way.

Part of their concern at that time was that AIDS was a fairly new phenomenon. Although HIV and AIDS had been around for a decade or so, neither Al nor Frank were clear about how people in the church would respond if Frank and Linda showed up and it was announced that Steve had AIDS. Al remembered a pastor who'd said, "The first time I met a man with AIDS, I ran to the bathroom after our conversation and washed my hands—hard—as hard as I'd ever washed them." That pastor knew that it was an irrational act, that AIDS was contracted through an exchange of body fluids, not casual touching such as shaking hands, but he couldn't help himself.

Al and Frank were afraid that if people knew the details, they might withdraw from Steve and Linda and not embrace them warmly as new members of the church family. They might also say or do something that would offend or alienate them. Both men were concerned, too, about what might be said to Steve and Linda's children and whether parents would keep their own children away from them. Al and Frank had heard of this happening in other places. They concluded that it was best to keep Steve's situation quiet, especially since that was the agreement Al had with Linda.

The next Sunday, Steve, Linda, and the children came to church and were greeted warmly by several church folk. But Al observed at one point that one couple looked at Steve with a mixture of concern, fear, and revulsion. It was a quick look, but Al thought it was unmistakable. *Can they really tell just by looking at Steve,* Al wondered, *that he has AIDS?* But nothing was said as introductions were made.

From talking with Frank and Joyce, Al learned that Steve and Linda indicated they'd like to become members of the church. They had attended several Sundays, were enjoying the worship services, were reading their Bibles regularly, and were growing—as Frank expressed it—"by leaps and bounds" in their new faith as Christians. Frank and Joyce were meeting with them regularly for Bible study. And they were pleased to see their children excited about church and making wonderful friends with the other children.

When Steve and Linda asked Al if they could join the church, Al responded, "I think it's a fine idea." He arranged for Steve and Linda to meet with the board of elders for the required interview. In the meeting, Steve and Linda gave their testimonies about their faith in Christ and how they appreciated the faithful and patient Christian witness of Frank and Joyce over the years. Frank, who was present as an elder, smiled broadly. And they expressed gratitude that Al was "the right man at the right time" in visiting their home.

During the interview, nothing was said about Steve's having AIDS, and no elder followed up with any question, either during the interview or after Steve and Linda left the meeting. A couple of times during the interview, Steve had coughing spells, but the elders simply waited for him to continue. The board was more than satisfied with their testimonies and indicated to Frank that he must be thrilled over their faith. It was a unanimous decision to accept Steve and Linda as members. Al quietly thanked the Lord in his heart that the board was so affirming of them and was relieved that no one asked anything about Steve's health.

The following Sunday, Steve and Linda were welcomed into the membership of the church. It was a warm and caring fellowship of people who easily gave hugs to one another. Al noticed, however, that on this occasion few hugs were extended to Steve and Linda. He thought that people perceived that Linda was shy and might not welcome a hug and that Steve was so frail. But people seemed happy enough to welcome them as members. The church was growing in attendance, and new members were always welcome. That was the prevailing attitude.

During the worship service a few Sundays later, Steve experienced a deep and prolonged coughing fit. Several people sitting in the nearby pews began to look at Steve. Some even craned their necks to see what was happening. Some of the people looked concerned; others looked irritated. Still others glared as if to say, *Do something besides just sit there!*

The coughing finally subsided, but after the service one woman came up to Steve and said with irritation in her voice, "If you have the flu, you should stay home—as much for our sake as for yours." Steve and Linda were crestfallen, afraid that their worst fears were coming true—that if people knew Steve had AIDS they'd have nothing more to do with them.

After that, Steve and Linda arrived for worship a few minutes late and sat in the foyer of the church, where they could hear but not be seen by everyone. That way, if Steve had a coughing fit, they could easily leave. And each Sunday they left the building as the final hymn was being sung. Their children protested arriving late and leaving early, but Steve and Linda explained that it was the best thing to do since "Daddy wasn't feeling well."

In the weeks following Steve and Linda's commitment to Christ and church attendance, Al read a great deal about AIDS. He wanted to understand the disease in order to better minister to Steve and Linda. One thing he learned was the importance of touch to someone who has AIDS. The literature explained that AIDS victims are often shunned by many people and are made to feel untouchable. People with AIDS also know the loathing expressed toward them, partly over the way they often look, and partly over the ways people think they might have contracted the disease. Some people are so repulsed by the thought of AIDS that they'll have nothing to do with a victim of the disease no matter how it was contracted.

Al also read about the fear of healthy people when they're around someone with AIDS, a fear that the disease might be contracted through touching or coughing, and a feeling of uncertainty about how to respond to the person with AIDS. But Al was a hugger, and he resolved to give Steve a hug every time he saw him. It was easy to do this, anyway, he reasoned, because it came naturally for him. And he knew that Steve needed hugs. Furthermore, he hoped that his giving hugs to Steve would be a good example for the church people to see and perhaps respond in kind.

Part of Al's core belief system was a deep conviction that Christians should love and reach out to people in need, no matter what the circumstances and no matter how people's own culpability had contributed to their own situations. It was what Christ did, Al would often say, and the followers of Christ should do no differently. He admitted having a low tolerance for Christians who were prejudiced against people of color, against foreigners, or even people who held different beliefs than the Christian faith.

He would debate endlessly and congenially with anyone who held a belief different from his, and he was known for his friendly discussions with other Christians about matters of doctrinal differences. But if he ever sensed prejudice from anyone toward someone different, he was quick to rebuke or challenge the prejudice. "I have little patience," he would say, "with people who don't follow Jesus' style of working with sinners." Jesus invited those whom the Pharisees rejected—"the poor, the crippled, the lame, the blind" (Luke 14:13)—to the banquet table of the Messiah and that was the model that Al tried to follow. He not only taught it to his congregation but also practiced it in his own life.

Now, facing his first test case with someone who had AIDS, he was almost too eager—*Is that possible?* he wondered—to extend hugs to Steve and

Linda and tell them that he loved them. And he was hypersensitive to how other people in the church were treating Steve. On more than one occasion, he thought about the irony that, on the one hand, he wanted people to embrace and include Steve in their lives, but on the other hand, he hadn't told anyone about the particular need. He realized the contradiction, but since no one asked about Steve's condition, Al kept his silence.

One day, Al was reading his denominational paper and was attracted by a particular item. A church in a nearby city, the paper said, had invited a Christian man who had AIDS to speak there. The man had contracted AIDS through illicit sex when he was in military service. Later, he became a Christian and was now engaged in a public ministry, telling people about not only his new life in Christ but also the necessity of living a moral life. His message was well-received everywhere he went.

With the approval of the board of elders, Al invited the man to come to his church to speak. In addition to announcing the meeting to the congregation, Al invited people in the medical community and civic leaders to attend the forum. The meeting was well attended by not only church members but also doctors, nurses, and community leaders. It was billed as an AIDS-awareness forum. Both the man's testimony of faith in Christ and his challenge for listeners to lead a moral life were clear. He also talked about the importance of touch and the need to reach out to people with AIDS rather than avoid them. "It's what Christ would do," he said.

Al was pleased with the turnout and was thankful to God for the clear and helpful presentation. After the meeting, he gave the speaker a big hug. He noticed Steve and Linda slipping out a side door from their usual seats in the foyer, and he was glad that they had come. Still, nothing was ever said publicly about Steve's condition, and no reference was made about his need for tangible expressions of love from Christians.

Four months after Al had first met Steve, his condition worsened, and he was no longer able to leave home. Shortly after that, Steve was placed in hospice care and died a few weeks later. Al conducted the funeral, at which both the family and the congregation could grieve Steve's death. It was a time, too, of celebration of Steve's new life in Christ and his resurrection to new and eternal life as a whole person. But, again, no reference was made to Steve's having had AIDS.

In the weeks following the funeral, Al visited with Linda several times for follow-up pastoral care, as was his usual practice. At times, Linda would cry and say how much she missed Steve and was afraid to go on without him, but she knew that the children needed her to be strong for them. The children seemed to be making a good adjustment to life without their father. Linda had few friends outside of Frank and Joyce and, being a private person, she seemed to Al to be quite lonely.

In retrospect, Al often wondered, *If I'd said something public about Steve's having AIDS, would the church people have poured out more love and offered more help to Linda?* On the other hand, he also thought it possible that people might have turned away from her, thinking that Steve got what he deserved. Or they might have said something crude or thoughtless to her or the children. Uppermost in Al's mind at the time was his desire to protect the children from potential taunts and ridicule had Steve's situation been disclosed. Now it was all a jumble in his mind, but it had seemed the right response at the time.

Now, ten years later, Al was facing a new situation involving someone with AIDS. This person wanted to attend the church that Al was now serving. Al thought that he needed to approach the whole situation differently than he had before. For one thing, he reasoned, there's now a great deal more understanding about AIDS than existed a decade ago. The public is now more aware of what causes AIDS, and some of the fear factors had dissipated. Also, better treatment programs and medicines were now available. *So*, he thought, *how people respond to meeting someone with AIDS today is likely to be more positive than it used to be.* Further, he thought that most people had likely met someone with either HIV or full-blown AIDS, and would thus be more comfortable around such people than might have been the case earlier.

For another thing, Al had thought long and hard about not publicly disclosing Steve's situation. It seemed to him like a conspiracy of silence in which he had willingly participated—for good reason, he thought—to protect Steve's children and because Linda had wanted it kept a secret. *But are secrets ever really secrets?* he wondered. Perhaps people did know about Steve's situation and they, too, were participants in the conspiracy of silence. Al couldn't get the fear out of his mind that he might not have handled the situation with Steve in the best way or most redemptive way to care for Steve, Linda, and the children.

Desiring to be open in regard to the case that now faced him, Al decided to confide in the chairman of his elder board. This man was sympathetic to the needs of AIDS victims and was understanding of Al's concern that there be no secrets in church, except to protect innocent people in cases of the most confidential nature. But the elder wasn't at all sure how the church people generally would respond. He related that a nearby church had removed a pew in the sanctuary to accommodate a member who used a wheelchair. When word got around that this church welcomed wheelchair people, before long, the church had several rows of people in wheelchairs attending the service.

The elder quickly added, "Of course, there's nothing wrong with this! I've listened to your preaching about Christ accepting broken people. I know that Jesus reached out to those in desperate conditions and I know we need to be like that. We have an opportunity now to act on what we've heard and believe. But," the elder paused, as if to express his next words carefully, "we should be prepared to receive more than one AIDS person into the church. He might bring others with him over time. I don't know how the church will respond to it. We need to think about what we're getting into. And how do we let people know what we're thinking? Should we seek counsel from the whole congregation, or inform them after we've done some work ourselves?"

Al thought about this man's comments for a few seconds and then replied, "I think it would be best to discuss the matter with the whole board of elders." The elders were a cohesive group of mature Christians. Al thought that their response would be a good barometer of how the whole church would respond. He knew that a great deal was riding on this. It could be a make-or-break time for his and the church's ministry to those in need in the community.

That conversation with the board chairman had occurred a week ago. It was now time for Al to prepare his presentation for the board's consideration. Taking his note pad, he thought about how he would approach the matter. He began listing the questions that should be raised and how he might answer their concerns.

Discussion Questions

1. Should the whole church be told if one of the parishioners suffers with AIDS?
2. Does the way in which AIDS was acquired change the way you think and feel about the person who has AIDS? Does this knowledge change the way a church should minister to the person? If so, how?
3. How can church leaders help parishioners overcome fears and prejudices about AIDS?
4. Are there any church activities for which it might be wise to limit participation by AIDS patients? If so, give examples.
5. How can the church minister more effectively to AIDS victims and their families?

6

GRIEF

Conquering the Last Enemy–Death

Henry's thoughts kept turning to the appointment he had later in the morning. He was in his church study, working on his Sunday sermon, but Sarah, the seminary student intern who was working with him, had asked to meet with him.

Two years earlier, Sarah's husband of fourteen months had died in a tragic car accident. She was now falling in love with a fellow seminarian, and it looked like their relationship could lead to marriage. Sarah wondered if it was too soon after her husband's death to think about marriage again, and at times she still grieved his passing. She viewed Henry as someone to whom she could talk about her own conflicted feelings, because he'd experienced grief over the loss of a teenage son, Mark, in a car accident. It seemed to her that very few Christians, especially those who'd never experienced the death of a loved one, understood how grief might affect a person for a long time after the funeral.

The internship director of the seminary that Sarah attended had suggested to her that she do her internship at the church where Henry was pastor. The director thought Henry would be sensitive to the grief issues with which Sarah was dealing. Henry was delighted to have Sarah as an intern. He needed the help plus, in helping Sarah process her grief, it would give him and Catherine, his wife, another opportunity to process theirs. He was puzzled, though, that the director had suggested to Sarah that she work with Henry. The director was typical of most clergy and church people, as Henry and Catherine saw it; he had seldom inquired about how they were doing, either at the time of Mark's death or now, fourteen years later. The director, and everyone else, seemed to assume—both then and now—that Henry and Catherine were doing fine.

As he thought about Sarah and looked back on his experience as a pastor, Henry realized that much of his ministry had been with people who grieved. There seemed to be no way he could get away from it—not that he wanted to. What puzzled him most was how Christians often seemed not to want to talk about death. When death came for a loved one, other people seemed to assume that those who grieved the loss would get over it in a short time and life would return to normal.

These thoughts led Henry to ponder the last twenty years. He had been a professional firefighter years ago, a job he greatly enjoyed and at which he excelled. Nevertheless, as a Christian with strong faith roots in a stable family, he'd often thought about being a minister. He and Catherine had five children, and with the demands of being a husband and a father, he had put the notion of seminary from his mind when the children were young. Providing for the family was his first priority. Besides enjoying his career as a firefighter, he took seriously his job to protect lives and property as a Christian duty. He saw himself as a Christian firefighter who desired to honor God in all he did. And he, Catherine, and the family were always active in church anyway, engaged in many activities and outreach programs. They all took seriously the catechism they'd been taught: "The chief end of man is to glorify God and enjoy Him forever." This was their goal in all of life.

But the thought of attending seminary and studying to be a minister never completely left Henry's mind. When the two oldest children left home, it seemed like a good time to make the move. Catherine had a good job with a Christian organization that specialized in reaching out to people with mental and physical problems. Her income, although modest, would provide financial support for the family.

In applying to seminary, Henry learned that, in addition to attending classes, he'd be placed as a part-time pastor in a church within his denomination. In that position he would receive some remuneration, which would help him and Catherine financially. Then, too, he was given a tuition scholarship that the seminary reserved for second-career students, so his educational expenses would be met. Thus, with the family's blessing and encouragement, Henry gave up his job as a firefighter and began his seminary studies as a middle-aged student.

When Henry began seminary, Mark was seventeen. Two other children were still at home—Tim, a fourteen-year-old boy and Betsy, a preteen girl. The family quickly got caught up in seminary life. It was a hectic time with studies, pastoral work, and children who were involved in many activities, but the family was happy and enjoyed their lives.

Mark especially enjoyed a close friendship with several seminary students. A group of them had formed a musical group that played at seminary functions and in churches throughout the area. The band focused especially on a ministry to young people, and although the music was a little loud and raucous for Henry's and Catherine's taste, they were thankful that Mark was a Christian and was happy in his music ministry.

For his part, Mark was a likable kid. People were drawn to his personality. Several times in the weeks before he died, he remarked to Henry and Catherine how thankful he was that they were his parents. It warmed their hearts when he told them how much he loved them. And he loved life.

Just a week or so before he was killed, Mark told his parents that if he died before they did, he wanted certain songs sung at his funeral. He even teased his dad about whether Henry would be able emotionally to conduct the funeral. Even though they laughed about it at the time, they also told Mark to stop being so macabre.

By this time, Henry was in his final semester at seminary and was looking forward to graduation. All over the house, sticky notes were stuck on furniture, doors, and walls in anticipation of the upcoming commencement. It was going to be a great day.

One week before Henry's graduation, Mark left the house after supper to visit a friend and practice music together, something that he often did. On this particular night, Catherine awoke a little after midnight and discovered that the lights were still on, an indication that Mark was not yet home. She was somewhat concerned because Mark had said that he'd be home early, and on the occasions when he was detained for some reason, he always called his parents to tell them he'd be late. This was standard procedure, even if it meant that he called after Henry and Catherine had gone to bed. But there was no phone call that night.

Worried, Catherine called the friend who Mark had gone to visit, but he told her that Mark had left hours before. Catherine then woke Henry and told him what she'd learned. Henry immediately called the police to see if they knew anything. The officer who answered the phone said that two policemen were on their way to the house at that very moment. Years later, Henry could still remember the awful alarm that went off inside of him when he heard those words. But he calmly asked, "Is it bad news?" Rather than answer directly, the officer simply replied that the policemen on their way would inform them of the situation. Braced for the worst, Henry and Catherine waited.

When they saw the police cruiser pull up in front of the house, they opened the front door and received the news that no parent ever wants to hear. Mark had died in a car accident. Mark's car had hit a tree, and he'd been thrown from the car, breaking his neck. There were no skid marks, but speed might have been a factor as indicated by the amount of damage to the front of the car. There was no evidence of alcohol or drug use, and the police theorized that Mark fell asleep and went off the road.

In the small town where they lived, the police knew Mark and his car, and they were quite sure that it was he who had been killed. Not only did they recognize him but also his billfold had several items of identification. They had taken him to the hospital, where the coroner had verified his death from a broken neck. Later, Henry and Catherine learned that he hadn't a scratch on him.

Henry and Catherine were stunned. How could their lovely nineteen-year-old son be dead? Although during his years as a fireman Henry had seen plenty of people killed in tragic accidents or fires, he was completely unprepared for the death of his own son. Catherine immediately sat down and cried. Henry quickly joined her in a sobbing embrace.

The policemen knew Henry from his days as a firefighter, and they knew Mark, but it was a requirement that Henry or Catherine go to the hospital morgue to give positive identification. They decided that Henry would go to the morgue and Catherine would stay home to be with the younger children. They wouldn't wake them until it was confirmed that the body was, indeed, Mark's.

As a fire and police chaplain since he enrolled in seminary, Henry had accompanied several distraught parents or family members to the hospital morgue to identify the bodies of loved ones. He never expected to be the one someone else would accompany. It was a short distance to the hospital but in many ways a very long ride.

At the morgue, Henry made the identification that the body was, in fact, Mark's. Feelings of numbness and horror overtook him, and he suddenly found himself hugging Mark's lifeless body and crying. The policemen hung their heads in respectful silence. In the midst of his own grief, Henry made a mental note that the next time he accompanied someone to identify a body, he'd stand close to them and put his arms around them. Never had he felt so lonely.

According to the police, no one had witnessed the accident. Another motorist driving by the scene later saw the car smashed into the tree. Curious, he got out of his car to see if anyone was still in the car and almost stumbled over Mark's body. He then called the police on his mobile phone.

The doctor who examined Mark at the hospital told Henry that death had come quickly for Mark. "He probably never knew what happened," the doctor said. Somehow that was a great comfort to Henry and Catherine. They couldn't imagine the suffering Mark would have experienced if he lay on the ground and lingered even a few minutes in pain. Thus, in the midst of their own pain and grief, they saw the grace of God.

The range of emotions that people often experience when a loved one dies overwhelmed Henry and Catherine and the children.

They were *angry* that death took a bubbly kid in the prime of life, depriving them of seeing him grow up.

They were *depressed* over the profound sense of loss they felt. Nothing like this had happened to them before, and they couldn't have imagined the depth of hurt they felt in their souls.

They reviewed with God, in a *bargaining* kind of way, that they'd given up a great deal to go into full-time Christian ministry. Was this their reward?

They felt *guilty* that Mark hadn't heeded their words of caution about fast driving. And they wondered whether they should have done more.

But through it all they felt a deep sense that God was there for them, that He had not abandoned them, that He knew all about death, having given His own Son in death to redeem them. They were confident that God would sustain them by His grace and would redeem the situation for His glory. It was an *acceptance* of the reality they were facing.

In the days that followed Mark's death, Henry recognized in his own gyrating emotions what the textbooks described as grief feelings. He and Catherine had them all. Back and forth they went. It was a crazy time.

Nor did it help when people made thoughtless and insensitive remarks. They happened to see a man who'd belonged to the church where they'd been members before Henry went to seminary. The man said to them, "Now do you realize it was a mistake to go to seminary? If you hadn't been there, this never would have happened!"

The remark not only hurt Henry and Catherine to the core but also stunned them in its irrationality. *Of course, it might not have happened,* they reasoned, *but other things could have happened had they not gone to seminary, or this could have happened to Mark where they'd lived before. And what kind of theology did this comment reflect? Was God unjust? Did He punish people if they weren't in His will?* Henry and Catherine believed in their hearts that even when a Christian was not walking closely with God, God was still with that person to bring him or her back into close fellowship with Him. And it was their fundamental belief that God used seeming tragedies in ways that human beings could never fully understand. This truth sustained them.

Nevertheless, the man's comment stung them. At least it was an honest statement, Henry and Catherine concluded as they talked about it. Much of the response of people from the church where Henry served as part-time pastor was not discernable. No one said much of anything. No food or meals were brought to the house, and no flowers came from the church. It was hard to figure out what people were thinking. "Perhaps they think a pastor doesn't grieve the same way that they do," Henry said to Catherine.

The response of the seminary community was different. Students, faculty, and staff reached out to the family with many gestures of kindness and with an outpouring of sympathy. And three days after Mark's funeral, Henry graduated with the M.Div. degree. The seminary had given him the option of not attending, but the family wanted him to have the experience of participating in graduation. Deep down, Henry did, too, but he didn't know how he'd get through the service. He was not in the mood for celebrating.

As it turned out, the commencement ceremony itself seemed a little subdued as Henry and Catherine compared it to previous ones they'd attended. When Henry's name was read and he stepped forward to receive his degree, the audience stood as one and applauded loudly. Henry and Catherine had trouble fighting back the tears, and many others did, too. Although they appreciated the sympathy that people felt for them, they hoped that their grief didn't dampen what was a celebratory time for others.

In one of the many ironies Henry was to face in that week of the funeral and graduation, a man in the church where Henry was pastor died on the same day as Mark. When this man was dying of throat cancer, he joked with Henry in the hospital days before he died. "I'll try not to die on the day of your graduation," he'd said, "so as not to mess up that great day for you." As it turned out, this man's body and Mark's body were in adjoining rooms at the funeral home. Henry slipped back and forth between the two rooms, extending pastoral care to people in one room and receiving it from others in the next room. He was not only a pastor but also a father in need of pastoral care.

Mark's funeral was conducted in the seminary chapel with several seminary faculty and administrators participating. A large crowd was in attendance. Denominational officials were there along with the seminary community, and it was a time of weeping and laughing. Participants told and enjoyed funny stories about Mark and the zany things he occasionally did. The next minute brought tears as someone told something about Mark that would be sadly missed.

In the three years that Henry had attended seminary, he'd conducted thirty-seven funerals of parishioners or people in the community of the church he served. Catherine had assisted as the church organist. He didn't know if that was a record, but people in the seminary community teased him about being the person to turn to for a funeral.

Now Henry and Catherine saw how different it was, sitting in the congregation, grieving, rather than up front leading the service. This time their grief was different. This time their grief was for their own son.

The day before Mark's funeral, Henry conducted the funeral of the man in his church who'd died of throat cancer, and Catherine played the organ. A large number of people from the church attended that funeral held in the church sanctuary. But during Mark's funeral, Henry and Catherine looked around the seminary chapel. Later they read the names signed in the book of remembrance during the visiting hours at the funeral home and later at the funeral service itself. They were surprised that not one person came from the church where he was pastor, not even to the funeral home. They were not only surprised but also hurt.

After the funeral for Mark, Henry and Catherine talked about it and wondered if perhaps people at the church couldn't handle two funerals in one week. Or perhaps they saw the seminary community as Henry and Catherine's "church family." Whatever the reason, it bewildered them that not one of their own parishioners attended Mark's funeral. Not one person from the church sent food, flowers, or a sympathy card, or even telephoned to ask how they were doing.

Weeks later, someone at church would occasionally ask Henry or Catherine or the children how they were doing, but it always seemed that the question was done more out of duty than as a genuine inquiry into their well-being. During one particularly stressful period, Henry conducted five funerals in rather quick succession. No sooner had he finished one funeral than a phone call summoned him to offer pastoral care to the family of another deceased person.

Feeling burned out and in need of rest, Henry spoke to the lay leader of the church to request some time off. He cited the several funerals he'd conducted in recent days and how that had been especially hard in light of his son's death. The man replied, "But conducting funerals is what we pay you to do as our pastor." He said further that he didn't think it was a good idea for Henry to take any time off. "The church is full of hard-working people," he said. "They're people who have to put up with a lot of difficulties in their lives. They won't understand your taking time off. They don't get that kind of privilege. They're apt to think you're being wimpy to take time off from doing what you're supposed to be doing, especially now when we've just arranged for you to become our pastor full-time instead of part-time." Henry didn't take any time off.

It was true that the church had just made a momentous decision to take on Henry as their full-time pastor. The congregation was composed of mostly blue-collar working families. For three years the church had been compelled out of financial necessity to accept money from the denomination, enabling them to graduate from having a part-time pastor to a full-time. It wasn't easy for them to admit their financial need, as a matter of pride. They were hard-working people who paid their bills as they went along. Accepting money from the denomination was like taking out a loan. They saw it as bad business. But, in the end, they had accepted the salary subsidy and had begun to refurbish the run-down parsonage so that Henry and Catherine and the children could live in a nice home.

As part of the renovation of the parsonage, the church had started to redo the basement area for Mark because they thought that he, as a nineteen-year-old, might like more privacy. This was a thoughtful gesture that the whole family, especially Mark, appreciated. The work on his living space was begun before he died, but it was never completed after his death. For the three years that Henry, Catherine, and the two children who were still at home lived there, the renovation begun in the parsonage basement area remained as it was the day Mark died. And nothing was ever said about it. To the family, the unfinished room was a constant reminder of Mark's death.

Another oddity for the family occurred when they moved into the renovated parsonage a few weeks after Henry graduated from seminary. No one from the church was there to greet them or to help unload the U-Haul truck. No one brought food. Nor did the lay worship leader say anything about it the next Sunday, although a brief note was included in the worship bulletin that the pastor's family was now in the parsonage and could be reached at the given phone number.

Henry and Catherine laughed about it. They reasoned that since he'd been the part-time pastor who was now full-time, the simple change of status needed, from the congregation's perspective, no further recognition. But Henry and Catherine couldn't get over the feeling that they were somehow considered "outsiders" who didn't quite belong.

Soon thereafter, Henry asked the board of elders if they thought of having an installation service for him as their pastor. When he'd first started part-time, they'd had no installation service but, under the circumstances, Henry thought that was all right. Now that he was there full time, however, he thought it would be an occasion for the church to celebrate. And it might encourage the congregation further that good things were happening in the church. He was unprepared for the board's response.

"Why should we do that?" responded one elder. "You've already been our pastor for three years. I think people would think it strange now if we had some kind of installation something or other." Other board members nodded their heads. The idea was dropped immediately. But Henry and Catherine continued to puzzle over the attitude of the people in the church.

What bewildered them most, however, was how other pastors responded to them in the weeks and months following Mark's death. A total of sixteen churches within the denomination were located in their geographical area. Monthly clergy meetings were held for fellowship, continuing education, and dissemination of denominational information. Henry enjoyed the fellowship with the other pastors and was faithful in attending the meetings. Of those sixteen pastors, only one, Phil, ever asked Henry how he and the family were doing. Phil's inquiries were sincere, and he genuinely wanted to know how they were responding to Mark's death. He became a "soul friend" to both Henry and Catherine in processing their grief over the weeks and months.

Phil recommended that they participate in a grief recovery group run by a community service agency. He'd referred to the group a number of people in his own church who were grieving. "I think you'd find it quite helpful," he said. "It's helped several people from my church, and I participated myself when my first wife died. God used other people who were grieving to minister to me, even though many of them weren't Christians."

Shortly after that, Henry and Catherine joined a new grief recovery group that was forming at the community center. The group was led by a Ph.D. student who was a bereavement counselor and was skilled in group dynamics. As had happened with Phil, God used this group, composed of mostly non-Christians, to minister to them. The group shared experiences, acknowledging and accepting one another's feelings. Henry and Catherine were helped to feel normal and accepted. No one looked down on them or thought it strange that a pastoral couple would be in the group. Henry and Catherine began to realize that it's hard for a congregation to understand the personal needs of their pastor and the pastor's family. The pastor is the one who gives pastoral care to them, not the other way around.

One of the topics discussed seriously during the sessions was how to get through the holidays. Thanksgiving had been a nightmare for many, and most people in the group expressed their dread over trying to get through Christmas without the loved one there. At the end of the group sessions, which lasted six weeks, someone suggested that they have a Christmas party. Another suggested that they all bring a favorite food of their deceased loved one. Henry and Catherine brought Mark's favorite, lasagna, saying that it was the first time they'd made lasagna in the seven months since he died. Others acknowledged that this also was the first time they'd prepared a favorite dish of their loved one.

Following the six weeks of group meetings, individuals and couples had an opportunity to engage in private therapy with the bereavement counselor if desired. Henry and Catherine took advantage of the offer and set up a series of appointments for themselves and also with their son and daughter. In these family therapy sessions Henry and Catherine fully realized how Tim and Betsy were dealing with Mark's death.

Mark's death and the family's grief were ongoing topics of conversation at home, and it seemed to Henry and Catherine that the children were handling their grief well. They were surprised, then, to hear Tim and Betsy talk to the counselor. Tim had shown little outward emotion at the time Mark died or in the weeks following. In the family therapy sessions, however, they learned that for weeks he'd cried himself to sleep every night.

Betsy had turned her grief to anger and was beginning to show signs of rebellion against the Christian faith and the values of her parents. The sessions were times of laughing, crying, honest communication, and deeper understanding of each other's processing of grief. God used the sessions to bring healing to them all.

As a result of the group and family therapy sessions—as well as the numerous funerals that Henry had conducted—Henry began to study the grief process more deeply. It seemed, too, that he was increasingly called upon to help people who'd experienced sudden or tragic deaths of loved ones. On one occasion, the police phoned to ask if he'd join them at a lake where a young man had drowned. The body had just been pulled from the water, and his teenage friends were still at the shore, shocked and distraught. Henry readily agreed to go, and the police cruiser picked him up.

Minutes later, he was at the beach, talking to a dozen or so teenagers. He told them about his own son and about some of the things they'd probably feel in the days to come. It also provided him with an unusual opportunity to talk about the gospel. Henry spoke to them about the hope that is in Christ. He explained that on the basis of Christ's death and resurrection, all who believe in Him by faith are assured of resurrection to eternal life. Several of the teenagers started attending his church afterward.

On another occasion Henry, as volunteer chaplain to the police and fire departments, was called to speak to a man whose wife and child had just been killed in a house fire. He said to the grieving man, "I think I know a bit about what you're feeling." Before he could explain what he meant, the man responded angrily, "You're probably a nice minister, but you're full of it. You have no idea how I feel!"

Henry told him briefly about Mark's death and what he and his family went through. Upon hearing this, the man grabbed Henry in a bear hug and broke down in heaving sobs. It became another opportunity to minister the grace of Christ through the "ministry of presence" to someone at a time of intense need.

For her part, Catherine found music to be a good outlet for processing her grief. In playing the organ, she could "let it rip" if she felt like it. She could choose to sing along with the congregation or, if she didn't want to sing, keep silent while playing. She also found that she could cry while playing the organ and no one would notice. Music was the therapy that God used to bring peace to her soul.

Henry served at this church for six years—three during the years when he was in seminary; three after being called as their full-time pastor. The church grew in numbers and was able to support a full-time pastor on their own, no longer needing the denominational subsidy. But there seemed to be some discontent in the church over Henry's leadership. He was happy, therefore, to accept a call from another church in his denomination. The move would be good for him, he thought, and it would be good for his current church.

Henry and Catherine helped to organize an informal farewell party a week before they left. They knew that even if the church people didn't think of it, some kind of celebration was needed to bring closure to Henry's ministry with them. One of his seminary professors had said, "If you don't say 'good-bye' when you leave a church, you can't say 'hello' in the new one. And if the church doesn't say 'good-bye' to you, they'll never be able to say 'hello' to the new pastor."

So, on Henry and Catherine's last Sunday as pastor, they had a reception in the fellowship hall of the church. In the middle of greeting people individually and saying thank you and good-bye, one woman said to them sharply, "I'm glad you're leaving. I'm sick of all this church growth stuff!" It was true, Henry had talked a lot about church growth, and the church had grown in numbers partly, Henry concluded, because of his emphasis on reaching out to people and "growing the church." He also felt that he'd served the church well and God had blessed the ministry. Henry and Catherine laughed off the woman's crude comment and focused on the many expressions of gratitude and well-wishes from other people.

Henry and Catherine were thankful to move to the new church. As a man in his middle years, Henry realized that God's hand was involved in his finding another church in his denomination. He didn't have the pastoral experience of most men his age who'd started out as a pastor earlier than he. So, with fresh energy, they made a new beginning at a different church, hoping that some of the pain of the past could be put behind them.

In the new church, several people wanted to know the story about Mark's death. Telling the story again provided further opportunity for Henry and Catherine to process their grief. When a family in the church experienced the sudden death of an infant, Henry conducted the funeral and Catherine played the organ. As Henry was giving the meditation, he began to cry, as did Catherine. Soon, most of the congregation was in tears. Although Henry was surprised and embarrassed by his tears, people afterward said that it helped them release their own grief. Henry realized that even several years after losing Mark, he was still fragile and could cry easily when he thought of death.

As part of his pastoral ministry to the church, Henry organized a grief seminar for parishioners. In it, he talked about the stages of grief and taught from the Scripture about death as the enemy overcome by Christ's resurrection. The seminar was held one night a week for four weeks. For one session, Henry asked the director of a local funeral home to address the group. He talked about what services are offered by funeral homes, how the body is handled, how cremation is done, and what were typical expenses. People found this information very helpful.

In the last session, people were asked to preplan their own funeral, writing out what passages of Scripture they'd like read, choosing hymns to be sung, and selecting people they wanted to participate. After discussing their plans with their family, they could leave a copy with Henry for the church files if they so desired. The plans would be a reference that Henry would use if he conducted their funeral. If he'd already moved on when the funeral occurred, his successor would have the plan to follow if needed.

The grief seminar was intended to help people think about issues related to death before they encountered it suddenly with a loved one and found themselves overwhelmed and fragile. In his final comments, he said to those gathered, "We live in a culture that avoids talking about death. People think it's macabre to talk about death, but it happens and we need to be prepared for it. Sometimes we feel afraid of death, so we don't talk about it. It's okay, though, to be afraid of it. Death is the last enemy to be destroyed by our resurrected Lord, but it *is* an enemy. The resurrection of Christ, however, has overcome this and all other enemies of our soul, so we can face even death with hope." To his surprise, people applauded when he finished.

His student intern, Sarah, attended the grief seminar. At one point, Henry saw her crying and assumed that she was feeling again the pain of her husband's death. Sitting next to her was her new boyfriend, and Henry observed that he looked a little uncomfortable. Henry made a mental note to talk to him, wanting to help this young man understand how Sarah might grieve the loss of her husband while still being able to love someone again.

One of the things about which Henry wanted to talk to Sarah and her boyfriend concerned the lack of sympathy that church people tend to show toward pastors in a pastor's time of need. Sarah was called by God to be a pastor and had obvious gifts for ministry. Her boyfriend seemed like a solid man who would be a good life companion for her. But Henry thought they needed to know that clergy are sometimes isolated from their congregations and are seen as different. *How can I help them see this reality without scaring them away from the ministry?* he wondered.

He also continued to be puzzled about the response of fellow clergy to his loss. Henry and Catherine had spent hours talking about this subject. Only Phil, who himself had suffered the loss of a loved one, had reached out to them in any way. This lack of sensitivity was manifest even at the luncheon following Henry's graduation from seminary, where the new graduates and their families were honored. On that occasion, one of the denominational leaders mentioned that pastors often go through difficult times themselves. But he noted that they cannot let that slow them down. At one point in his remarks, he looked squarely at Henry and Catherine and said, "Some of you have recently experienced tragedy, but you have to get on with life."

Henry and Catherine felt the sting of that remark and wondered if their feeling devastated by Mark's death was bad or wrong, or if they'd expressed their grief in some inappropriate way. After the luncheon, however, several faculty members expressed their sadness and anger over the insensitive remarks made by the speaker. Henry and Catherine were reassured that their feelings of anguish were not bad and that God loved them. Several people put their arms around them and said, "We're praying for you." Those people had no idea what an encouragement that was to Henry and Catherine.

Catherine also reflected on how the coworkers at the Christian mission where she worked hardly ever referred to Mark's death. These people were doctors, nurses, counselors, and social workers, but they said little or nothing to Catherine in the days and weeks following Mark's death. The only acknowledgment of how Catherine might be feeling came from her boss, who told her that she could take off as many days as she needed. She appreciated that, but some hugs and words of comfort from the Christians who worked with her would have helped, too. Catherine and Henry rationalized that the staff were busy, working at a hectic pace, and were dealing with huge problems in people's lives. But at the same time they sensed a subtle message from them that the caregiver never needs care.

* * *

Henry must have spent at least an hour thinking about all of these things as he prepared to meet with Sarah. She would be coming soon for their weekly supervisory session. He thought that he'd begin their discussion with some reflections on 2 Corinthians 1:3–4, where Paul said, "Praise be to the God and Father of our Lord Jesus Christ, the Father of compassion and the God of all comfort, who comforts us in all our troubles, so that we can comfort those in any trouble with the comfort we ourselves have received from God." *Would this be helpful to her?* he wondered. What else should he say to her?

Discussion Questions

1. Why do some people in the church assume that pastors are immune to grief?
2. How can pastors communicate their own grief to parishioners without negatively affecting how people might view them as leaders?
3. What are some of the ways churches can minister to a person or family who is experiencing grief? Would these same responses be effective for pastors who grieve?
4. How can a pastor minister to others when he or she is personally struggling with grief?
5. Is it true that our culture avoids talking about death? If so, why? And what can pastors and churches do about it?
6. How can your own experience of grief benefit your own ministry?

7

SPOUSE AND CHILD ABUSE
Conspiracy of Silence

K imberly was broke. She was behind in paying the rent. The utility companies were threatening to cut off electricity and disconnect the phone. The oil company refused to deliver any more heating oil until she paid something on the outstanding balance. And there wasn't much food left in the house for Kim and her three children, ages six, three, and sixteen months.

But her greatest fear was that Matt, her ex-husband, would return and hurt her and the children again. He knew where she lived. In addition to beating Kim and abusing the two oldest children for years, he'd threatened to kill Kim and had actually attempted to do it several times in the past, although not in the last year. But Kim feared that Matt might try something again. Although she committed her well-being to the Lord and trusted Him for protection, at times she was afraid that Matt would appear suddenly at the door and the abuse would start again.

Kim and Matt met in college. They had the same major and, thus, several classes together. Both of them were Christians, which drew them together in one of the Christian organizations on campus of the state college they attended.

They began to date and enjoyed each other's company in studying together, taking walks, and attending campus events. Kim noticed that Matt would occasionally be jealous if she took a walk with one of her many girl friends, but he explained that he wanted to be with her so much that he didn't want to share her with anyone else. He made it sound as though he wanted to be with her more than she wanted to be with him, causing her to feel guilty. So she gradually dropped other friendships and devoted her time exclusively to Matt. He had few friends other than Kim, but she thought nothing of it at the time.

One time when they left class together and were going down the stairs, Kim turned quickly to speak to Matt, who was behind her. In doing so, she accidentally elbowed him in the crotch. He yelped in pain and raised his fist as though he were going to hit her. He didn't, but his face showed fierce anger. Kim apologized profusely, but Matt ignored her and walked on. Other people saw it happen and looked at Kim with alarm. She was utterly embarrassed by the whole thing.

Later in the day, when they were together again, she apologized for accidentally hitting him. He apologized for being angry and stated that he would never hit her. She believed him, of course.

Kim then noticed that when Matt was feeling pressure, writing a paper or studying for an exam, he would be abrupt with her and was generally on edge. On one occasion when he felt stressed, he and Kim were on a double date and he got angry at something the other couple was doing. They were just being goofy with each other, but Matt spoke angrily to them with a slew of filthy obscenities. Kim and the other couple were stunned at such language coming from a Christian.

Matt never apologized for his language, but he explained later to Kim that he was feeling a great deal of stress. Kim asked how she could help. She had a higher grade point average than he did, and he replied that he'd welcome her help in studying and writing papers. His asking for her help surprised her because he sometimes resented her getting better grades than he in the classes they had together.

But she loved academic work and plunged into helping Matt with his studies. After a while, she was virtually writing his papers for him in addition to her own, and she prepared questions to help him get ready for upcoming exams as she studied for them herself.

Kim began to be more concerned about Matt's behavior, his need for her to help him frequently, and the fact that he wanted her exclusively to himself. When she had an opportunity, she asked her pastor what he thought about the situation. The pastor said that he thought Matt was just under stress and that it wasn't really a problem. He added that it wasn't unusual for young people in love to be possessive of the one for whom they cared. He thought that Kim worried too much about it. Matt himself assured Kim that it would be different when he finished college.

Their courtship lasted for three years. During that time, both Matt and Kim felt confirmed in their call from God to enter pastoral ministry together. And they were convinced that God had led them to each other and would bless their marriage. Kim put her misgivings about Matt's controlling behavior behind her, and the relationship grew.

When Matt finished his college degree, Kim still had five courses to go. She had worked part-time on campus during her studies and hadn't been able to take a full load of academic work every semester. But Matt assured her that she could take the classes at one of the colleges near where he planned to go to seminary. She could then transfer the credits back to the state college to receive her degree. After that, they planned for her to engage in seminary studies herself.

A few days after Matt graduated from college, they were married. After a two-day honeymoon, they packed up their belongings from college and moved to seminary. During the summer, they were able to live off the savings that Kim had accumulated from her work throughout college.

Matt began studying Greek in summer school, and Kim was allowed to sit in on the class as a spouse. She grasped the nuances and paradigms of Greek readily and was a big help to Matt, who found it tough going. The pattern thus continued that was set when they were in college—Kim doing much of Matt's academic work for him.

Not long after arriving at seminary, they learned that Kim was pregnant. From the timing of things, she seemed to have conceived the baby on their brief honeymoon. But Kim was strong, healthy, and young, and she threw herself energetically into seminary life and helping Matt with his studies.

By the fall, she'd found a job as an administrator at a social service center funded by the state. It was a demanding job with heavy responsibilities. Kim handled the administrative details of the center's daily operations while the clinic director supervised the social workers and counselors.

Throughout the fall and winter before the baby was born, Kim was busy working full time, doing all of the housework, and listening to the lectures that Matt had recorded in the classes he was taking. Every evening, although she was exhausted, she would help Matt organize his notes. Or she would do research on the topics he chose to write papers on. Eventually, she wrote most of the papers herself, but he affixed his name.

On the rare occasions when he wrote his own papers, he would get a lower grade than when Kim wrote the papers for him. This infuriated him, and he would yell at her, begrudging the fact that she was smarter than he. Sometimes when he lost his temper he would give Kim a shove or hit her with his fist. Kim would cry and ask him to stop behaving like that. He'd sulk and leave her alone, apologizing the next day, promising that he'd never do it again. But he did, and with ever-increasing frequency and intensity.

Kim came home from work tired, especially in the latter stages of her pregnancy. If she didn't have the energy to help Matt with his studies or didn't do it the way he wanted, he yelled at her and often threw things at her. She wondered what the neighbors thought because she was pretty sure they could hear him. On occasion, one of the neighbors would look at Kim with concern.

As the weeks went on, his angry outbursts intensified. Numerous wedding gifts were smashed—glasses, dishes, lamps. One night, he even jumped on the coffee table and broke it into pieces. It was something she'd bought with her own savings before they got married, and she especially liked the design of the piece.

On another night, when Kim was trying to sleep, Matt woke her and asked her to help him with his studies. She'd already done some research for him earlier in the evening and had to go to work in only a few hours. She pleaded to be able to continue sleeping. At that, he yelled, "You always ignore me when I need you!" Then he jumped on the bed and hit her in the back with his knee. The jolt was so hard it knocked the breath out of her.

When she regained her breath, her first thought was for the safety of the baby in her womb. She ran for the door, not knowing where she would go, but Matt blocked the door in a menacing stance. She then ran for the telephone, but he beat her to it and yanked the cord out of the wall. Kim was crying and begging Matt to let her go, but he would not. She sat on the floor and sobbed, saying over and over, "Please don't hurt the baby, please don't hurt the baby." Matt finally calmed down and walked away but kept his eyes on Kim and the door.

The fetus, it turned out, was unharmed, and Kim gave birth to a healthy baby boy a few weeks later, almost nine months from the day they were married. They named him Chad. Kim had worked right up to the day she gave birth and, after taking only two weeks' pregnancy leave, she was back at her job full-time.

The clinic director allowed Kim to bring Chad to work with her. She just worked an hour longer each day to make up for the time she interrupted her work to feed or care for the baby. She was thankful to have a boss who allowed her to do this and for having a job where she could both work and care for the baby. Otherwise, she wasn't sure what she would have done.

Matt was taking a full load of courses, determined to finish his M.Div. in three years. He had little time to care for Chad, and Chad's arrival not only complicated life for Kim but also made it worse. She was now a full-time mother, a full-time employee, and in effect a part-time student, helping Matt with his academic work. Kim did all of the housework—cleaning, washing, cooking. The only thing Matt did to help with household chores was manage the money, all of which Kim earned. She was thankful, however, that at least he handled the checkbook.

Matt did nothing to care for the infant. In fact, he grew increasingly resentful of the time Kim had to spend with Chad. It meant less time for her to spend with him. Although Chad was an unusually good baby, he did cry from time to time, as babies do. More than once, Matt slapped Chad when he was crying. Although Kim spoke sharply to Matt about it, he only glared at her and raised his fist to her in a menacing gesture.

Later, when Matt had calmed down, Kim would ask him never to slap the baby or hit her. One time when she said this without anger but with firmness, he turned to her and shouted, "I'm the man of the house. I'll do what I ____ well please. And don't you ever forget it."

When Matt was angry at Kim not long after that incident, he hit her and then started to hit Chad. Kim grabbed the baby and ran for the door. But Matt caught her and shoved her hard into the wall of the front entrance. She hit the wall so hard that the impact knocked a two-foot-square hole in the wallboard. As she gasped for breath and was examining Chad to see if he was hurt, Matt grabbed her purse, removed the car keys and credit card. With steel in his voice, he looked at her and said, "If you ever try to leave me, I'll kill you." Kim had never felt such fear within her soul. She believed he would do it.

After Matt calmed down, Kim asked what should be done about the hole in the wall. He told her to tell the landlord that she stumbled and fell into it. It was true that she had stumbled on an object on the floor, but mainly she was shoved into the wall by Matt. With embarrassment, however, she told the landlord what Matt required her to say. In her mind, she knew it was a lie, but she didn't know what else to do.

Matt continued to make more and more demands on Kim, especially in his academic work. By his last year in seminary, she was writing all of his papers for him. Sometimes he didn't even read the papers but just turned them in with his name on them. She even did much of his textbook reading. He rationalized that he could honestly say on reading reports that he'd read the required books since he and Kim were husband and wife and would be entering ministry together. Years later, she would tell an acquaintance, "I did all of the work for his M.Div. but got none of the credit."

On rare occasions, Matt would thank Kim for her help and apologize for hitting her. As he did before they were married and in college, he said that when he was out of seminary he would feel less stress. He assured her that life would be better then. In her heart, she wanted to believe him.

Matt had grown up in a church affiliated with a denomination whose polity was similar to that of Baptist or Congregational churches in observing local church autonomy in a fellowship of regional churches. And he continued in that denomination throughout his seminary studies, including doing his field education at a church in his denomination. It was not Kim's background or choice, but she joined the church, knowing that Matt planned to serve in the evangelical wing of the denomination.

Matt had a supervision session with the pastor of the church where Matt did his field education. Afterwards, Matt told Kim that the mentor had asked if he'd ever hit Kim. Kim asked how that came up in the conversation. Matt replied that the pastor asked about Matt and Kim's relationship, and something Matt said caused the man to ask the question about abuse. Matt said that he'd told the pastor that he'd hit Kim but added, "It's not a big deal." He went on to explain to the pastor that he did it only when Kim aggravated him. The pastor looked at him and said, "Well, don't do it again."

Kim was incredulous that the matter had even come up in the supervisory session. She asked the pastor about it the next Sunday, waiting until he'd greeted people following the worship service when no one was around. The pastor just smiled at Kim and said, "I don't think he'll do it any more. I told him not to. He's under a lot of stress with his studies."

Kim started to say, "So am I." But she said nothing. At the time, she found it incredible that someone else was aware that Matt hit her, but all he would say was, "I don't think he'll do it any more." If someone knew about it but did nothing, Kim concluded that it would be of no benefit to tell anyone about the extent of Matt's abuse. She had few friends in the church or seminary to tell anyway. Her life and schedule were too hectic and demanding to make friends. Even when people asked her with concern, "Are you all right?" she always replied, "Yes. I'm fine. I'm just quite busy." But she often wondered if people suspected something when they asked about her welfare.

During seminary, Matt had remained active in maintaining connections with his denomination, including placement options. In his final semester, he had an opportunity to candidate at several churches in the denomination and was called by a church that wanted an evangelical minister. The day after he received his M.Div. degree, Matt, Kim, and Chad moved to his first church. He would last there for three years. And, contrary to his promise to Kim, the stress of pastoral ministry was even greater than that of being a student. His abuse of Kim increased.

Matt had grown up in a family in which the father, Alex, was very controlling. Thus, Matt picked up that pattern quite naturally. Alex, a successful businessman, was also competitive. When Matt told his parents that he wanted to pursue pastoral ministry as a vocation, his father decided to engage in a lay training program that would qualify him to be a bi-vocational pastor in the denomination. Alex was the part-time pastor of a small church in the state where Matt was called to serve. Matt's new church was, in fact, about an hour's drive from Alex's church, and Alex had "pulled some strings" to get Matt placed in the church that called him.

For her part, Kim had grown up in a close family where love and respect abounded. Her mother died when Kim was only ten, but she had fond memories of the tenderness and care her parents had for each other and for her. She had no experience with spouse abuse. She, in fact, didn't recall ever knowing anyone who was a victim of abuse. Now she was being abused regularly herself. Many times she wanted to talk with her father about it, but he had a weak heart after having survived several heart attacks, and his doctor had warned him to live a low-stress life. Kim wondered what would happen to him if he ever found out what she was experiencing.

Once settled in the home church, the reality of her situation set in for Kim. She came to accept that Matt was an abuser and that he would continue his abuse of her and Chad. Stress, living conditions, her or Chad's behavior had nothing to do with Mat's abuse. She began to think seriously about how she could protect herself and Chad in the future.

Listening to Matt preach Sunday after Sunday was especially hard for Kim. The public man and the private man were very different, except that occasionally Matt would be close to losing his temper in front of the congregation or a committee. Kim observed that people sensed his anger just beneath the surface, but no one ever said anything.

The pattern that began in college and continued in seminary continued also in Matt's pastoral duties at the church. At first, Matt only demanded that Kim "help" him in preparing a sermon. Within a year, she was writing the entire sermon for him. He even sought and received approval from the church board for Kim to accompany him to various committee meetings. He said the reason was "so that she can help me organize my time." Kim did more than organize his time, however. She did virtually all of the behind-the-scenes work, but not because she wanted to. True, she greatly enjoyed the tasks and was good at administrative work, but doing what Matt wanted made life easier for her in the long run. She rationalized that if she did what Matt demanded, maybe he wouldn't abuse her so much.

At one point early in their ministry in the church, Kim, with Matt's approval, organized a Bible study for women. Before long, the study group had become popular and was growing in numbers. Matt then informed Kim and the women in the study that he'd do the teaching from now on. Unbeknown to the women, however, he still required Kim to prepare the material, which he then taught. But after a few weeks of Matt's teaching the class, attendance dwindled drastically—a fact not lost on Matt and for which Kim paid dearly.

Kim found great comfort for her soul in studying the Bible and in having private devotions. These were times of peace for her and closeness to the Lord, and helped her cope with the abuse. Matt then stopped her from having devotions on her own, but she had to continue preparing his sermons and Bible studies—and only when he was present to observe her. Still, even these were times when she felt her own soul refreshed, although she'd never let on in front of Matt that such was the case. On occasion, when Matt was in a deep sleep, she'd get out of bed and read the Bible in the kitchen in the middle of the night. If she heard Matt coming on the creaky floors of the old parsonage, she'd hide the Bible and be drinking a cup of hot chocolate when he demanded to know what she was doing. She hated lying to him, but it was better than being hit.

Whenever Matt wanted sex, which was frequently, they did so regardless of whether Kim wanted to. Sex had long ceased to bring pleasure to Kim, but she never revealed her true feelings. The price for being honest in this area—or any other area of their lives for that matter—was too high to pay. Kim had hoped not to get pregnant again, but Matt controlled the use of contraceptives. A little girl was born to them early in Matt's second year in the church. They named her Cheryl.

In the weeks following Cheryl's birth, Kim was still convalescing from the delivery, which had been long and difficult. On a night when the church deacons were meeting, Matt wanted her to accompany him. She simply could not and, to her surprise, he accepted it. But apparently he took out his anger on the board. When he came home from the meeting, he told Kim that he talked with the deacons about the lack of church growth. He told her that he'd said, "This church isn't growing because the people in the church 'suck.'"

Involuntarily gasping, Kim thought their ministry at the church was over at that point. She couldn't imagine his speaking to church leaders like that. Nor could she imagine their accepting it. Apparently they did accept it, however, because nothing ever came of it. When Matt did leave the church less than twenty-four months later, Kim then learned that the deacons hadn't fired Matt on the spot at that meeting out of respect for her and the newborn baby. But they never forgot it.

But before Matt was asked to leave, that conflict was neither the first nor the last the deacons had with Matt. The first occurred when Matt and Kim had been at the church for only a few weeks and Matt informed the board that he'd take his four-week vacation soon. The board said that they thought it was too soon for him to take the full four weeks off after being there for such a short time. Matt looked at them and spoke very slowly, "I said I was going to take my vacation soon, and that's what I will do." The board decided not to press the matter further, but several members wondered then if, as they told Kim later, the church had made a mistake in calling Matt to be the pastor. They weren't used to a pastor who was as controlling as Matt.

The biggest conflict, however, was over changes Matt introduced into the worship service. His father had been to a conference where he was exposed to a contemporary "seeker-sensitive" style of worship. Not only was he enamored with it but also he cajoled Matt into adopting the different format at his church. It was characteristic of Matt that when he decided to do something, nothing would stop him. So he announced one Sunday that a new style of worship would be instituted as soon as a "worship team" could be trained.

After that service, the deacons had a quick meeting and asked Matt to join them. They wanted more information on what changes would be made. When he gave them details of what he had in mind—a praise band, no choir, occasional drama, new music, dispensing with hymnals—the deacons said flatly that the plan would not work. The organist who'd been asked to sit in on the meeting quit on the spot. The deacons said they were open to talk with Matt about how the service could be changed, but stated flatly that what he was proposing could not be done. Under the unified and firm stand of the deacons, Matt backed down. But he never dropped his plan to eventually change the service.

Matt continued to push the idea with the deacons and, eventually, a compromise was reached. A new service at 8:30 A.M. would be offered using the contemporary worship style that Matt was proposing. The 11:00 A.M. service would remain traditional in format. With great fanfare, Matt announced that the new service would begin on a specific date. He was convinced that the new format would attract visitors and enable the church to grow. Kim helped recruit and train the worship team and praise band.

At the first 8:30 service, only six people came. There were more people on the platform than in the pews. But Matt persisted in pushing the service for weeks. At the highest point, however, only eight people were in attendance, and they were all members of the church. No visitors came, even though the service was widely advertised in the community.

Matt was furious over the seeming failure of the 8:30 A.M. service. And he took it out on Kim and the church. One Sunday he shouted and yelled in the sermon for forty-five minutes, departing from the notes that Kim had prepared. "You're all a bunch of deadbeats," he yelled, adding, "I seriously question whether some of you are even Christians." He went on to berate them about almost everything, saying, "I'm the only one who does any work in this church." Kim was so frightened by his words and tone that she was frozen in her seat, scarcely breathing. It seemed to her that this also was true for the rest of the congregation. But in her mind she laughed, *What do you mean that you do the work? I do all the work.* The church emptied quickly and quietly that Sunday morning after the service.

At home, things worsened. The beatings continued, and Matt's threats to kill Kim increased. One time, Matt was so rough with her, Kim thought that he actually would kill her. Were it not for the two children, Kim thought she might take her own life as the only means of ridding herself of the suffering. But she knew she had to stay alive for the sake of the children.

Matt had long before ensured that Kim did not have any credit cards, nor did she have a set of keys to the car or house. At the time, she had never heard of Help for Abused Women and Children (HAWC). Nor did she know of any other help or what to do. In one of his angry rages, Matt had destroyed the two mobile phones they had, and he scrutinized every phone bill to see if she'd called someone he didn't know. Kim had become a prisoner in her own house.

But she grew in her resolve to find a way to escape. Two things happened that helped her in making plans. The first was a credit card offer that arrived in the mail one day. She applied for the card in her name—and then she prayed. She prayed that it would be accepted and would arrive on a day when she could open the mail before Matt came into the room. It worked the way she prayed it would.

The second thing was Matt's asking her to get a second set of keys made for the car. He wanted a spare set handy if he misplaced one set, as he occasionally did. She actually had two sets made, keeping one for herself, and lied to Matt when he grilled her about whether she had had only one set made.

Matt looked through her dresser drawers regularly—ransacked might be a better way of putting it—to see if she had any garments he didn't know about. He even controlled the amount of underwear she was allowed to have. But when he approved of her replacing a piece of clothing, instead of throwing a garment away, she hid articles of her and the children's clothing in the attic in black trash bags, praying that Matt would never look for anything there. She also hid the credit card and the car keys there. This kind of planning went on for several months.

Then one night when Matt roughed her up, he went to the toolshed to get a hammer, threatening to kill her and commanding that she stay in the house. Usually Kim would have obeyed him, but this time she was afraid of what he would do with the hammer. With speed that amazed her, she scrambled to the attic and grabbed the plastic bags. Then she ran to the children's bedroom, grabbed one in each arm, and ran out the front door as Matt was coming in the back. By the time he realized what was going on, Kim was backing the car out of the driveway. As she pulled down the street, Matt came running alongside the car yelling and banging on the car with the hammer. She sped away as Matt threw the hammer and it bounced off the car trunk.

After driving around for an hour, crying and shaking but assuring Chad and Cheryl that they were going to be all right, she pulled into a bank parking lot. Not knowing if the credit card would work, she went to the ATM to get cash. To her delight, it worked.

Next, Kim called the psychiatric unit of the regional hospital, something she had thought about doing if she ever had opportunity to escape from home. She briefly told the counselor on call what had been going on. The counselor told Kim that she'd have to let Matt know where the children were; otherwise, in the state where they lived she could be charged with kidnapping. Before Kim called Matt, however, she phoned his parents and told them what was going on. At first, they didn't believe her, but they drove to see Matt and arrived at the house an hour or so later.

When they asked Matt if the story Kim told them was true, he said yes. But he also defended his behavior by saying that Kim deserved it. His parents requested him to come home with them and he agreed. Meanwhile, Kim had called to say that she had the children and they were all right, but he didn't seem to care. So she didn't tell him where she was, nor had she planned to if he'd asked. She spent the rest of the night at a motel.

The next day, Matt's parents suggested that he see a psychologist, at which point he lost control and started screaming and yelling obscenities. They ended up calling 911, and an ambulance came to take him to the hospital. At the psychiatric unit admission desk, they were informed that, because Matt was married, only he himself or Kim could admit him, not the parents. And the mandatory in-hospital stay was only seventy-two hours. At his parents' urging, Matt finally agreed to have himself admitted. In his mind, he thought he would stay the seventy-two hours for the evaluation, and then he'd leave and deal with Kim.

Told by Matt's parents that he was in the hospital, Kim went to see him there with the understanding that she'd be safe. Through clenched teeth Matt said that he'd be out soon and would find Kim and kill her. She left the room and told the hospital attendant what Matt had said. A doctor immediately went to see him, and Matt confirmed in a matter-of-fact tone that he intended to kill Kim and the children and then kill himself. With this information, the doctor was then able to hold him in the psychiatric unit for an indefinite period of time. This gave Kim peace of mind that she hadn't had in a long time.

Next, Kim phoned the area minister to tell him what was going on, and the minister quickly arranged a meeting with her. She expected him to help her through the coming days. But he was, in fact, no help at all and ended up making matters worse. His primary concern seemed to be how things would look to the community. He instructed Kim to tell no one in the church about any details of the abuse. Nor was she to say what Matt was being treated for in the hospital. When Kim asked, "But what do I say if people ask me what's wrong?" he replied that she could say one of three things: (1) Matt was getting better; (2) he is the same; (3) he is still undergoing tests. She was aghast and again stated that she wanted to tell people what was happening. The area minister then flatly stated that she was to say nothing to anyone. He implied that he could make it difficult for Kim if she didn't follow his instructions. His firm demeanor resulted in Kim's saying nothing to people, which was not hard to do because she'd already borne her suffering in silence for a long time.

The weeks that followed were a blur. Kim moved back to the house with the children because Matt was in the hospital. The area minister made arrangements for pulpit supply at the church, preaching occasionally himself. The only information given to the congregation was that Matt was ill and needed to be hospitalized. Many people asked Kim what had happened, and she replied vaguely that tests were still being done. After a few weeks of her noncommittal responses, people stopped asking her about Matt. Kim sensed that people felt awkward about the whole situation, but she felt powerless to do anything because of the "gag order" given her by the area minister.

Speculation abounded, however, that Matt had experienced some kind of a breakdown. Some people in the church said that he must have had a heart attack as a result of his pent-up anger. A few people who tried to visit him in the hospital learned that he was in the psychiatric unit and could not receive visitors. That's when most people were convinced that he'd had a breakdown of some kind.

The psychiatrist treating Matt also met with Kim many times. He helped her understand the nature of spouse and child abuse. In doing so, he told her that abusers fit into ten categories with three or four characteristics usually present in any one person. In Matt's case, the doctor thought that he fit all ten categories and would never change although medication would help to suppress his anger. Treatment, however, was tricky because Matt was also diagnosed as bipolar with a narcissistic personality disorder. The best treatment plan for Matt, the doctor concluded, would be for him to be hospitalized for the rest of his life, but this would not be possible given the state laws pertaining to the mentally ill. At some point, the doctor said, he would have no choice but to release Matt.

That day finally came, and Matt was released to the custody of his parents. He didn't return to the church or the parsonage. By this time, the area minister, after arranging for an interim pastor to serve the church, decided to declare the pulpit vacant and inaugurate a search for a new pastor. He then decided that the best course of action would be to call a congregational meeting to explain that Matt would not return as their pastor.

Kim had little contact with the area minister during Matt's hospital stay. Then she heard the announcement in church one Sunday that the area minister had declared the pulpit vacant and was calling for a congregational meeting. She phoned him, saying that she thought it was time for her to tell the whole truth to the church.

She'd been meeting regularly with a woman minister for encouragement and help. Arranging for this support was the one good thing the area minister did to help Kim. Her talks with this pastor had helped her not only in her perspective on abuse but also on how to stand up for herself. She insisted that she be allowed to speak to the church.

The area minister said that he'd allow her to do so but only if he could approve the statement in advance. She agreed, albeit reluctantly, to this condition. He edited the statement by deleting the more stark descriptions of abuse, which Kim accepted because it was still clear that gross abuse had occurred.

At the meeting, which was well attended by church members, the area minister reported that Matt's health would not permit him to return as pastor and that a search committee for a new pastor would need to be formed. He then announced that Kim had a statement to make. He stated further that he was committed to helping the church through this difficult time. Then he invited Kim to read her statement.

As Kim read her statement, the room was deathly quiet. Kim could hear her own heart beating. One thing Kim noticed, however, is that no one looked surprised. No one gasped or appeared distressed when she described in general terms the abuse that she and the children had received at the hands of Matt. She concluded that no one was surprised by what she had to say.

The only surprised look was on the face of the area minister—and Kim knew that he was merely acting. When Kim sat down, he announced that this was the first he'd heard of the abuse. Kim couldn't believe what she heard, but she sat frozen in her chair. Later, she said that she wished she'd jumped up and screamed, "That's a lie!"

The area minister then stated the meeting was adjourned. But before anyone got up to leave, a woman called, "But what about Kim? Can she stay in the parsonage?" A brief discussion ensued and, in the end, a motion was approved that allowed her to stay in the parsonage for six months.

Someone then asked about salary for Matt and Kim. The area minister replied that the denomination's insurance plan would cover the salary at two-thirds' level under provisions of the long-term disability (LTD) coverage. He then dismissed the meeting and went into an adjacent room to meet with the board of deacons. Kim never learned what happened in that meeting.

When the congregational meeting was adjourned, several people came by to express their concern for Kim. Some of them said they weren't surprised to hear about the abuse, that they suspected it was happening but didn't know what to do about it. Others expressed anger that Kim had not said anything about it before now. Most people just left without saying anything.

All of that had occurred a number of months ago. A few days before Kim had escaped from the house to avoid being beaten by the hammer, she and Matt had sexual intercourse, and Kim became pregnant. The very week she delivered the baby, another boy, whom she named Connor, the six-month grace period ended that allowed her to stay in the parsonage. She hoped that she could stay a little longer since no new pastor had been found. The church clerk phoned her a week before the six months ended, however, and reminded her that she needed to vacate the parsonage.

Even with a five-year old, a two-year-old, and a newborn infant, she managed to find a place in town to rent. Finances, however, were in short supply. The LTD benefit was sent to Matt, not to her. Although the court had ordered Matt to pay child support, he never sent anything to Kim. On the advice of the psychiatrist and the minister who counseled Kim, she obtained a divorce from Matt, but she was constantly apprehensive about what he might do to her and the children.

In the following months, Kim's financial situation became bleaker still. With three young children, she had no possibility of working. Food stamps, meager welfare money, and help from the area Women, Infants, and Children (WIC) program were nowhere near what she needed to live on, even on a poverty level. And she had no parents to help her. Her mother had died when Kim was ten; her father had died several months ago of a heart attack, a few days after he learned about Matt's abusing Kim and the children.

She had little money for rent and utilities, for counseling for her and the children, or for a car or health insurance. And the church gave no assistance. Kim had felt awkward in going to the church after the truth was known. She felt as though the people would rather she not be there, so she left quietly. That was months ago, and only a handful of people had called to ask how she was doing or to offer any help.

Kim was aware that she might be put out on the street at any time because of unpaid rent and overdue bills. But she didn't know what to do. She was attending another church in town, and the minister there took time to talk with her and pray with her, but the church was small and had limited means to assist her financially. Still, that church did what it could, but it was not enough to make ends meet.

As Kim reflected on her plight, a host of questions swirled in her mind. It seemed as though she'd lived in a conspiracy of silence—her own, the church's, the area minister's. How could it have been handled differently by everyone, including her?

How would she make it financially? Where could she turn for help? The children sometimes didn't have enough food to eat, and the diet on which they all lived was not healthful. How could this change, given their financial plight?

Should she do anything to protect herself and the children from Matt if he should suddenly appear at the door?

At one time, she had felt a call to ministry herself, but without a college or seminary degree would she be accepted by a church or Christian ministry? Should she even think about this as a possibility?

Would her divorce prevent her from being accepted and employed by a church in the future if she were able to get a seminary degree someday?

As she thought about these questions, she reminded herself that God loved her and always would. She thought, however, that the church did not, and she didn't know what to do about it.

Discussion Questions

1. From your perspective, how pervasive is the problem of abuse in the church today?
2. If you are aware of or suspect spouse and/or child abuse in your church, what should you do?

3. What Scripture passages come to mind as you think about a Christian response to spouse and child abuse?
4. How can preaching help people who face abuse but who never come forward with the story? What are some of the things churches can do to aid victims of abuse?
5. How do you evaluate Kim's handling of the situation?
6. Why do victims tend to stay in abusive situations for so long?
7. What kind of help would you give to Kim and the children? To Matt?
8. As you see it, would Kim's situation prevent her from entering ministry?
9. Evaluate how the church and area minister handled the situation.

ALCOHOL ABUSE
When Change Doesn't Happen

David sighed. He wondered if the cycle with Keith was about to be repeated. He had just finished a phone call from Keith, a member of the church where David was senior minister. Keith was an alcoholic who would remain sober for months but then would "fall off the wagon." This looked like one of those times.

In a way, David didn't mind extending pastoral care again and again to Keith. He, in fact, enjoyed their times together. What he found perplexing, even frustrating at times, was that Keith continued to struggle with alcohol years after he'd become a Christian. Keith seemed sincere in his repentance whenever he'd sober up after a binge, and he'd beg for God's help to overcome his desire for alcohol. But nothing seemed to work. The question in David's mind as he'd talked with Keith over the years was whether Keith would ever find complete victory over alcoholism in this life. But David determined to keep meeting with Keith, encouraging him to maintain his contacts with Alcoholics Anonymous and assuring him of God's grace and forgiveness.

Grace and forgiveness were concepts that Keith had trouble accepting. He simply couldn't understand God's unconditional love. "How can God love or forgive me," he often asked David, "when I fall so short of His expectations?" Even joining the church was a big effort for Keith because he thought he could never measure up to people's expectations. A decade of David's talking about grace and eternal life with Keith didn't seem to get through to him. He simply couldn't understand God's grace and saw himself as unworthy of it. David wondered if Keith's not embracing grace or accepting God's forgiveness might be contributing factors to his occasional bouts of binge drinking. But he also knew that Keith was an addictive personality and manifested instability in other areas of life as well.

Keith was in his mid-forties, but David knew little of his background. Keith didn't want to talk about that, and his reluctance to reveal anything caused David to surmise that it wasn't good. Keith wasn't married, although he'd been engaged several times. The women to whom he'd been engaged broke off the relationship when they learned that he was an alcoholic and would binge drink.

Currently, Keith was dating Sandy, a woman in the church. As far as Keith was concerned, it was a serious relationship, and he'd even asked Sandy to marry him. But Sandy wanted to proceed slowly. She herself came from a family where alcohol abuse was present, and it had left its mark on her. Although she understood alcoholism and had vowed never to get involved with anyone who was an alcoholic, she was drawn to Keith. But she was also wary.

Their relationship almost ended when Keith was arrested for driving under the influence of alcohol. But Keith was deeply remorseful afterward when he and Sandy met with David. They had all prayed together for God's help to give Keith victory, and Sandy agreed to continue the relationship. She wasn't yet ready, however, to accept his proposal of marriage. David encouraged them to take whatever time was necessary before getting married. He'd seen enough marriage breakups in his twenty-five years of ministry to know that it took stable commitment on the part of both the husband and the wife to keep a marriage together.

David wondered what would now happen to the relationship. Keith had just called about a binge drinking episode that had resulted in another DUI arrest. It had been more than a year since the last DUI arrest, but this new one might push Sandy over the edge and cause her to break off the relationship altogether.

Other indicators also showed that Keith was not stable. He'd been unable to hold any job for a long period of time. In the ten years he'd been attending David's church, he'd had four or maybe five different jobs. He lost some of the jobs because of his alcoholism, but other jobs were positions that Keith had left on his own. He just couldn't settle down to any one job over the long haul. It was clear that Keith had a restlessness about him, and Sandy indicated that it, too, was a factor in her caution about marrying Keith.

The one thing at which Keith excelled was working with the church's sound system. With a background in electronics, he'd designed the system now used in the church sanctuary. David greatly appreciated Keith's skill because he'd attended churches where the sound system was in bad shape. He knew how frustrating it could be for the preacher and the listeners when the sound system wasn't good. Too, David's current church, at which he'd been pastor for eighteen years, was located near a major university. Students, staff, and faculty attended the church in large numbers, and they had high expectations for a well-crafted and high-level worship service. David had seen attendance at worship on Sundays grow to more than nine hundred in three morning services. David was a good preacher and senior minister, and he appreciated a good sound system, as did the people of the church. They had Keith to thank for that.

Another contribution Keith made to the church was initiating an Alcoholics Anonymous group. Other churches in town had AA groups, but the initiative for the group had come from AA, not someone in the churches. And in those cases most of the attendees came from outside the congregation, not from the church where the meetings were held. In this case, however, Keith had asked David if the elders might support an AA group's being started at the church. It would be open to anyone who wanted to come, whether from within or outside the church, because it would be listed with other AA groups meeting in the city. But Keith hoped that anyone in the church who had an alcohol problem would find it not only convenient but also helpful to be in a group with other church members. He reasoned that their fellowship and accountability *as Christians* would be strengthened.

David took the request to the board of elders, and they held a lengthy discussion. They debated the costs to the church in terms of heat, lights, and janitorial services. After a review of liability issues and, after ascertaining that no additional rider needed to be added to the church's umbrella insurance policy, the board unanimously approved the request. The only restriction placed on the group by the board was that no smoking could be done in the building. This was a common policy observed by other churches where AA met.

The AA group had been in existence at the church for over two years now and was a successful outreach ministry of the church. A few church members were involved as participants, but it was composed mostly of people from outside the church. Some of these people had started attending worship services at the church as a result of AA's meeting there. Those members who weren't already Christians, David prayed for, and he was convinced that, in time, they would become Christians.

When the AA group first started at the church, David and the elders wondered if the congregation would be concerned or displeased about it. An announcement was placed in the church bulletin for two or three weeks in advance of the first meeting, but no one said anything or raised a question. And even when the meetings continued to be included in the weekly schedule, no one ever said anything about it. David was relieved that no problems had arisen, and he was glad to see the group use the church. He was especially glad for Keith's involvement.

David now thought back to when he first met Keith. Ten years ago Keith had started attending David's church through the influence of a coworker at Keith's place of employment. At the time, Keith said that he'd become a Christian a long time before he started attending this church, but he'd always struggled with the notion that God would forgive sinners. He thought that he had to get his life straightened out before God would accept him. Then he'd be good enough to come to church. The coworker assured him that the church was for sinners who needed constant forgiveness from God. "What better place to be with fellow sinners than in the church?" he asked Keith. "Especially a church that takes seriously the good news of forgiveness from God and eternal life through Christ." Keith expressed a bit of surprise that someone would actually refer to church people as sinners. For some reason, he thought that church people viewed themselves as beyond sin, so he thought that he could never be part of a group like that.

When Keith first started coming to church, his attendance was sporadic. He would come for two or three Sundays in a row and then be gone for weeks. Keith's coworker had introduced Keith to David, so David knew who he was. And the church used a system whereby attendees recorded their names on a loose-leaf notebook in each pew. David, however, didn't look at that information regularly. An elder was responsible for reviewing the attendance record and kept the pastoral staff and board of elders informed of patterns. This is how Keith's sporadic attendance was first noted.

But when, at Keith's initiative, he and David started meeting together regularly, Keith began to attend worship more consistently. David wasn't trained as a pastoral counselor, but he was known as a good preacher with a solid understanding of biblical teaching. Thus, he talked with Keith from a theological perspective, fulfilling his calling as Keith's pastor and enjoying pastoring Keith. He also enjoyed talking with Keith about the very real grace and mercy of God, about how Christ's death atoned for sins, there being no way that any human being would ever be good enough to achieve salvation through his or her own efforts. David repeatedly stressed to Keith that eternal life is given to believers on the basis of Christ's perfect sacrifice on the cross, not human goodness or perfection.

Keith understood these truths on one level. But most of the time he was so overwhelmed by feelings of guilt and inadequacy, it seemed that the message was, indeed, "too good to be true." The major stumbling block to Keith's fully embracing God's grace and forgiveness was that he continued to struggle with alcoholism. He pleaded with God time and again to give him victory over his desire to drink, but if that didn't happen, he prayed that God would at least help him be disciplined enough never to take another drink. He knew that once he had even one small drink, his thirst for alcohol would not be assuaged until he'd had too much. When this happened, it only increased his feelings of unworthiness and failure before God. In a vicious cycle, he saw himself letting God down—but he also felt that God had let him down.

Still, David never tired of talking with Keith about grace and forgiveness. On more than one occasion, he reminded Keith of the apostle Paul's "thorn in the flesh" and how the answer for Paul was that God's grace was "sufficient" to help him live with whatever the thorn was. On one level, Keith found comfort from this sufficiency, but he also longed to be rid of his "thorn" in *this* life. It was hard for him to think that full deliverance would occur only in the new life to come in God's heavenly kingdom.

"If you fall," David always reminded Keith, "seek God's forgiveness and believe on the basis of what Christ has done for you that you are forgiven. Then get up and go on with your life, knowing that you are forgiven." David had repeated this phrase so often that when he began to say it again, Keith would finish the sentence. They'd laugh about it. Keith would then sigh and say something like, "I just wish I could be different *now*, in *this* life." David said that he wished the same thing for Keith, but inwardly he sometimes wondered why repentance and a genuine desire for change didn't always yield the results believers wanted. The hard truth, David realized, is that genuine repentance and desire to change don't always bring about actual change, especially with an addiction such as alcoholism.

David saw his role with Keith as that of a theological friend and pastor. Whenever Keith had another bout with alcohol, they would meet several times and talk about grace and forgiveness and would pray for Keith to be disciplined not to take a drink in the future. Then weeks or months would go by with no sessions because Keith was sober at those times.

Keith was also faithful in attending AA meetings, sometimes several meetings a week. David strongly supported Keith's involvement in AA, and when they counseled together, David always asked Keith if he was keeping up with his accountability partner. Keith would always say *yes*, but that didn't keep him from slipping occasionally—a reality of which both of them were keenly aware, but they continued to hope for change.

In the past, David had recommended that Keith seek help from a professional counselor, but Keith said, "Been there, done that. Didn't work." He'd rather talk with David as his pastor and continue his involvement in AA. David never pushed the matter further.

Another ongoing situation that continued to concern David was Keith's tendency to lie. Several times David had caught Keith in a lie about something in his personal life or church activity. Sandy had observed Keith's tendency to deceive, which added to her reluctance to make a commitment to marry him.

The frequency of Keith's deception, however, had decreased measurably over time. One reason was Keith's high level of trust in David. He would gently confront Keith about his lying but never stopped talking to him or even considered breaking off the relationship. Another reason was Keith's desire to continue the romantic relationship with Sandy. She'd made very clear to Keith that she couldn't continue in the relationship if she couldn't trust him. "You simply must be truthful with me all of the time," she insisted. "Otherwise, our relationship is over."

Deceit and falsehood were so ingrained in Keith's way of living and talking that it was hard for him to change. Although Keith showed signs of improvement in this area, neither David nor Sandy was fully persuaded that they could always believe what Keith said. They were happy to acknowledge progress, but they also knew that deceit was simply a way of life for Keith. Nonetheless, they continued to hope that progress in this area would lead to complete change.

David also observed that commitment—staying power—was an ongoing trouble spot for Keith. Keith not only jumped from job to job every year or so—apparently often of his own doing—he was also inconsistent about showing up where and when he'd promised. Whether for a church meeting or a pastoral counseling session, David had learned to have a "plan B" ready if Keith didn't show up. Although Keith was more responsible now than when he first came to the church, he still manifested a pattern of not showing up when he was expected.

Keith's issues related to commitment were a factor, too, in his taking two or three years to finish the classes required to become a member of the church. The classes were offered for six weeks, three times a year. Keith would come for a class or two and then not show up again, only to continue with the classes he missed when the course was offered the next time around. But he finally completed the required classes and joined the church.

The two activities, however, to which Keith was able to maintain a commitment were attending AA meetings and running the sound system at church. On Sundays, he was in the sound booth at all three morning worship services. David appreciated Keith's professional help, and occasionally joked that Keith could preach the sermon at the third service because he'd already heard it twice.

When just this past Sunday, then, Keith didn't show up, it triggered an alarm bell for David. He wondered if something had happened to Keith. Other assistants were able to oversee the sound system in Keith's absence, but David wasn't surprised when Keith phoned to say that he'd been arrested on a DUI charge and spent the weekend in jail. Keith asked if he could come by to talk with David, and they had set an appointment.

Sandy phoned David shortly after Keith had called. She asked if she could join the session, and David was quick to say that she was welcome. She often accompanied Keith to the sessions with David, so nothing about her request was unusual. But David detected a note of sadness in her voice this time. He wondered if it meant that Sandy was giving up completely on the relationship.

In addition to Keith's steadfast commitment to AA and being the church's sound engineer, he had always been committed to pursuing Sandy. Although she wanted to go slowly in the relationship, she was open to the possibility of marriage if Keith could remain sober over the long haul. David wondered if Keith's falling again would be the last straw for her. If so, it would be a huge blow to Keith. But he also wondered if Keith's fall would be a huge blow to Sandy.

On the one hand, David looked forward to talking with Keith and Sandy again. He expected that they'd discuss grace and forgiveness and admission of failure and sin, then the need to grasp forgiveness and move on with life. But David had begun to wonder if this was enough. A number of questions were on his mind. *Was AA and the pastoral care that David extended to Keith enough? Should David insist that Keith go to a professional counselor? If Keith agreed, what would David's role with Keith be then? If Keith refused to see a counselor, what should David do? Should he break off the relationship and risk losing Keith altogether, or hang in there in hopes that Keith might eventually seek professional help?*

David knew a little about aversion therapy, where medication was taken that caused a person to be violently sick if alcohol were consumed. *Would this work for Keith?* he wondered. *Or would Keith simply not take the medication if he wanted a drink? How long would it take for the medication to get out of Keith's system if he wanted a drink badly enough?*

David also thought about the congregation's role with Keith. Because the church was so large—more than nine hundred people in Sunday worship—it was easy to be invisible. Much of the congregation was highly educated and Keith hadn't gone beyond high school. Thus, he didn't feel comfortable in the small groups the church organized. The one place where David thought Keith might find fellowship and friendship was a men's group that met regularly. This group embraced the type of inspiration and commitment experienced at Promise Keepers' meetings. But so far Keith hadn't been interested in participating in the group. *Should I push harder for Keith to join the group?* David wondered. *And if he refuses, what should I do?*

Other questions came to David's mind. *What was the congregation's responsibility toward a fellow believer who was hurting?* David surmised that most people didn't even know that Keith was an alcoholic. *Should it somehow be made known? Would Keith allow David to make some kind of discreet disclosure to selected people or even a larger group in the church in hopes that fellow believers would be of support and help to Keith?*

David also thought what Sandy's reaction would be to Keith's latest slip. If she broke off the relationship, David would need to be sensitive to the hurt that both Keith and Sandy would experience. Sandy, too, might be angry with Keith, and David had observed that Keith didn't cope well with anyone's anger toward him; it reinforced his feelings of inadequacy and worthlessness. *But if Sandy decided to continue in the relationship with Keith, what would she need from me as her pastor?* he wondered.

The fundamental question in David's mind, though, related to how repentance affects change in behavior. He knew that God's grace and forgiveness were there for Keith, but he asked himself, *Why does Keith's repentance not result in change for him? How do repentance, grace, and change fit together? Does repentance mean that something has to change? Why does victory over something in this life not always happen when it seems so right and good? Perfection and holiness will come in the next life, that's for sure, but why can't it happen now when it seems to be the best thing and is so desperately desired? Can one never be free of addictions in this life?*

As these questions raced through his mind, and not for the first time, David also contemplated his role as pastor. Praying for guidance, he wondered once again how he might be used of God to help redeem this situation.

Discussion Questions

1. How can addictive behaviors such as alcoholism distort one's understanding of God's grace?
2. Why don't genuine repentance and forgiveness always produce complete victory?

3. When is it time for a pastor to insist upon professional counseling for alcoholics?

4. What forms of therapy are appropriate for alcoholics, including aversion therapy? In the therapy process, how can a pastor be of help?

5. Is it appropriate to set restrictions on the kinds of church activities in which an alcoholic can participate? If so, what are some examples of such limitations?

6. Who in the church has a right and/or responsibility to know about an addictive problem of a parishioner? How can this information be disclosed appropriately?

7. How can a church minister to alcoholics who are both inside and outside the church?

9

ADULTERY

One of Life's Deepest Wounds

This was to be Clayton's final Sunday as pastor of the church. As he sat on the platform, listening to the organist play the prelude music, he surveyed the congregation. *The people look despondent and troubled,* he thought. *Is it because I'm concluding my ministry at the church? Or is it because of the news that Barry committed adultery with Pam?* Barry was one of the leading members of the church, Pam the church secretary. *Maybe,* Clayton thought, *it's a combination of both.*

Trying to concentrate on the worship service that was about to begin, Clayton couldn't help noticing Barry sitting by himself at the back of the church. Barry looked as though he was about to cry, maybe crying already. Toward the front of the church, Barry's wife, Alice, sat with two of their three children. The sixteen-year-old son looked angry. It was hard to discern what the five-year-old daughter was thinking. Confused, perhaps? The one-year-old infant was in the nursery. Alice looked gaunt and distressed.

Clayton scanned the congregation looking for Pam. But he didn't see her anywhere. So many thoughts were flitting through his mind, but the prelude had ended and the choir was singing the introit. It was about time for him to lead God's people in worship on this, his last Sunday as their pastor.

Only a few weeks earlier, Clayton had accepted a call to be pastor of another church. He'd been the pastor of his current church for several years, and he'd increasingly sensed that it would be good for both him and the church if he were to seek another call. The district superintendent was helpful in arranging for him to interview at another church in the denomination he served. The interview and candidating process had gone well, and Clayton and his wife, Janet, thought he was a good match for the needs of the new church. That church did, indeed, vote to call him to be their pastor. After a week of praying about it and discussing it with his wife and the leaders of his current church, Clayton accepted the call to the new church.

When he and Janet returned from the final interview at the new church, he learned of the adulterous relationship between Barry and Pam. When Clayton came into the church office on his first day back, he was surprised that Pam wasn't in the office; as church secretary, she was always at her desk. A telephone message in Pam's handwriting lay on his desk, stating that Alice had called. The slip was marked "urgent."

Clayton phoned Alice. "My husband is having an affair with the church secretary," she said, her voice strained.

"Are you sure?" Clayton asked, dumbfounded.

"Quite sure," Alice responded. "If you'd been here the past few days, you would've read about it in the newspaper."

This statement surprised Clayton even more. "What happened?" he stammered.

Alice asked Clayton to come to her house to talk about it, preferring not to discuss it over the telephone. He quickly agreed to come as soon as possible and called Janet to ask her to pray for him, especially at this time. He hurriedly told her what he'd learned.

As he drove to Alice's house, he surmised the reason Pam wasn't at her desk in light of the news he'd just heard. But he still had trouble believing that Barry and Pam were having an affair. He thought he knew Pam pretty well and couldn't imagine her being unfaithful with another woman's husband. On the other hand, she was always so dependable, her not being in the office and not leaving a note gave credibility to the news. *Was she too embarrassed or ashamed to come to work?* he asked himself. *Or had something else come up?* It wasn't like Pam not to leave a note if she wouldn't be there when he returned. But perhaps her way of informing Clayton was her urgent note to phone Alice.

At Alice's house, the story tumbled out. Although she'd suspected her husband, Barry, might be having an affair with Pam, she wasn't sure until just a couple of days earlier. Barry had come home later than usual and broke the news that he'd been arrested and suspended from his job. He then revealed the affair to Alice.

Both Alice and Barry were police officers, he for the town in which they lived, she a part-time officer in one of the suburban communities nearby. They had met, in fact, at a police event, had fallen in love, and Clayton had had the privilege of officiating at their wedding. It was the first marriage for both, although Alice had a son born outside of marriage some years before. When Alice and Barry got married, her son was six years old. Barry adopted him and was happy to be the adoptive father. After Alice and Barry tried unsuccessfully to conceive a child of their own, they made arrangements to adopt a baby girl from Russia. That was two years ago. Shortly after adopting their daughter, Alice conceived, and the new baby was now a year old.

Alice and Barry gave every appearance of being a happy couple. Barry was known as a good police officer; Alice enjoyed being a good mother to the children, now ages sixteen, five, and one. The whole family was active in church. Clayton, in fact, considered Alice and Barry the primary leaders of the church. And their son was one of the spark plugs in the church youth group.

The Christian testimony of both Alice and Barry was well-known in the town. Both had been instrumental in organizing a Bible study and prayer group among their fellow police officers. Barry had spoken at high school events on matters of police work and crime prevention, and had always been able to include appropriate comments about his Christian faith in those talks.

But other police officers, especially headquarters' supervisors, were suspicious of how Barry used his time. Another police officer, for instance, had seen Barry in a restaurant with Pam. That officer inspected the log at the end of the day, and noticed that Barry hadn't recorded his being at the restaurant. *Every* activity while on duty was supposed to be noted in the log, but the log didn't indicate that Barry had even visited the restaurant while on duty. The officer reported the omission to Barry's supervisor.

As Alice was telling Clayton these details, Clayton recalled a time when he, too, came across Barry and Pam in a restaurant. Clayton came over to greet them and noticed they appeared uncomfortable, but he chatted with them for a few minutes and left. He thought it strange that Pam said nothing about it when she returned to the office after lunch, but he assumed nothing was amiss and thought no more about it—until now.

When he mentioned this incident to Alice, she replied with some embarrassment that she'd heard similar reports from other people. That's when she'd begun to suspect that something was going on between Barry and Pam. Alice said that she even called Pam one day to ask if anything was going on, and Pam, with some degree of hesitancy, rather nonchalantly indicated that nothing was happening between her and Barry. But she had seemed a little flustered to Alice, and Alice said to her rather icily, "You'd better stay away from my husband." Pam had said nothing in response, which only added to Alice's suspicion.

The police, however, after the omission in the police log was discovered, initiated a surveillance team to monitor Barry's activities. He was tailed, and on many occasions was found going to Pam's house, frequently while on duty. These visits, though, were never noted in the police log. The visits to Pam were not short, and on the night when he was caught, the police stormed the house and found him and Pam together in bed.

It was a rather dramatic entrance on the part of the police, but the supervisors were anxious to keep goodwill with the community. Police ethics, especially on the part of one who was a Christian, were uppermost in their minds. It was, in fact, standard police policy for officers on duty to practice good moral ethics. Barry was arrested, taken to the very police station where he himself was assigned, and booked on charges of engaging in adultery while on duty and of falsifying police reports. He was immediately suspended with pay while the official investigation took place.

A very broken man, Barry came home to tell Alice about it. He cried, asked for forgiveness, and said that he'd do anything to make it up to her. He indicated that he didn't want to lose their marriage and that he'd never see Pam again.

"That will be hard to do," Alice retorted, "She's the church secretary and you deal with her all the time." In her own anger and despair, Alice asked him to leave the house immediately. As he gathered a few belongings and left, both were crying.

Never had Alice felt such a crush of emotions. One minute she was so angry that she thought her head would explode. The next minute she was weeping uncontrollably. Then she wanted to scream her head off and break things. Deep down she felt a hurt that she'd never known. Her husband had broken his covenant vows to have her, and no one else, as his wife. He'd betrayed her. *Death would be better than this,* she said to herself, adding, *His death, not mine.* She wanted to hit him.

In the agony of that night, Alice also wondered if she'd contributed to his affair with Pam. With the demands of keeping the home running smoothly, parenting three children with their multiple activities, caring for the incessant needs of a one-year-old, and working part-time as a police officer herself, she didn't have much energy left for intimacy and activities with Barry. Church involvement consumed much of their free time as well. She kept asking herself, *How much of this affair is my fault?*

In the morning, after a sleepless night, Alice made herself a cup of coffee and retrieved the morning newspaper from the front porch. There on page one was a picture of Barry with policemen on both sides of him holding his elbows. The caption read, "Well-known police officer arrested." The accompanying article gave details of what had happened and indicated that the mayor had promised a full inquiry into Barry's conduct. Alice dissolved in tears.

Alice had wanted to call Clayton and seek his counsel immediately, but he was away. She didn't know at the time that he was candidating at the new church; it had been announced in church only that he was taking a few days of vacation. So there was nothing she could do but wait.

When the children awoke, she told them that their father had been arrested because of some "bad behavior" but that it had nothing to do with them. She explained that he'd be living somewhere else for a time while she and he sorted things out. She also emphasized that she was there for them, and although their friends would know that something happened, they should go on about their activities as best they could.

The five-year-old couldn't fully comprehend what was going on, and accepted her mother's explanation with little comment. She trundled off after breakfast to get ready for her half-morning of kindergarten. The son, however, was full of rage. "How could Dad do this?" he exploded. His anger only intensified as he read the newspaper. When Alice saw him fighting back his tears, the dam burst for her, and she melted in her own tears.

Her big, strapping son embraced her and said, "It's okay, Mom. We'll get through this."

Although Alice told him that he could stay home from school if he wanted to, he opted to go. "I think I'd like to see my friends," he said. But he was anxious to know that his mother would be all right, and after she assured him that she would, he left for school.

Watching him walk down the sidewalk, Alice could think of only one word: *embarrassment*. Having a son out of wedlock sixteen years ago was bad enough, but she'd gotten through that difficult period and was thankful for the wonderful son he turned out to be. She thought that her life was on a secure track—and now this happened. Never had she felt such humiliation, such profound embarrassment. It was one thing for her husband to have committed adultery; it was another thing for it to be plastered on the front page of the newspaper for everyone to see. *What will people think?* she wondered.

It didn't take long to find out. A handful of friends from church began to stop by the house, having read the newspaper story. In every case they hugged and cried with her, telling her how sorry they were that this had happened. Others phoned with similar messages of encouragement. To her surprise, a few admitted that their husbands, too, had been unfaithful, but they'd gotten through it and their marriages were now stronger than before. Alice hadn't known about these affairs until the women told her. But in at least one way her case was different—it was very public.

Pam herself was nowhere to be seen when the newspaper story broke. In her early thirties, she was almost twelve years younger than Barry and was a very attractive woman who looked younger than her years. She'd been married to a man named Ray but had divorced him a year ago. Ray didn't contest the divorce, which she initiated. In telling Clayton and others at church the reason she sought the divorce, she cited Ray's uncontrollable anger, which she said deeply frightened her on occasion. She also revealed his addiction to pornography.

Ray and Pam had a five-year-old son at the time of the divorce. Although the divorce had proceeded uncontested, some unpleasant moments occurred around the division of furniture, household goods, and property. And, in an effort to gain custody of the son, Ray accused Pam of having affairs with other men, a charge that she denied and Ray could not prove.

In the end, she gained custody of the son, and Ray wasn't heard from once the divorce was final.

When the scandal about Barry and Pam broke, however, Ray somehow obtained Pam's e-mail address list. He sent everyone on the list a blistering letter about Pam and her "dirty deeds." People who knew about the custody battle thought that Ray might be trying to get custody of the son and was attempting to drum up public support for his cause. The effort backfired, however, in that most of the people on the list were close friends of Pam. They saw Ray's ploy as a "cheap shot."

Clayton didn't know how all of this would turn out, or even what the best thing might be. To further complicate matters, though, Ray and Alice were siblings. Alice, in fact, had introduced Ray and Pam and had encouraged them in their courtship. Ray and Alice had grown up in a strong Christian home, enjoyed a close relationship as brother and sister, and were well-taught in the Christian faith by their godly parents. But Ray had never married, and Alice thought that he and Pam would make a great couple. She was delighted to introduce them to each other and was even more delighted when they eventually got married.

When Pam and Ray first met, Pam was still feeling the effects of her first divorce from a man whom she married when he was a seminary student. Although both that man and Pam were Christians, their marriage was a disaster from the beginning and did not last more than a year or so. Friends who knew them were not surprised when they divorced. Not long after that, Pam met Ray, and a new romance began. Although Pam was cautious at first because of her previous divorce, the relationship with Ray matured, and they eventually married, bringing them not only joy but also support from many of their friends.

Alice now wondered if Pam had made up the stories about Ray's uncontrollable anger and addiction to pornography. In the past, on the few occasions when Alice tried to talk to Ray about it, he refused to say anything. Alice even pleaded with him once, saying, "You're my brother. Talk to me!"

He replied calmly, "I love you, Sis, but I'm not going to talk about it." And that was that.

Now Alice wondered if Ray had refused to say anything because he suspected something was going on between Pam and Barry. *Was Ray trying to protect me?* Alice wondered. She longed to talk with him about it and vowed she would do so eventually. Meanwhile, it was all she could do to get through this day, the next day, and the day after that.

As friends stopped by to offer comfort and support to Alice, the conversation turned inevitably to Pam's way of speaking and relating to people. People were confused about her. Something about her didn't come together for them, although they admitted they'd never talked about it to anyone. Pam would often be the first to speak up in a group setting, whether it was a Bible study, committee meeting, or congregational meeting. She was full of opinions, strong-minded, and seemed to be self-confident. One person described her as "full of God-talk." On the surface, she was perceived as one who cared deeply about spiritual matters, but now people were questioning their own judgment. Pam was an enigma to them.

Clayton had been unable to talk to Pam after the scandal broke. Rather than telephone, Pam simply sent a note to Clayton resigning as secretary, effective immediately. With his moving to a new church shortly, he fretted over whether there was any way he could contact Pam and provide any pastoral care for her. But she didn't answer the phone at her home, and no one knew where she was. In the end, Clayton saw his best option as simply praying for Pam and committing her to God.

It was a different story with Barry, however. Barry had seen Clayton for pastoral care many times since the affair became public. He was a broken man, one who seemed to Clayton to be genuinely repentant. "I can't believe I've been such a fool," he said over and over. And he repeatedly expressed his desire to save his marriage. Barry and Alice were talking to each other, but Alice was still wary of having Barry return home. Trust had been broken, and Alice didn't know whether she could get it back. In talking to her, Clayton could tell how deeply she was hurt, and he surmised that she would need time to regain her trust in Barry. But Clayton thought it could happen. At least he hoped it would, and he prayed to that end.

In one conversation between Barry and Clayton, Barry revealed that sexual intimacy was not as frequent between him and Alice as he would have liked. The more they talked, Barry revealed that it was, in fact, quite infrequent. According to Barry, Alice was "always tired" when he hoped they would have sex, and this frustrated him. But he also acknowledged that his way of handling it was "stupid." Clayton pointed out that given her many responsibilities, it was likely that Alice actually was tired much of the time. He suggested that if Barry and Alice were to make it together, they should look at their busy lives and make some tough decisions about what they could do to spend more time together.

Although Barry genuinely regretted his affair, he also showed ambivalence in his emotions because of his genuine enjoyment of sex with Pam. "She was always ready for me to make love to her," he said. "Alice never wanted to have sex. In fact," he added, "Pam said that she'd marry me in a minute if I were available and asked her. She told me she loved me, and I told her I felt the same toward her. Now I don't know. I've been such a fool."

Silence followed this statement. Then Clayton quietly said, "I think you know the right thing to do."

"Yes, I do," replied Barry, "at least I think I do. But I wish you were going to be here to help me."

Clayton felt a quick pang of guilt but simply said, "Me, too."

On the Sunday following the public disclosure of the scandal, Clayton of course made no reference to it in the worship service. In his pastoral prayer, however, Clayton did ask God for help and wisdom in dealing with life's hurts, and humbly asked God to draw near to those with broken hearts, to bring His comforting peace and presence. After the service, Clayton observed several small clusters of people talking in hushed tones, and he had a pretty good idea of what they were talking about.

Clayton and Janet had talked about what they should say to their own children, who were old enough to understand what was happening. Their dilemma was soon answered, however. Their fourteen-year-old daughter came home from youth group and said that Barry and Alice's son had told the group about what had happened. "Oh, Mom and Dad, it was so sad. We were crying for him." She described how the group had surrounded him with love and support, thus making the experience a teachable moment for the youth group. Their daughter's description of the son's anguish was also an opportunity for Clayton and his wife to have a frank conversation about sex and fidelity in marriage. They talked about the pain of adultery being about the worst kind of pain a human being could endure. Their daughter listened as they had never seen her listen before.

In the midst of all of the turmoil, Clayton thought the situation was a blessing in disguise, giving the young people in the church an opportunity to talk about the issues surrounding adultery. *In this sex-obsessed world in which we live,* he ruminated, *it's good for youth to see first hand the pain of sexual infidelity.* He realized, however, that teachable moments sometimes come with great pain surrounding them.

Another matter that concerned Clayton was how Alice and Ray's parents would respond. The parents, now in their early seventies, were "pillars of the church." Hardworking and self-sacrificing, they were virtually revered in the church. It was they whom God had used to help hold the church together through rough periods in the past. Then, when Ray and Pam got divorced, it just about broke their hearts. And now with Barry and Pam's affair, it was almost more than they could take. But they rallied around Alice, and continued to embrace Barry at every opportunity, assuring both Alice and Barry of their continuing love and prayers. Their Christian grace in the midst of their own pain was a remarkable testimony to everyone.

The congregation responded to the whole situation by showering Alice's parents with love and support. Clayton observed that a benefit of the scandal's lack of secrecy was the congregation's Christian response to the parents, and to Alice and Barry for that matter. They surrounded them with love and encouragement. Clayton felt sure that such a response would remain a beautiful picture in his mind as he looked back on his years as pastor of the church.

The final worship service was over. The good-byes had been said. The farewell party had been given. Now, as Clayton finished packing the books in his study and prepared for the move to his new church, he had some unanswered questions.

Foremost in his mind was what his role should be with Alice and Barry in the coming weeks. The church had just begun the process of forming a search committee, and the board of elders was looking for an interim pastor. Although he knew that he could no longer be their pastor, at moments he felt as if he were abandoning them. *What is appropriate for me to do for Barry and Alice until an interim pastor arrives?* he wondered.

Also very much on his mind was how to tell people in his new church about adultery. He wanted to shout from the rooftops, "Don't do it!" *But a lot of good that would do,* he chuckled. As a pastor, he observed that when it comes to sexual behavior, people tend to act first and think later. Still, he carried a heavy burden, wanting to warn people that infidelity caused such misery for everyone concerned that it simply wasn't worth it, as well as being just plain wrong. How much could he say in his new church about what had happened with Alice and Barry? Anything? Nothing?

He was taking his confidential files with him when he left to go to the new church. These records were his private property. But he wondered what information, if any, about Pam and Barry's affair he should leave for his successor. The church had not yet found a replacement for Pam, although part-time volunteers from the church were handling necessary office matters. Then, too, Pam also needed pastoral care. *What could be done for her now and in the future?* Clayton wondered.

"What a muddle!" Clayton said out loud in his empty office. "How will it all end?"

Discussion Questions

1. How would you compare the pain of adultery with other problems that people face?
2. What can a pastor do to minister to those involved in or affected by adultery?
3. How can the pastor and the church address the needs of children affected by adultery?
4. How can a church handle the publicity of adultery? If it's not publicly known, should anything be disclosed to anyone outside of "those in the know"?
5. How can the church be educated about the consequences and prevention of adultery?
6. How is the situation in the case complicated by the pastor's leaving for another call? Should he do anything in the interim to help the church and those affected by the adultery?
7. What might be done in the case that would lead you to predict a good outcome for all concerned? If that is not done, what is the worst you think might happen?

10

CHILD MOLESTATION
The Sins of the Fathers

I can't believe this is happening," Paul muttered aloud in his empty study. "I thought I did the right thing in allowing Bill to join the church. Surely it's what Christ would have done. But right now it seems to have backfired!"

Paul had just finished a phone conversation with Don, a husband and father from one of the young families attending the church where Paul was the pastor. Don had informed Paul that he and his wife and young children were moving to another church.

Paul had missed this family at church the last couple of Sundays and had called to see if everything was all right. His worst fears were confirmed when Don said with some hesitation, "We just don't feel safe at the church anymore, not since Bill started attending regularly. Now he's even become a member."

"But we've put strict conditions on Bill when he's at the church, to ensure that children will be safe," Paul countered.

"I know that," Don said, "but we think it's too risky. We're responsible for our children, and we won't deliberately put them at risk."

Paul could barely contain his frustration. The church needed young families like this. Further, he and the elders had carefully—and prayerfully—thought through the implications of what they were doing. And it seemed so right.

It all started when Bill began attending church through the influence of Ed, a member of the church who worked in a prison ministry. While incarcerated, Bill became a Christian through Ed's witnessing, and once Bill got out of prison, it was natural that he'd wanted to attend Ed's church.

Bill was a convicted child molester. He'd admitted to two offenses; one against a four-year-old and the other against a two-year-old. The offenses were not brutal in that no physical harm was done. Bill had touched the children's genitals while he masturbated. But who knows what lasting harm was done to these children in the long run? These incidents happened when Bill was eighteen, about ten years ago.

Paul didn't know how the crime had been discovered or how the victims were doing now, a decade later. But, as a father, he could only imagine the rage and grief that he and his wife would have experienced had this happened to one of *their* children. So he had some degree of sympathy for families in the church who were uncomfortable around Bill.

After Bill had started attending the church—spasmodically at first and then more regularly—he approached Paul and asked if it would be appropriate for him to become a member. Bill had informed Paul that he was a convicted child molester, although Paul had already learned of it; the prison minister had informed Paul of Bill's background. Such disclosure was appropriate and even recommended in cases involving child molestation. Bill had to register as a sex offender, so it was a matter of public record.

Child molestation wasn't the only offense that had led to Bill's incarceration, but it was the worst. The other offenses were minor misdemeanors, mostly petty theft. The result was that Bill had been in and out of prison for most of his adult life. Now, as a Christian, however, he wanted to live a clean life, and seemed to be making good progress in doing so. No other child molesting charges had been pressed other than the two a decade ago, nor had he engaged in any other illegal activity since his release from prison.

Paul decided to allow Bill to attend the membership class but also told Bill that attending the class was no guarantee that he'd be accepted as a member. Paul also indicated that Bill would need to discuss the matter of his membership with the board of elders.

Bill said that he understood but would like to pursue membership if there was even a possibility of his being accepted as a member. A primary reason Bill wanted to become a member concerned the polity of the church; it restricted participation in the Lord's Supper to those who held church membership somewhere. And Bill was not a member anywhere, but he wanted to observe communion with God's people because he'd become a Christian.

In conducting membership classes, Paul always spent time with each candidate. He thus got to know the person better, hearing that person's testimony of faith in Christ, and ensuring that all of his or her questions about the church were answered. He decided early on to meet with Bill and learned a great deal about him and his background.

Bill came from a dysfunctional family. He didn't know who his father was; when he was four, his mother gave him up for adoption. He hadn't seen her since. No one adopted him, however, and he became a ward of the state. From then on, he was in and out of various state institutions.

One of the reasons he wasn't adopted might have been that he seemed to be mildly retarded. He could look after himself in many ways, but he was easily distracted, had a very short temper, and became belligerent when he couldn't get his own way. He was a hyperactive child who lived daily in front of the TV set or played video games.

He began to act out as a child, and most of the adults who worked with him saw him as incorrigible. By the time he was a teenager, he was getting into all kinds of trouble, and was in and out of state juvenile detention centers or state hospitals. With the advent of Internet availability, it wasn't long before Bill was hooked on pornography in its early stages of easy accessibility. When at age eighteen he molested the two children, he was sent to prison as an adult.

Knowing all of this, Paul felt a burden for the church to be a redemptive community for Bill. He'd never experienced any stability in his life, and at least the church could be the family that Bill never had, Paul reasoned, and could help him follow the way of Christ in daily living.

As he got to know Bill, Paul had two basic questions: Would it be at all right to allow Bill to become a member? Should the congregation be informed about Bill's background? If so, when? At this point, only the prison minister and the board of elders were aware of Bill's being a convicted child molester. And they had agreed to keep the matter confidential until a decision was made about whether Bill could actually join the church. The board also suggested that Paul get more information about Bill, that he find out if other churches had faced similar situations and, if so, what was done in those cases.

Paul had learned from the prison minister that Bill's criminal file was a matter of public record. So Paul went to the courthouse, where records were kept, and read Bill's file. It was a thick file, full of all sorts of information about Bill's misdeeds and the history of his treatment at the hands of the state. Reading the file, Paul thought, *I can't believe that in this day and age we can't do a better job of caring for needy people.* He alternated between anger and sadness as he read the material. *Sure,* he thought, *Bill has done some dumb or bad things, but somewhere the system failed to help him.* As Paul closed the folder, he vowed that the church would be a place where Bill would not only be accepted but also find a caring, forgiving, and helping community to assist him in his life as a Christian.

This was Paul's first experience of looking at a court record and finding out the rules and regulations pertaining to sex offenders. In Paul's state, the law requires that sex offenders register with the authorities wherever they live. Also, the law requires public disclosure of the sexual offense, done by mailing letters to residents in the area surrounding where Bill chose to live. Apparently, no one from the church lived in the vicinity of Bill, so church people were not aware of his status as a registered sex offender. At least no one in the church had said anything to Paul about it.

Helpful clerks at the courthouse also said that sexual offense cases were extensive. One person told Paul that as much as 25 percent of the population in America are victims of sexual abuse. It was a figure that Paul found difficult to believe or comprehend. But the prison minister confirmed the figure, not from any statistical study of which he knew, but from his own experience as a prison chaplain.

In response to the elders' other request, Paul talked to a minister in his denomination who'd faced a similar situation. Paul put two questions to this pastor: (1) Do we accept Bill as a member? (2) Do we inform the church about Bill's past? The other minister responded with a resounding *yes* to both questions.

The *yes* to the first question reflected the minister's theology—the church comprises forgiven sinners, and where else could forgiveness and accountability be experienced better than in the church? The *yes* to the second question was based on Bill's record being public, and anyone could find it if they wanted to do so—and would find it if Bill lived near them. Disclosing the information up front would help to build trust among the congregation toward the pastor and church leaders. *Not* to disclose the information when the likelihood was high that it would become public anyway might appear as though Paul and the leaders were trying to hide something, and that would destroy trust.

In talking with this minister, Paul learned of another church that had faced a similar situation. The pastor of that church listed several reasons contributing to his and the church leaders' deciding to allow a sex offender to become a member of their church. Two basic convictions undergirded his action: (1) God wants people to worship Him in the *company* of other believers; worship is not a private experience. (2) Believers need to be with other believers for fellowship and growth in the faith. Accountability is found in a group, not within an individual.

This minister said, too, that he and his leaders put several restrictions in place to safeguard children and families in the church. The basic condition was that the recovering sex offender would not be allowed to attend any church service where children would be present. This meant that the sex offender was not allowed to attend Sunday morning worship but was welcome to participate in the Saturday night service, which was usually attended by only adults. The Saturday night service emphasized worship and healing and celebrated the Lord's Supper. But even at that service, if any child under the age of fifteen was present, the offender would have to leave immediately. There could be no violations of this policy or the individual would have to leave the church. The pastor reported that so far this policy had worked, although it was quite restrictive due to the serious nature of the offense.

Paul asked this minister, "Might the policy eventually be made less restrictive if the offender stayed 'clean'?"

The pastor replied, "I suppose there could be leniency in the future, but I doubt it. I've studied this issue since the person came to our church, and I've learned that predatory sexual offenders seldom change. They can't regulate themselves, so others have to set the standards, and those standards must be high, hard, and unyielding."

What Paul learned from these conversations confirmed his own perspectives and gave him a sobering picture of what he was facing. He reported his findings to the board of elders. In making his report, Paul stressed five points:

1. The church is for sinners. Bill was a forgiven sinner like every other person in the church.
2. Bill's profession of faith was credible, and he was growing as a Christian.
3. Bill would need to complete the membership class and then be in some kind of accountability relationship with a church leader for a period of time before he could join the church.
4. The congregation would have to be informed soon of Bill's background. Following the public disclosure, some kind of forum for discussion would have to be set up and include anyone concerned about the matter.
5. The conditions that would be imposed upon Bill would be "high, hard, and unyielding," and the congregation would be informed of these conditions.

Following Paul's presentation, the board voted to allow Bill to complete the membership class and then go through a probationary period, during which he would be called a "member candidate." During the probationary period, Paul was to meet with Bill on a regular schedule and keep the elders informed of discussions and issues arising from those times of pastoral care.

The final condition imposed was that one of the elders must be with Bill anytime he was in the church. He would not be allowed to enter the church for any service or activity by himself. A rotation order was set up with each elder assigned to a specific week, and Bill would be informed to call this elder beforehand if he planned to come to church. The elder would then meet him in the parking lot and accompany him throughout his time at the church. The elder on call in any particular week was also to spend time with Bill in a discipling relationship.

Before working out the details of the plan, the elders prayed for wisdom and pure hearts as they acted. They asked God to lead them in their decision and for Him, following their decisions, to redeem the situation for His glory. They asked, too, for His protection for the people of the church and that the congregation would respond to the plan in redemptive ways.

They determined that Paul would reveal the plan to Bill. If Bill agreed to everything, as they hoped he would, an announcement would be made the following Sunday calling the congregation to a special meeting to discuss an important matter. But the exact topic to be discussed would not be disclosed when the meeting was announced.

Paul met with Bill the next day and outlined the course of action to be followed. At first Bill was put off and even got a little huffy. "This doesn't sound like forgiveness to me," he said.

Paul quickly replied, "Oh, but it is. We're accepting you into our fellowship, and we're setting up a process that we think will help you not only grow in your Christian life but deal with any temptation you might have along the way. And we think it will give the congregation confidence in how we're handling things. We need their trust to make this work. After several months, we'll review things with you and consider membership at that time. Until then, you'll be called a 'member candidate.'"

"Has this ever been done before?" Bill asked.

"No," Paul replied, "but that's not the point." He reminded Bill that the few other churches he'd visited, when they discovered his background, had subtly let him know that he wasn't welcome. "We're not just giving you a chance," Paul said, "we're committing ourselves to come alongside you as your brothers in Christ and support you every way we can."

At that point, Bill softened and agreed to all of the conditions, including the public disclosure at a special church meeting. The only thing he asked to include in the public statement was that he was attending Sexaholics Anonymous regularly. He thought this would illustrate his commitment to go straight.

After Paul and Bill talked, Paul called the elders and told them that Bill had accepted the plan. The following Sunday, Paul announced the special congregational meeting to discuss an important matter. He gave no other details, except to state the date and time, set for later in the week. Maybe it was the way Paul announced it, the tone of his voice as he talked, or the lack of detailed information, but Paul sensed immediately some wonder bordering on tenseness within the congregation as he made the announcement. After the service, several people asked what it was all about, but Paul responded lightly, "Come to the meeting, and you'll see." Although in saying this Paul didn't intend to dismiss people, he observed that several people seemed not to appreciate his response.

Letters were sent to church members informing them of the upcoming meeting. The letter, signed by Paul and the chairman of the board of elders, simply indicated that an important issue would be discussed but no congregational action would be taken. The meeting was for informational purposes only.

At the meeting, which Bill was told not to attend, Paul reported the whole situation, including what he'd learned about Bill's background and the experiences of other churches who'd faced similar situations. Then the chairman of the board of elders reported on the conditions that had been set up to hold Bill accountable, aid his discipleship, and protect the congregation. Both Paul and the chairman stressed that Bill was a "member candidate" and that an evaluation would be made before the board determined whether to make him a member. Following these presentations, the floor was open for discussion.

A few seconds of silence passed before anyone said anything, and many people looked stunned at the news they had just heard. Finally, Carl, a young husband, spoke. "We have young children in the church, and although my wife and I need to talk about this together, I can say right now that I'm not comfortable with the direction you're taking. I think we should have been informed before now about Bill. This whole thing makes me nervous." With that comment, the dam burst.

In rapid succession, more people spoke, several of them trying to speak at the same time. One woman, on the verge of tears, said, "I'm afraid now I can't let my children out of my sight when I'm at church." When the board chairman pointed out that an elder would always be alongside Bill when he was at church, she answered, "Well, that's good, but what if he finds out where we live and comes by our house when the children are playing outside? I'm very upset about this!" Her voice trembled as she spoke.

More comments from some of the younger families came rapidly. No one spoke in favor of the plan for monitoring Bill. But Paul observed that a majority of the people said nothing. *That's a bit unusual*, Paul thought, and he wasn't sure how to read it. He did notice, however, that many people nodded their heads slightly when others talked about their fears and concerns.

Toward the end of the meeting, Paul and the elders assured those present that they would monitor the situation closely in the coming days and would keep the church informed. Although Paul acknowledged the legitimate concerns that people had raised, he talked about the church as a redemptive community and said, "Surely this is what Jesus would have us do." He then closed the meeting in prayer.

The following Sunday, Paul noticed that one of the younger families was not at worship. This was a key family who were faithful in attendance. Usually the husband or wife would let Paul know if they were going to be away, but he hadn't heard anything this time. So Paul called them later in the day and was told that they'd visited another church that Sunday. The reason given was that they simply weren't comfortable with Bill's being in the church. Paul asked if he could discuss the matter further with them, but the man gently said, "Pastor, I think this is an issue we're not going to agree on." So he saw no need to get together.

As the weeks went by, the plan seemed to be working. Eventually the board voted, allowing Bill to become a member, and then informed the congregation of their action. After that, several more young families were not in attendance at Sunday worship. Paul followed up with every couple and heard the same thing as he'd heard from the first couple who left. Some people said that it was acceptable for Bill to attend the church but that he shouldn't have been allowed to become a member. This made no sense to Paul. Another mother explained that she didn't want to take communion in the service with Bill. When Paul asked why, she gave a vague answer: "I'm just not comfortable with the idea."

It didn't help matters any when Bill was jailed two times after he'd become a member candidate. One time was when he moved his residence, as he often did, but didn't report the change of address to his probation officer within the required thirty-day period. On the other occasion, it was a case of mistaken identity in a crime of theft, and although it was proven that Bill was innocent, some church people still held him responsible.

In the long run, the plan of action with elders discipling Bill and accompanying him to church didn't work as designed. Bill would often call the elder too late to be met at the parking lot. The result was that Bill would sometimes enter the church alone before an elder caught up with him. Also, elders found it more stressful to be his "shadow" at church than they'd expected. As the elders talked about it, several of them admitted that they were increasingly uncomfortable around Bill. "He's different in some ways," they said. "He intrudes into conversations and says off-the-wall things."

Others acknowledged that their families weren't happy when it was their turn to accompany Bill. On those occasions, they couldn't visit with their friends, and their families weren't happy with Bill's sitting with them. "It's just weird," one family member said. Although the elders said that they wanted to continue the monitoring process, they were asking if some adjustments should be made.

Paul sensed a kind of weariness setting in with the elders. He understood, because at times he felt weary with it himself. Accommodating someone like Bill took a great deal of time, energy, and planning. Besides, there was the whole church to think about. The church was not large—around one hundred seventy-five members with an average attendance on Sundays of ninety-five. The congregation consisted of mostly older people. The few families in the church who were young and had young children were crucial to the church's future, yet it was they who were most disaffected with Paul's and the board's decision about Bill.

The church had been declining in membership for several years. The downtown neighborhood in which the church was located had undergone change as well. The church had a noble history as an evangelical witness to the community, and when the congregation called Paul to be their pastor, they had great hopes that he'd help the church to grow. He was young and inexperienced, but was highly regarded by everyone who knew him. This church was his first pastorate out of seminary and he threw himself into the work of ministry with joy and energy. His wife was deeply committed to the ministry as well.

And Paul had been instrumental in bringing younger families into the church. He worked much the same as a church planter would in calling on new families moving into the community. He would share with them a vision for the church as a redemptive community worshiping the one true God and seeking to be a faithful witness to the gospel. He was now in his third year at the church and was grateful for the young families who'd become part of the church. The older members of the church rejoiced with him in this new growth.

But then Bill came to the church. And in the ensuing fallout, four young families had already left. Now Paul learned on the phone that another one was gone as well. Only one of the families who left took the time to talk with Paul about their concerns. The others just quietly slipped away, and Paul contacted them to see what was happening. Each family indicated that Bill was the reason they were looking for a new church home.

The one couple who did take the initiative to talk with Paul before leaving was quite adamant that other young families would soon be leaving as well. "You and the elders have badly mishandled the situation," the husband said to Paul. "You don't seem to realize how afraid we are for the safety of our children. Especially in this day and age, we have to be vigilant."

"But I have young children, too," Paul rejoined, "and I think it's possible for us to safeguard our children *and* include Bill in our church."

"Many of us don't agree with you," the man said.

Something in the man's tone caused Paul to ask, "Have you and other couples been talking about this?"

"Oh, yes," the man said. "It's been a nonstop conversation for weeks, ever since the church meeting."

"But why haven't you talked to me?" Paul asked. "I feel like I'm fighting against something that I can't see until it's too late."

"It's because we know where you stand," the man explained. "You've made your position very clear. We see it differently, and we don't want to argue with you about it. Our only alternative is to leave." And his prediction about other families leaving was proving true.

At a ministerial meeting of fellow evangelical pastors, Paul shared a little of what was going on and talked about his frustration. To his surprise, the other pastors also indicated that they thought Paul had made a mistake. "You've sacrificed the whole congregation for the good of one person," one of the ministers said. Another one added, "It would be better to sacrifice Bill than the young families. You're not listening to their hurts and fears."

Other ministers commented on the volatile climate created by the sexual molestation scandals in the Roman Catholic Church and, to a lesser extent, even in Protestant churches. That current climate dictated a harsher approach to a sexual offender than Paul and the elders of his church had taken. Paul thought of the comments made by some of the families who'd left the church, referencing his behavior as paralleling the cover-up actions of church leaders in the Roman Catholic Church. But, to Paul, the way he was handling the situation was night and day removed from any kind of cover-up.

Nevertheless, the words of his fellow pastors stung. *Have I made a mistake?* he wondered. *Did we get ahead of what God wanted to do, or is the Devil impeding the work? Can we go back and do things differently? Should we? What does it mean to be forgiven by God for our sins? If, as God promised, He forgives when we confess and ask for forgiveness, what does it mean? Should people trust a child molester who has sought God's forgiveness and is trying to deal with his unholy desires? And doesn't the church have a responsibility to help forgiven sinners through love, support, prayer, and accountability?*

In the midst of all of these questions tumbling through his mind, Paul asked himself, *What do I do now?*

Discussion Questions

1. How would you characterize the fears of people in the case regarding a child abuser becoming a member of the church?

2. Is there a connection between forgiving a sinner for past sins and trusting them to "go straight" from then on? In other words, how are forgiveness and trust linked?

3. If a church accepts for membership a child abuser as a forgiven sinner, is it fair to establish limits on what the person can do? Why or why not?

4. Were the questions raised by the pastor in the case—namely propriety of church membership and public disclosure—good questions to be raising? How would you evaluate the pastor's handling of the situation? Was he thinking through the questions carefully?

5. Was the process that the board established realistic? Why did it end so badly?

6. What would you advise the pastor and leaders to do now in light of people's actions?

7. How would you answer the questions the pastor raised at the end of the case?

8. How can the church address the problem of child abuse?

$$\boxed{11}$$

SEXUAL DEVIATION
Sexuality and the Church

I suppose we shouldn't be surprised at what we're now seeing in the church." Ted, the senior minister, was speaking at their weekly pastoral staff meeting, "But I must admit . . . some of this stuff just blows my mind! What's going on?"

The pastors had been talking about matters relating to sexuality, which they were encountering in increasing numbers in the church. To some of the older pastors on staff, the sexual issues confronting them bordered on the bizarre and surely, they thought, would be classified as sexual deviations.

As they talked, they wondered if the size of the church played a factor— the larger the church, the more possibility of attracting deviants who could remain anonymous more easily than in a small church. But in the situation they were discussing, the problem centered on people not wanting to remain anonymous. Except for one case of an exhibitionist, who was desperate to keep his indiscretion secret, the men with whom the pastors had recently dealt all wanted to make a public statement about their sexuality.

Even in the case of the man trying to hush everything up, his exhibitionism was itself rather public, at least to one person. So maybe even he was making some kind of public statement. Pastor Mike said, "Maybe a large church gives sexual deviants a broader platform in which to make a statement."

"The problem is," Pastor Jerry countered, "what we're calling 'sexual deviation' is not seen as deviation by much of the culture today."

"Yeah," said Pastor Samuel, "we sometimes think we're the majority but, in fact, we're not."

Pastor Larry asked, "So, how do we deal with all of these problems?"

Ten full-time pastors were on the staff of First Baptist Church. Another seven full-time and part-time directors of various ministries made up the professional ministerial staff, although these seven people didn't participate in the weekly pastoral staff meetings. All totaled, the paid staff of the church, including full-time and part-time people, was sixty. First Baptist Church was indeed a large church—a megachurch—with multiple ministries to a wide variety of people. The church was known for its evangelical witness.

The discussion at this particular staff meeting about current issues relating to sexuality was initiated by Ted. He related some of the situations he'd recently encountered in the church. Without revealing names, he first talked about a situation in which a man had apparently taken a picture of himself masturbating and sent it to a teenage girl in the church.

The only ones dealing with the situation at this point were Ted, his secretary, the minister of pastoral care, the youth pastor, and the Christian education minister. They had agreed to keep the matter confidential until further information had been obtained. One other staff person knew about the case—Gail, the computer technician in charge of the church's Web site. She was a whiz at fixing computer problems for all of the church staff, and she played a key role in the case involving exhibitionism. But Ted, in talking with his colleagues at this point, kept his remarks general.

The case in question began when Ted received an e-mail from Amanda, a sixteen-year-old girl in the church, saying that Merle, her Sunday school teacher, had sent her a picture of himself naked and masturbating. In her e-mail, Amanda said that she was frightened and wanted to know what she should do.

Because Ted received several hundred e-mails every week, his secretary, Pat, screened his messages, weeding out extraneous material from the essential matters he needed to see. Pat immediately printed the one from Amanda and brought it to Ted, saying as she handed it to him, "Be careful. This gal can be trouble. I know her, and she's a bit flighty."

Upon reading the message, Ted immediately called Ian, the minister of pastoral care on staff, and asked to meet. The two of them looked at the message and determined that Ted should phone Amanda and request that they meet as soon as possible. Then, after he got more information, he could involve other pastors who would be more directly involved with the people concerned. But for now, they reasoned, it would be better for Ted to make the initial response since the e-mail had been sent to him.

When Amanda met with Ted, she was nervous at first. Fidgeting in her seat and moving her hands rapidly, she talked about how frightened she was when she got the picture. She talked about how she was afraid that her parents might see the picture, since she hadn't deleted it from her computer in case it would be needed for some kind of evidence. She'd printed the picture, however, which she produced when Ted asked if he could see it.

As Ted looked at the picture, he thought, *This looks like Merle, all right, but what in the world is he doing sending this to a teenage girl in his Sunday school class?* The whole thing seemed preposterous. Now Ted didn't know who was more embarrassed—him or the girl. He was sure that his face reflected his shock, but he quickly regained his composure. "I'll need to keep this picture," he said, and Amanda nodded her assent.

Then they discussed the next step. Ted indicated that he would confer with the minister of pastoral care and that probably the youth pastor and Christian education minister would need to be involved as well. And, of course, Merle would be contacted for conversation. Amanda's primary concern was keeping her own name out of it as much as possible. "I don't want any of my friends to know about it," she said. Ted assured her that nothing would be said to her friends. In the back of his mind, he hoped that none of her friends had received similar photos.

"I . . . don't get along with my parents," said Amanda, so she didn't want them to know about it either. Ted recalled Pat's saying that, from what she knew, Amanda came from an unstable family.

Ted replied that at some point it would be necessary to inform her parents because she was legally a minor. "But," he added and smiled, "I need to do some further checking first."

This statement seemed to unsettle Amanda. "My parents will take away my computer if they find out about this," she muttered.

"Maybe not," Ted responded, "especially if they think we've handled the situation well."

Next, Ted and Ian met. Ian looked at the picture of Merle and said, "Wow! This is hard to believe. How could anyone be so stupid?" The next step was a phone call to Merle to arrange for an appointment.

When Ted and Ian met with Merle, the whole story was laid out, and they showed the photo to him. As Merle looked at the picture, both thought that he was too calm, almost overcontrolled. They thought, *If this were a picture of me in such a compromising position, and I was innocent, I'd strongly protest in no uncertain terms.* But Merle simply looked at the picture and said calmly, "This is my face, but that's all. Someone must have used computer technology to put my face on someone else's body." Merle laid the picture on the desk. "Someone's trying to embarrass me or get at her. I wouldn't do something like this."

Ted said that the girl was very frightened by the picture. And before he could go on, Merle interrupted, "Frightened? Ha! She tried to blackmail me. She's not frightened. She just didn't get her way."

"What?" both Ted and Ian exclaimed simultaneously. Ted quickly added, "Did you already know about this?"

"Oh, yes," Merle replied. "Amanda called me one day and said she had the picture and that if I didn't give her a specific sum of money—a rather large sum, I might add—she'd report it to you, Ted. I told her I didn't know what she was talking about and hung up."

"That's it?" Ted asked. "You didn't pursue the matter further?"

"No," Merle replied.

"Did you tell anyone about it?" Ted queried.

"No," Merle replied. "I'm innocent. Why should I talk about it?"

For a few seconds, no one said anything. Then Ted suddenly had an idea. "Since Amanda is a minor," he said, "we'll have to do an investigation, starting with an examination of your computer. I'd like you to go home and get it right now."

Merle hesitated a moment, then said, "I'd be happy to do that, but . . . well, frankly, it feels like you don't trust me."

"The investigation is necessary to protect you," Ted replied, "as well as Amanda, and the church."

Merle left to get the computer and, while they waited, Ted and Ian outlined a course of action. Ian would follow up with the girl and bring the youth pastor and the Christian education minister into the loop so that they could minister to the girl and her parents as needed. They would also be ready to help Merle's wife and children if needed. Ted, as senior minister, would pursue the investigation. He contacted Gail, the computer technician on staff, and said that she was needed in Ted's office immediately.

It took longer than Ted or Ian expected for Merle to return with his computer. Merle explained that he'd run a few necessary errands on his way home, causing some delay. When Ted asked if the computer was available to the whole family, Merle replied that this particular computer was kept in his home office and that the family used another one. He further indicated that he would need the computer back as soon as possible because he did some of his work from home.

Merle was in his forties and was a successful business man. He and his wife, Bernice, were very active in the church, both regarded as model Christians. His wife was perceived especially as a godly woman. And Merle had taught the high school Sunday school class for the past two years. He was one of the "go to" leaders of the church.

When Gail examined Merle's computer, she found great amounts of pornography still on the hard drive in the spot where deleted materials were kept. She could also tell when the material had been deleted—about an hour ago. This explained Merle's delay in bringing in the computer. *Errands, huh?* Ted mused.

Ted and Ian met again with Merle and told him what they'd found. Again, Merle didn't seem upset and said nonchalantly, "Someone else must have downloaded the pornographic material." Then he added, "Young people from the Sunday school class are at my house frequently and one of the group had probably accessed the pornography."

"Our computer tech says that one piece of pornography was deleted only an hour before you brought the computer in," Ted remarked.

Merle stated, "The technician must have made a mistake."

Ted then said he would have to pursue the investigation further. Meanwhile, Merle was to immediately stop teaching the Sunday school class and ask the substitute teacher to take over. Merle agreed with no protest.

Next, Ted and Ian met again with Amanda to get more information. She again told them that she didn't get along well with her parents. They were not churchgoers. Furthermore, she said that she and her boyfriend had been "rather close" and she had sent an e-mail to Merle asking for his advice. He'd invited students in the class to contact him this way if they ever had questions about anything. She also asked Merle about how to get along better with her parents.

They began a frequent exchange of e-mail messages in which she talked frankly about her relationship with her boyfriend. Then suddenly Merle sent the message asking if she would enjoy looking at the attached picture, the one in which he was masturbating. Amanda thought he must have done that because of the information she'd shared with him about her relationship with her boyfriend.

Amanda admitted that she'd phoned Merle, demanding money, but she realized afterward that it was foolish, and that's when she contacted Ted. She also admitted that she'd told a couple of her closest friends about it. They were "horrified," she reported, but they also wanted to see the photo. She hadn't told her boyfriend, however, saying, "He'll kill Merle if he finds out."

Next, Ted met with Merle and his wife, Bernice. Merle confirmed that he frequently exchanged e-mail messages with students in the class as a way of keeping in contact with the young people and giving advice when they asked. Merle's wife indicated that he'd told her about the accusation from the girl, and she was eager to meet with Ted to assure him that the accusations were false. Bernice acknowledged that Merle spent a great deal of time at the computer sending e-mail messages to students, "But," she added with intense feeling, "there's no way Merle would do anything like that. Never."

Ted then showed her the photo. She glanced at it, turned away quickly, and said, "That's disgusting! It may be Ted's face, but anyone can superimpose a face on a body if they know how to do it." The whole situation was very upsetting to her, and she let Ted know it. She couldn't believe that Ted would take a young girl's word against Merle's.

Meanwhile, the computer technician had taken the photo and Merle's computer to an expert in computer technology. The expert's opinion was that no one had tampered with the photo in question. An examination of the computer itself—where the picture was still located among the deleted materials—confirmed this expert's opinion that the photo was genuine.

With this evidence, Ted and Ian met again with Merle and confronted him with what they'd learned. Merle again denied the accusation. Ted then said that he'd have to contact the authorities because the girl was a minor, and the evidence would be turned over to the Department of Youth Services. Merle paled at this but said nothing. Ted also indicated that the girl's parents would now be informed of the situation. At this, Merle simply got up and walked out. That was the last time Ted and Ian saw Merle; Merle and his family stopped coming to First Baptist Church.

A number of weeks had gone by since that last encounter with Merle. The investigation by the civil authorities was proceeding, and Amanda's parents had not gone berserk as she had feared. They had, in fact, responded to their daughter with support and love.

Shortly thereafter, Ted received a letter from another church in the city requesting a "letter of transfer of membership" for Merle and his wife. *Now what do I do?* Ted asked himself. Such requests were handled by the board of elders, and transfers of membership to the new church were usually done with the board warmly commending such people as "members in good standing." But Merle was not a member in good standing. Merle might even be facing a criminal charge of exhibitionism to a minor. Did FBC have a right or a duty to disclose that information to the church requesting the letter of transfer?

To further complicate matters, Ted and the other ministers who knew about the situation had not told anyone else about it, not even their wives. Nor had the board of elders been informed. Ted had followed the written policy of the church in handling allegations of malfeasance, except the step of informing the elders. That hadn't been done for two reasons. First, one of the elders was known for not keeping confidences. Ted had cautioned him about it, but the man had not become more circumspect. Ted was waiting for this man to complete his term as elder, and if his name was again put forward by the nominating committee, Ted planned to request that his name be withdrawn. Ted feared that if he informed the whole board of the exhibitionism, this particular elder would disclose the information inappropriately.

The second reason Ted hadn't informed the board was that another elder was not supportive of Ted's leadership as senior pastor. Although this elder had been unsuccessful in building a coalition of like-minded elders—he, in fact, stood alone in his opposition to Ted—he'd managed to gain the support of Pastor Jud, one of the other pastors on staff. Ted simply didn't want to give them any ammunition for the cannon they had trained on him.

Pastor Jud was eager to be the senior minister himself, although he had no support from any quarter except the one elder. He'd been especially unhappy with how Ted had handled the situation involving Cliff, the seminary intern working under Jud's supervision. The incident occurred when the computer technician updated the software on all of the computers used by the church staff. When Gail worked on Cliff's computer, she found a great deal of pornographic material.

Cliff was working with young people, so Ted immediately removed him from his internship and recommended he seek counseling. Cliff should have been an example of righteous behavior, thus Ted did not want any problem to arise if people found out that the intern was involved in pornography but had been allowed to remain in the internship program.

The young man admitted his addiction to pornography and readily agreed to seek help. Not only was his repentance genuine but his wife was also standing with him in love and support. Both of them were in counseling together, and Ted had every reason to believe that in due course the student could be restored to ministry.

Jud, however, wasn't pleased. He objected to Ted's insisting that Cliff be removed from the internship until he could demonstrate that pornography would no longer be a problem. Jud claimed that because Cliff had repented, there was no need for him to step down as an intern. Since that time, Jud seemed to use every opportunity to make disparaging remarks about Ted to anyone who'd listen.

But now Ted was faced with a dilemma: What to do about Merle's request for transfer of membership as a member "in good standing" at FBC. Merle was definitely not a member in good standing, but for Ted to deal with the matter honestly he'd have to inform the elders and thereby run the risk of their questioning how the whole situation had been handled. He decided to postpone an immediate decision until he could confer with the other pastors who knew about the situation. Then he would act, but at this point he didn't want to predict what would happen.

Two other episodes of a bizarre nature had consumed pastoral staff time and energy, and had generated several serious discussions with the elders in recent days. One concerned Gene, a man who was a transvestite. Although Gene wasn't a church member, he was a frequent attendee at worship services as well as other of the many activities and programs run by the church. He was involved in the music industry as a career and had occasionally asked if he could help with the music ministry at FBC. So far, the pastors, with unanimous support from the elders, had been successful in holding him off from involvement with church music.

But the major problem came when this transvestite used the women's restrooms at the church. He claimed this was his right, but it made a large number of women extremely uncomfortable, and they insisted that church leaders do something about it. The pastors and elders insisted that Gene use the men's restrooms, but he said that this made *him* uncomfortable. A separate restroom in a secluded area of the church was then made available to him for his exclusive use, but he claimed that he was being discriminated against. He threatened to sue the church, but so far he'd done nothing.

It was possible that the transvestite had left the church. At least he hadn't been seen for several weeks. Many church people expressed relief that he was gone and were praying fervently that there would be no ongoing problem or lawsuit.

The other bizarre incident was, in the minds of the pastors and church leaders, even more serious. This case had to do with Terry, a man who was a transsexual. He'd been a member of the church, but moved to another state and transferred his membership to a church there. While he was a member at FBC, Terry gave no indication that anything was amiss with his sexual identity. He was in his thirties, married, and had two children.

Suddenly, Terry was back at FBC and meeting with Ted. He informed Ted that he was a transsexual and had been undergoing hormone treatment for the last six months to develop his breasts and to stop facial hair from growing. As a result of his decision to go public with his desire, his wife had divorced him and remained with their children in the state to which they'd moved.

Terry had joined the local Gay/Lesbian, Bisexual, and Transgendered Alliance, which encouraged him to continue his church involvement and to press for change in the church. He explained that he enjoyed the fellowship he experienced with likeminded people at the Alliance, but that he didn't want to cause trouble for the church. He continued to affirm his faith in Christ as Savior and said that he was learning to "rejoice" that God had made him the way he was.

Terry did, however, request that he be allowed to use the women's restrooms. Ted replied that it would not be allowed and that Terry would have to use the men's restrooms while at church. Fortunately, Terry agreed to abide by the decision, but he also said that Ted would likely have to change his mind after Terry had his sex change operation and legally changed his sex from male to female. In a few weeks, he was going to Sweden to undergo the surgery; upon his return, he would finalize his legal status as a woman.

The conversation was very calm and matter-of-fact on the part of both Ted and Terry, although Ted admitted later that his "insides were jumping up and down." As a devoted husband and father, he couldn't imagine why this man wanted to change his sex. The man replied, "Oh, it's easy. God made me this way. It took me years to figure it out."

Ted responded, "No, God made you a man and brought you to a one-man, one-woman relationship in marriage, and that's where you need to stay."

The man sighed and replied, "I don't suppose you'll ever understand."

When the pastoral staff were processing and discussing these issues, Ted had said, "I suppose we shouldn't be surprised at what we're now seeing in the church. But I must admit . . . some of this stuff just blows my mind. What's going on?" The discussion moved on to what the church could and should do about such matters.

Questions swirled around the discussion, one pastor after another giving voice to them. *Should the church do more by way of educating the congregation to contemporary sexual issues? How could the church help parents be more comfortable in talking frankly about sexual issues with their children? How old should children be before being exposed to instruction about sex? What does the Bible have to say about sexual matters? In our pluralistic world, how do we uphold biblical standards when the culture in general is moving toward much more tolerance about what used to be called sexual disorders or sexual deviancy? Today, many people, including Christians, see these "disorders" as normal options for people. And what would FBC do if they were challenged legally by someone over church policy about sexual matters? Although all new members signed assent forms to the printed "Church Discipline Guidelines," and members who'd joined the church before the guidelines were written had approved their adoption, what would happen if the local Gay/Lesbian, Bisexual, and Transgendered Alliance held a protest at the church on a Sunday morning, as had been threatened, or brought a lawsuit against FBC, accusing the church of intolerance and discrimination? And what should be done about the specific cases currently facing the church?*

Another question, too, was on Ted's mind. Without divulging any details about Merle, Ted asked his colleagues a general question: "How would we handle a situation if someone involved in sexual sin tried to transfer membership, but hadn't really dealt with his problem?" No one responded immediately.

"Okay," Ted said to his colleagues, "we've asked more than enough questions. What's our first step?"

Discussion Questions

1. Do you think there's an increase in the number and kind of sexual issues being faced today by people in the culture? Why or why not?

2. Is the size of a church a factor in attracting people who may be facing issues related to sexuality? If size is not a factor, what might be the explanation for some churches' having to deal with more sexual issues than other churches?

3. In the case study, how does another member of the pastoral staff's being at odds with the senior minister complicate matters? Did the senior minister handle the situation with the staff minister appropriately?

4. How can the church respond to what it perceives as sexual deviations when the modern culture says, "God made me this way," thus implying that a particular sexual proclivity is not a deviation in need of treatment?

5. How would you answer the questions that the pastors raised at the end of the case, especially the questions dealing with upholding biblical standards in a context in which litigation, or at the least a possible public demonstration against the views of the church, is a distinct possibility?

6. How would you advise the pastor in the case study regarding the request for transfer of church membership? What, if anything, should be disclosed to the other church about the member's background?

12

MISCARRIAGE AND STILLBORN BABIES
Death in the Womb

Nelson and Lisa were almost giddy with joy. At long last, after two miscarriages in their ten years of marriage, Jacob, a healthy, ten-pound son was born. They had dreamed often of this day in the last nine months, but were afraid to get their hopes up because of what had happened in the past.

But this was a great day, and they rejoiced in the goodness of God in granting them a son. Their families also were glad. It was the first grandchild on either side of the family, so the news of the baby's birth was announced with great joy.

Nelson and Lisa reviewed their pilgrimage to this point. They'd met at a state university at a meeting of InterVarsity Christian Fellowship. It was almost love at first sight. A few weeks after they graduated from university, they were married.

In his sophomore year at university, Nelson had sensed a call to ministry, particularly pastoral ministry. When he met Lisa, he shared his desire with her, and she enthusiastically supported his call. After they graduated, Nelson worked as a campus minister, employed by the church in the university town where they lived. Lisa completed work on a master's degree in higher education.

Two years later, following Lisa's graduation with an M.A. degree, they moved to seminary, where Nelson began his M.Div. studies and Lisa found work on the support staff of the school. The months flew by, and Nelson graduated with an M.Div. degree five years later. He'd worked part time while in seminary, and Lisa had worked a job and a half, enabling them to leave seminary debt free. This had been their goal, and they didn't mind that it had taken five years to do it. At least they were not in debt, as many of their friends were.

All along, Nelson was affiliated with the Presbyterian Church in the USA. In his final year at seminary, he completed the ordination exams required of PCUSA ministers and accepted a call to a small Presbyterian church in a rural area of the upper Midwest.

Two hundred fifty names were on the membership roll of the church, but the average attendance when Nelson began his ministry was only around forty. Nelson and Lisa were the youngest couple the church had called as pastor in almost fifty years. Nor had there been any children in the manse in that time. Most of the people in the church were well over fifty, many of them in their seventies and eighties.

The people of the church, though, were delighted to have a young couple in the manse. During the candidating process, Nelson and Lisa had stated that they hoped to begin a family after they got settled at the church. The search committee was pleased to hear it, and the news quickly spread through the church. In fact, when Nelson and Lisa moved into the manse, a pair of knit booties was hanging on the door of one of the bedrooms. Nelson and Lisa giggled when they saw it.

At the first dinner to which they were invited in a member's home, as they were sitting at the table the wife asked, "So, when are you going to have a baby? This will be the first baby born in the manse since most of us can remember, and we're sure excited about it!" Nelson and Lisa stammered that they'd be trying soon. "Well, you better get started," the woman said. "You're not getting any younger."

At age thirty-one, Lisa knew that her biological clock was ticking, but she also knew that many women had waited even longer and still gave birth to healthy children. She and Nelson had deliberately waited to start a family until they were out of school and settled in their first church. Now was the time to start, they reasoned, but they didn't expect public discussion of the matter.

On the way home from the dinner, Nelson and Lisa laughed about the woman's frankness. "Wow! She's worse than our parents," Nelson exclaimed.

"Yeah," Lisa responded. "I'm glad our parents haven't put much pressure on us, but I know they want us to get started, too."

Feeling that the time was right, Nelson and Lisa began trying to conceive a child. After several months of trying, Lisa did get pregnant; a pregnancy test confirmed it. But they waited for a few more weeks before saying anything to the church family. They did, however, tell both sets of parents, who were ecstatic at the news. The conception took place at a charming and romantic inn where Nelson and Lisa had gone for a minivacation. They'd talked and dreamed of trying to conceive a child in such a setting. And, to their delight, it happened.

But six weeks into the pregnancy, Lisa began to bleed seriously one evening and experienced severe cramping. Nelson was at a church meeting, and by the time he got home, Lisa had miscarried. He immediately took her to the hospital for treatment, and there the miscarriage was confirmed.

Both Nelson and Lisa were crushed. They held each other and cried. Nelson stayed with her at the hospital that night, but neither of them slept. They talked off and on, their comments punctuated by periods of silence. The initial shock wore off, and they reassured each other of God's love and providential care for them.

During their seminary days, Nelson and several of his fellow students once carried on a long discussion regarding babies who died in the womb. *Would they go to heaven? Or did a state of "limbo" exist for little children? And was there such a thing as an "age of accountability"?*

Nelson was convinced that their little one was in heaven. With this in mind, they gave the baby a name. Before the miscarriage, the ultrasound seemed to indicate that the fetus was male, so they gave the baby a boy's name.

In the morning, their doctor met with them and said that he saw no reason why Lisa had miscarried. But he scheduled several tests to see if anything was amiss. All of the tests came back normal, so the doctor encouraged them to try again, but to wait a few months before attempting to conceive to allow Lisa's system to stabilize.

Once home, they called their parents to tell them what had happened. Both sets of parents said that they were sorry to hear the news, but they said very little beyond that. They didn't ask any questions or even inquire as to how Nelson and Lisa were feeling about the situation. The lack of response hurt Nelson and Lisa a little.

Several months later, Lisa conceived again. The doctor was encouraging that everything was proceeding nicely, and Nelson and Lisa were cautiously optimistic that all would be well. This time, after Lisa passed the first trimester safely, they informed not only their parents but also the church family. Church people were excited and began to plan for a big baby shower. Early gifts began to pour in.

Late in the second trimester, during a routine physical exam at the obstetrician's office, the nurse couldn't detect a heartbeat in the fetus. The nurse quickly called for the doctor, and further examination revealed that the baby had died in the womb. Once again, Nelson and Lisa were crushed.

The doctor immediately admitted Lisa to the hospital, where she was induced. This time the baby would have been a girl. As before, they gave the baby a name and had a simple funeral service at the hospital chapel. Following the dilation and curettage procedure, Lisa was sent home.

Once again, they telephoned their parents with the news. And, once again, there was little response. Although both sets of parents lived within a day's drive, neither offered to come to be with them. It felt to Nelson and Lisa like a death; in fact, the loss of the baby *was* a death. *Why, then,* they wondered, *did no one seem to care?*

The following Sunday, Nelson informed the church about what had happened. He was fighting back the tears when he told the congregation. It was Advent season, and Nelson had planned to preach on Joseph and Mary that Sunday. But now he knew he couldn't get through that sermon, so at the last minute he prepared a different sermon, this one on trusting God in the midst of life's pain.

After the service, only a couple of people said anything to Nelson at the door of the church. The two who did comment said simply, "I'm so sorry." But their words sounded genuine and heartfelt, and Nelson appreciated their sympathy. Lisa was at home recuperating from the ordeal, but no one asked how she was or sent greetings to her.

The usual practice of the church whenever a death occurred in the congregation was to bring food to the house of the bereaved. Only two people brought anything to Nelson and Lisa's house, and one of them was cruel in her remarks as she handed the casserole to Nelson. "What are you two doing wrong?" was all she said. Nelson was so shocked that he said nothing. But as the woman walked away, he almost threw the dish at her.

A couple of Sundays later a woman approached Lisa at church. The woman told Lisa that she'd probably spent too much time near the microwave oven and that's what caused the stillbirth. Another woman tried to be nice in saying something comforting to Lisa. "Well, be glad it wasn't a birth with defects," said the woman. Lisa's mouth dropped open, and the woman quickly added, "I mean, it's possible there could have been serious problems or something, and this was better than that." She quickly hurried off, leaving Lisa standing with her mouth open.

Two or three people asked Nelson and Lisa what they could do for them. Nelson indicated that they'd really appreciate their prayers. One of the people responded, "Well . . . yes . . . but what else can we do?"

Nelson wanted to say, "Treat us as you would anyone else who's experienced a death in the family." But he said nothing.

In the days and weeks that followed, no one from the church phoned or sent notes or sympathy cards. Nor did they send any flowers. The usual things that church people did when someone died were not done. It seemed to Nelson and Lisa that the congregation simply didn't know what to do when a death involved the pastor's family. Or perhaps people didn't see the death of a child in the womb as being the same as the death of a child who'd been born and lived for some time. In either case, it would be death, Nelson and Lisa reasoned, but it's possible other people didn't see it that way.

One of the most perplexing elements surrounding the lack of response from people was the absence of any cards, letters, or phone calls from fellow clergy or presbytery officials. Nelson was active in presbytery meetings and affairs and was a regular attendee at the monthly clergy fellowship meetings. As one of the few evangelical pastors in the presbytery, he was often shunned by the more liberal pastors. This was especially the case after he'd taken a strong stance against abortion during one of the clergy discussions. Some of the more liberal clergy actually laughed at him, and one referred to him as "antiquated."

Did this have anything to do with the lack of response from fellow clergy? Nelson wondered. He'd informed presbytery officials of what had happened, and he thought something might be said about it in the monthly newsletter sent to clergy, but nothing was ever mentioned.

So Nelson and Lisa grieved alone. They had each other and experienced a special closeness to one another and to the Lord at this time. In addition to talking to each other at length, both of them found good outlets for their grief through physical activity. Nelson had always enjoyed working around the house, so he put his energies into painting several rooms and improving the washroom and storage areas. For her part, Lisa found cross-stitching to be a good release for her emotions. Both of them spent hours engaged in their projects.

The more Nelson thought about the lack of response from church people, the more two ideas kept going through his mind by way of explanation. The first was that perhaps people saw the pastor as only a caregiver, not as a care-receiver. They probably didn't know how to minister to the minister. People, Nelson knew, tend to put clergy in a class all by themselves. He and Lisa had occasionally laughed that churchgoers seemed to divide people into three genders: men, women, and clergy.

The second idea concerned age difference. He and Lisa were in their early thirties, but most of the congregation were at least twice that age. Nelson and Lisa's generation had learned to talk about feelings. The older generation had not. If true, Nelson wondered how to bridge the gap, encouraging people not only to minister to him and Lisa, but also respond appropriately within their own families should anything similar happen. He also hoped that the older generation could minister to younger couples whom the congregation wanted to attract.

Both hunches were confirmed to Nelson over the course of time. When several years later he left the church to go to another, one man at the first church said to him, "We know you went through some rough times personally here. We felt for you but didn't know what to do. You were the pastor, and we didn't think you needed help."

Also, months after the second miscarriage, a woman in the church confided that she'd miscarried in her youth. Back then, however, no one talked about it, viewing it as a private matter. Talking about it was, in fact, viewed as bad manners. "It just wasn't done," she said, "so I suffered in silence."

The woman was now in her seventies and told Lisa that she was the first person to whom she'd ever told this. Lisa was astounded.

She was even more astounded when, months later, her own mother revealed that before Lisa was born she, too, had suffered two miscarriages. Her mother's miscarriages were discovered after she and Nelson received the results of medical tests, indicating that all was well. So they prepared a genetic history for both sides of the family. When in conversation to obtain her mother's medical history, Lisa was told her mother's experience.

"Mother! Why didn't you ever tell me?" Lisa exclaimed. Her mother quietly replied, "It simply wasn't something anyone talked about. We kept these things to ourselves rather than burden anyone else with it. It happened to a lot of people, and we just accepted it and got on with our lives."

Lisa thought, but did not say, *Well, this explains the lack of response from you when I miscarried.* The information from her mother also helped her understand that a genetic but unknown factor might be contributing to her own miscarriages. Lisa also wondered if her mother's comment was a rebuke for how she was handling the loss. Lisa said nothing, but she felt hurt—hurt that her mother had never told her about her own miscarriages, and hurt for her mother's losses at a time when people were not so open with their feelings. She was further hurt when her father had said to her during a recent a phone conversation, "Are you over it yet?" The implication was that she should be.

She answered, "No, but I'm getting there."

One month after the stillbirth of the baby, Nelson's grandmother died. Although she was advanced in years, he'd been very close to her, and he was sad when she died. He told a friend, "She's the one who prayed me into the ministry and prayed for me every day since then." Grief was compounded by more grief.

Also, shortly after the baby's death, Lisa and Nelson packed up the toys, gifts, clothing, and furniture that were in the room they had prepared for the baby. They stored the items in the basement, not knowing if they'd ever use them. It was another occasion for tears.

Lisa then began to experience a mild postpartum depression. She felt tired and listless, was not motivated to do anything, and cried easily and often. She didn't attend to little things that she normally would have handled efficiently. Once, for example, she made muffins and, although she turned off the oven after the prescribed baking time, she forgot to take the muffins out. A week or so later, the muffins began to smell and that's when they found the source. They laughed about it, but it was definitely not like Lisa to do something like that.

Medication prescribed by the doctor and persistent expressions of love from Nelson resulted in a gradual lifting of the depression. Lisa's involvement in cross-stitching also helped, as did an appropriate use of humor on Nelson's part. Their sexual relationship, too, never waned during this time. Later, both credited their love for each other and their love-making as elements that God used to both lift their spirits and remind them of His love. Several times they reminded each other that they didn't get married to have children but to serve the Lord together.

After the second miscarriage, Nelson and Lisa were not sure they should again try to conceive a child. They looked into the possibility of adoption but decided to give themselves more time to think about it. Medical tests on both of them revealed no physical problems or abnormalities, so the doctors were encouraging. They thought the chances were good that Nelson and Lisa could ultimately conceive a child who would come to full-term birth with no problems. Her doctor did recommend, however, that she wait at least a year to eighteen months before trying to get pregnant again.

Nelson and Lisa committed their way to God and had peace that He would direct their steps. Neither was completely enthusiastic about adopting, and although they saw themselves as being potentially good parents, they were content with the possibility of being childless. They continued to pray for God's blessing and felt led to try to conceive a child once again.

Fourteen months after the second miscarriage, Lisa became pregnant. When the pregnancy was confirmed, they were unsure about who to tell and when. Some church people had asked kindly from time to time, "Are you going to try again?" It was a question of concern, not nosiness. Others, however, rather crassly stated, "You're not going to try again, are you?"

Although Nelson and Lisa wanted both their families and the congregation to know about the new pregnancy, they were apprehensive about public disclosure. Not only had their own hopes been dashed twice before, but they'd come to see that the expectations of their parents and the church family had been shattered as well. That such was the case was proven when Nelson and Lisa did go public with the news.

Their parents gave all kinds of advice to protect Lisa's well-being. Her father, in particular, took a keen interest in her welfare. He was convinced that his wife's miscarriages years ago were caused by her doing too much heavy work when she was pregnant. Thus, he continuously admonished Lisa to take it easy. "I can't bear the thought of it happening a third time," he said.

A few tentative souls in the church also made supportive comments. A typical one was made by a woman in her seventies. When she heard that Lisa was pregnant again, she said, "Oh, I do hope this works out, not just for you, but for the church. We had so been looking forward to a baby being born in the manse. Somehow it just seems to depict the future of the church." Others, however, were tightlipped about it, giving Nelson and Lisa the impression that they thought another pregnancy was a bad idea.

So it was a great day when Lisa gave birth to a healthy and strapping ten-pound boy, delivered by cesarean section. Not only did Nelson and Lisa give thanks to God for His wonderful gift, but also the church and the families breathed a sigh of relief and joined in the rejoicing.

But for some people in the church the rejoicing seemed to be done grudgingly. With the approval of the Session of the church, Nelson took a week off to help Lisa at home when the baby was born. The next week when he was back in the pulpit, one woman huffily said to him, "I don't know why *you* had to take a week off. In my day, husbands never did that. Young people nowadays . . ." and her voice trailed off. Nelson almost shouted, "Hallelujah, anyway!" but he just smiled.

In the midst of their joy at being new parents, Nelson and Lisa also looked for ways they could help other young couples who might experience the same losses they did. A few young couples were coming into the church, couples of childbearing age. During their losses, Nelson and Lisa had studied issues related to miscarriage. They discovered that instances of miscarriages might not be more common now than in a bygone era, but medical science can now confirm pregnancy and miscarriages more accurately than in the past. Some evidence suggests, too, that environmental factors may have a bearing on miscarriages. With this knowledge in mind,

Nelson and Lisa explored ways in which they could minister to others in circumstances similar to their own.

During their time of grieving after the second miscarriage, Lisa looked for written material by Christians for Christians dealing with miscarriages. She found very little. She was looking for spiritual help, not a how-to book. So she began to keep a journal describing her experiences, feelings, questions, and prayers. Gradually, the journal took shape as a book, and God used it to help bring healing to her soul. The book was never published, but Lisa eventually had it printed privately and used it with other women who had experienced miscarriages. A growing number of women sought her out to talk about their own losses.

At the suggestion of a friend at the time of their second loss, Nelson and Lisa had gone to a counselor who specialized in grief counseling. Both of them found it enormously helpful. As part of the therapy, they joined a group of parents who had recently lost children, some through miscarriage, others through tragic death after birth, and still others through abortion.

Nelson and Lisa quickly discovered the mistake of putting together people who'd experienced miscarriages with people who'd obtained abortions and were now grieving the loss. People who'd experienced miscarriages were ready to strangle those who'd gotten abortions, even if those people now regretted what they'd done.

Nelson and Lisa talked about the possibility of their starting a group for people who'd lost children in the womb. They realized that such groups would be a wonderful ministry of the church, open to anyone who wanted to come. They thought that their own experience could be helpful to others, and they'd seen how groups could aid those in grief. They'd be careful, however, to distinguish between those grieving from miscarriages or accidental death of children and those grieving from an abortion. Both circumstances brought grief, but a clear difference in circumstances existed that must be understood.

Two groups of questions were on their minds as they talked about starting this ministry. First, how they would get started? How would they get the word out about the group? Would they be qualified to lead such groups? Would non-Christians be put off by the focus of looking to God for comfort and peace at a time of loss?

Second, how would the congregation respond to their starting a grief group for parents whose children had died? The older people in the church had made it clear that "suffering in silence" was the accepted way to deal with the loss of a child. There was no need to call attention to it. Just "buck up" and get on with life was the prevailing attitude of the older generation. Also, for many of the older people, the loss of a child in the womb was a very private matter.

How, Nelson and Lisa wondered, *can we change this attitude? Did it even need to change, or could generational differences simply exist side by side? In an intergenerational church, as theirs was rapidly becoming, was there opportunity for dialogue on these matters, or at least respect and acceptance of others' needs? Or would change come only after the older generation was gone?*

Nelson knew that older people grieved, but their grieving was not as open as what Nelson and Lisa needed. When their son was born a healthy child, one church member cautioned them not to rejoice too publicly. "Remember," he said, "something could still happen to your child in the future."

Nelson just about lost it at that point but instead responded with determination, "We know that, and we're holding him loosely. He belongs to God. But we're rejoicing right now in the wonderful blessing from God."

That's it! thought Nelson. *How can we help the church rejoice with those who rejoice and weep with those who weep? It's not a private matter. But what can the pastor do?*

Discussion Questions

1. Why do different generations view and talk about miscarriages differently?

2. Does a Christian perspective make a difference in how one perceives a miscarriage? If so, why?

3. How can churches minister to couples who have experienced miscarriages?

4. When it comes to childbirth and miscarriages, how can pastors help their congregations "rejoice with those who rejoice," and "mourn with those who mourn"? How does public disclosure affect this process?

5. What resources are available for clergy who mourn?
6. Are pastors different from lay people in how they mourn? Why do churches tend to handle clergy's grief differently than they do other people's grief?

13

MURDER
When the Unthinkable Happens

D rew instantly sensed that something was wrong. It was a Wednesday night, Family Night at the church. The adults would be attending Bible study while the children engaged in all sorts of activities. As pastor, Drew had been reviewing in his mind tonight's lesson, and had just pulled his car into the church parking lot when he noticed a cluster of women standing outside the door adjacent to the parking area.

One of the women saw Drew getting out of his car, and she ran to him. "Eve is missing," she said, her voice tight. Kent, Eve's husband, had just called one of the women to say that Eve hadn't come home from her early afternoon jog and that a search for her was under way. The family wouldn't be at Family Night that evening, so the substitute teacher for Eve's children's class would need to teach.

Jumping back into his car, Drew told the woman to get one of the elders to lead a prayer service in place of the usual Family Night activity. He then left for Kent and Eve's house to provide pastoral support for Kent and the children. A jumble of thoughts raced through his mind as he drove along—wondering if Eve had had an accident or if something worse had happened, or if she'd simply lost track of time while doing an errand. But Eve was so organized and self-disciplined, it was unlike her to leave her family wondering where she was. Drew feared the worst.

When his cell phone rang, Drew pulled over to the side of the road and answered it. It was one of the elders. He told Drew that Eve had been found and was at the hospital. She was barely alive and in critical condition. Drew did a U-turn and headed for the hospital.

When he arrived, he quickly found Kent and the two children, Liz and Marty. Kent said in an emotion-choked voice, "She's dead . . . murdered!" Drew said later that he would forever remember those words. The next few minutes seemed to pass in slow motion. Kent related the details as he knew them.

Eve had gone for her usual afternoon jog. A devoted jogger, she went to a park near her home, which has a jogging path that many people use. People could set their watches by her regular pattern of exercise at the park. That's why when Liz, seventeen, came home from school she was surprised that her mother wasn't there. Liz had arrived home from high school minutes before her brother Marty, fourteen, came home from junior high.

Liz called her father at work to say that her mother wasn't home, nor was there any note of explanation. When she talked to her father, she said that she was frightened. Kent was able to leave work immediately and come home.

A quick look around the house made Kent realize that Eve had gone jogging. He expected that to be the case, so he first looked in her closet. The clothes she had worn that morning when Kent left for work were on the bed, and her jogging shoes and clothes were not in their usual place. Liz and Marty, too, had already noticed this.

Kent called the police and told them what they'd found. The policewoman who answered the phone said that nothing could be done until a person had been missing for twenty-four hours, unless there was evidence of criminal activity. In this case, the evidence at the house indicated no apparent crime.

"But you don't understand," Kent said. "This isn't like Eve. She's an extremely responsible person. She'd never leave the house without writing a note for me or the children."

"Oh, you'd be surprised at what people do," the policewoman responded. She indicated again that the police could do nothing at this point, except note in the log that a person was reported missing. She took down the details of Eve's height and weight, color of hair, and what she was probably wearing. And that was that.

Frustrated, Kent began to call Eve's closest friends, all of whom said that Eve was not with them. They expressed surprise that Eve had not left a note and that she wasn't there when the children came home from school. Eve was always there when the children returned from school.

Almost frantic now, Kent called a friend who worked in the mayor's office and told him what was going on. The friend said, "Let me see what I can do." A half hour or so later, two policemen showed up at the door to get more information on Eve. Obviously, the mayor's office had acted.

Kent and the children gave them more information about Eve and where she usually jogged. When the police arrived, Kent had been ready to leave for the park and look for Eve himself. They convinced him, though, to stay at the house in case she called. Some of Eve's friends whom Kent had called started to arrive at the house, as worried as Kent and the children. So Kent stayed behind to be with the children and the others while the police began the search.

Before long, the police called the house and told Kent that Eve had been found, badly beaten but still breathing, and was on her way to the hospital. Kent and the children took off for the hospital, followed by Eve's friends. Using their cell phones, the friends alerted others in the church about what had happened, and the church's prayer line was quickly activated. An elder called Drew to inform him that Eve had been found, and that's when he made his hasty turnaround.

When Kent poured out his anguished cry to Drew that Eve was dead, he added, "I didn't even get to see her or talk to her or anything. She was in the emergency room when I arrived, and I couldn't go in. I never got to speak to her to tell her how much I loved her." And he dissolved in tears.

Other friends arrived, crowding the small hospital room where they gathered. Some people cried softly and hugged each other. Others made phone calls. Drew asked for quiet and led in prayer, asking for the peace of God to be present in a special way. His voice broke as he prayed, and his own tears flowed.

One of the medical staff came into the room to ask Kent if he'd like to see the body. He responded that he would, and asked Drew to accompany him. It was not deemed wise for the children to come, nor did they want to. On the way to the room where Eve's body lay, the nurse told Kent that he needed to prepare himself for a shock, that Eve obviously had been badly beaten.

Nothing could have prepared Kent and Drew for the sight that met them. Saying nothing, but gasping, Drew thought, *Beaten? She looks like she was tortured!* Eve was recognizable, but barely. What once was a beautiful woman with fine and delicate features was now a mass of cuts, bruises, and swollen flesh.

Drew, who had stood at many hospital bedsides, almost lost it. His knees felt weak and his head light. He prayed for strength and wisdom to minister to Kent. Drew was fighting back tears, but Kent just stood in steely silence and looked at Eve. Then he took her lifeless hand and held it for a long time. Finally, he leaned over, kissed her tenderly, and said, "Goodbye, my love." Again, Drew almost broke down himself, but he stood with Kent in silence.

Finally, the silence was broken. "Pastor," Kent asked Drew in nearly a whisper, "is this part of God's plan?" Drew avoided a direct answer to the question at the time, and replied softly, "God is sovereign, and He's here right now." He prayed again, giving thanks for the life and witness of Eve, and asking the God of all comfort to bring His grace and peace to Kent, Liz, and Marty.

Back in the other room, Kent embraced the children and spoke softly to them, words that those around could not hear. Even Drew did not hear what was said, nor did it matter especially. He suggested that people leave the room to give the family some privacy for a few minutes.

The two policemen who'd come to the house were waiting outside the room when Kent came out. They asked if he felt up to talking with them then. He indicated that he did and waved for Drew to join him. The children also remained in the room.

The police had the doctor's initial report. There had been no sexual penetration, although Eve's jogging shorts were torn, raising the suspicion that her attacker had attempted to assault her sexually. She was badly battered and bruised but had fought her attacker viciously. Skin and blood, not hers, were under her fingernails and would prove to be valuable DNA evidence in the future. "She must have fought her attacker off, but had no strength left to get up," they said. They had found her in a wooded area about fifty feet off the jogging path. "We'll catch whoever did this," they said to Kent. He nodded and thanked them for what they'd done.

Although the police had been discreet and had chosen their words carefully, it still was upsetting to Liz and Marty to hear those details. It seemed too horrible even to imagine what had happened. Their mother had always been so careful, never jogging when it was dark, never wearing a headset radio so she could hear sounds around her, and even carrying pepper spray.

Before the police left, Liz asked them about the can of pepper spray. The police said they found it lying near the path, causing them to look more closely in that particular area. The can had been discharged, and there were signs of some kind of a scuffle from the path to the spot where Eve's body was found. As the police left, they said that a house-to-house inquiry of the homes near the jogging trail was under way to learn if anyone had heard or seen anything.

Kent looked at Drew and asked, "What do I do now? I don't know where to start."

Drew responded, "It's one step at a time now." He suggested that they return home, call other family members, and begin to make plans for getting through the next few days.

When they pulled up in front of Kent's house, reporters and TV crews were already standing in the yard, hoping to get information for the 11 P.M. news broadcast. "This is unbelievable!" Drew said to no one in particular as he jumped out of his car and raced to where the reporters and cameramen were standing. He pleaded with them to give the family some privacy at this point, and said that some kind of a statement would be made later.

The crews begrudgingly picked up their gear and left, but not before a couple of reporters were filmed outside the house, narrating details of what was known about the murder, done in broad daylight on a very popular jogging path. And they repeated the police request that if anyone had seen or heard anything to report it to authorities. The news media carried information about the story for days.

From Wednesday, when the murder happened, to Sunday, when the funeral would take place, Kent's house and the church were beehives of activity. The church had around five hundred members and was strategically located near the heart of a West Coast city in an area undergoing rebirth and upscale development. The murder was big news. Not only was the entire congregation stunned by Eve's murder, which took place not far from the church, but also the surrounding neighborhood was in shock.

Eve was beloved in the church. She was a bundle of cheerful energy and brought joy to everyone who had any contact with her. She had been a children's teacher in the church for the last ten years, the result being that a large number of children and young adults knew her and loved her for her wisdom, grace, and charisma. Such was the solid foundation that she laid in her teaching that many of them credited her with their understanding of biblical teaching. Again and again, people exclaimed, "It's not fair!" Accolades about her beauty and joy were frequently declared.

Drew attended to the usual pastoral tasks of helping the family deal with the initial shock and grief when a loved one dies. He focused his energies, too, on planning the funeral service, helping Kent decide on burial or cremation, what kind of casket to purchase, and cemetery arrangements. The very nature of Eve's death, however, required Drew to cope with public access and information, making pastoral care much more complicated.

Before becoming a pastor, though, Drew had worked as executive director for a social service agency. In that capacity, he'd gained experience in dealing with crises. Thus, he swung into action when Eve was murdered, setting up a crisis management team of volunteers to answer the phones at church and at Kent's house. Dozens of calls were coming in from media sources across a wide geographical area, wanting information directly from Kent.

The crisis management team responded to these inquiries, using a prepared statement that Drew revised each day. Each statement referred to Eve's faith in Christ and the Christian's hope of resurrection to new life because of Christ's resurrection. Broad information was given, too, about how the family was doing, about the funeral, and background information about Eve.

The pastoral staff at the church were also in high gear, comforting church members in their grief and assisting with the many details surrounding a high-profile funeral. Arrangements were made for meals to be brought to the family's house. The youth pastor spent time with Liz and Marty, who were responding to their grief in very different ways. Liz was withdrawn and didn't want to be with people. Marty got lost in video games. People were coming and going through the house, and the phone would not stop ringing. Kent himself seemed to be in a daze much of the time.

Many church volunteers were present at the house, handling dozens of details efficiently even as they also grieved. "It was," Drew said later, "one of the finest hours for the church. We functioned as one body. And though we grieved, it was not without hope. I think that was obvious to everyone."

Expecting a large crowd at the funeral in a sanctuary that seated only five hundred, Drew arranged for closed circuit TV to be set up in several classrooms. The church was prepared to handle one thousand people for the funeral, including civic leaders who planned to come because of the circumstances of Eve's death. Many more people than that actually came, crowding the halls and standing outside the building.

Media personnel were not allowed to be at the service, but did set up their broadcasting facilities across the street from the church. Drew was thankful that media personnel respected the privacy of the family, and they, in turn, expressed appreciation to Drew for the professional way he kept them informed. More than one reporter talked about the Christian faith that Eve embraced and noted the church's focus on resurrection hope. Eve's testimony and the hope of the church were broadcast far and wide. Even international wire services picked up the story.

On the Sunday of the funeral, which was scheduled for the afternoon, Drew preached to a packed sanctuary at the morning worship service. He spoke on 1 Corinthians 12:26: "If one part suffers, every part suffers with it; if one part is honored, every part rejoices with it." He commended the congregation for how they'd pulled together and had rallied to help the grieving family as well as attend to the many details surrounding Eve's death.

He also talked about what it meant to grieve with hope, the unique assurance that Christians have. He encouraged the church family not to doubt God. The sermon flowed from the heart and had been prepared in only two hours, in contrast to the usual fifteen hours he spent on a sermon. And the words hit home. Person after person left the sanctuary that morning saying only a simple "thank you" to Drew as they shook his hand. But their eyes and demeanor said much more.

At the funeral, Drew chose as his text the apostle Paul's reassuring words from Romans 8:35: "Who shall separate us from the love of Christ? Shall trouble or hardship or persecution or famine or nakedness or danger or sword?" Drew paused, then added slowly and deliberately, "Or murder? No! Nothing! Nothing!" He made the point that God had not abandoned Eve, and He would never abandon any of His followers even if all seemed dark. As with the morning sermon, the message flowed freely from his heart and was prepared in record time in light of so many other pressing needs during the previous days. Drew quietly thanked God for His grace to him in the last ninety-six hours.

Drew was also thankful for his wife, who cared for his needs through meals, love, and prayer support. It was as though she could anticipate everything he was thinking or needing, and she was there for him. And in the coming days, when Drew himself was tempted to doubt God's grace and presence with His people, his wife was there, praying patiently for him and reminding him gently of his own words of assurance to the church and to Kent, Liz, and Marty.

The church had committed itself to provide meals for the family for a number of weeks following the funeral. And Drew had made a commitment to spend more time with Kent and the children than he normally would have done. He *wanted* to do it, and he sensed that the family needed it. All of the public attention had subsided, but the family's grief continued, perhaps more freely now after the furor had dissipated and they could think about what happened.

During one of Drew's pastoral visits to the house, Liz was especially upset. She kept going over that terrible Wednesday in her mind. She had sensed that something was wrong when she came home from school that day. Having discovered her mother's jogging shoes missing from their usual place, she thought that something must have happened while she was jogging. She now wished that she'd gone out immediately, looking for her mother. Hearing that her mother was alive when she was found, Liz kept thinking, *If I'd found Mom three hours earlier, maybe she'd still be alive today.*

Drew listened while Liz poured out her thoughts. Then he read Psalm 139. He spoke of David's assurance in confessing that God was always with him and knew his thoughts even before he spoke. David's assurance of God's presence and acceptance of him in spite of his failures and questions were realities that people today can experience; it was not a truth for only David. Liz seemed to take comfort from Drew's words.

God also used a woman in the church whose mother had committed suicide to help Liz deal with her feelings. The woman had worried for years that her lack of sensitivity had contributed to her mother's death, and she felt guilty that she didn't do enough for her mother when she was alive. Liz was helped by the words of this woman describing her own thoughts.

Marty was helped as time went on by the youth pastor who befriended him and would just hang out with him from time to time. Marty didn't talk about it much, but was sad over what happened to his mother. To the youth pastor, Marty seemed overwhelmed by all of the attention the family received immediately after his mother's death. So the minister wanted to give him space but also be available as needed. This seemed to be the right balance for Marty.

Drew was most concerned about Kent. As an accountant, Kent lived in a world where order prevailed. Two plus two was always four. Numbers were logical and always added up right. But nothing about Eve's death added up right. He couldn't get his mind around what had happened, couldn't make sense of it. It seemed to him so pointless, so needless. Eve had never hurt anyone. On the contrary, she had brought joy to everyone she met. The whole thing just wasn't logical. And it certainly wasn't fair. He began seriously to question the providential care of God for His children.

Kent couldn't get the image of his bruised and battered wife out of his mind. And he couldn't shake off the growing feeling that God had abandoned her when she was attacked and didn't care that she'd suffered.

Kent had fallen in love with Eve from almost the first moment he met her. She was a lovely, petite, joyful, and utterly charming woman. Their love for each other was deep, and they rejoiced that God had led them to each other. Then, when the children were born, they were an utter delight, with Liz evidencing many of the traits of her mother and Marty those of his father. They were among the most involved families in the church. Their Christian faith was clear, and their testimony of God's grace to them was evident to anyone who met them.

And now this. "Where was God when Eve was attacked?" Kent asked repeatedly. The question burned deeper and deeper into his mind and began to crowd out the truth that he previously confessed—that in spite of difficult circumstances God would always be present with His people. Although he knew that bad things happened to good people—and just because one is a Christian doesn't mean that one is protected from trag-edy or suffering—the truth he once embraced about God's always being with His people began to slip from his grasp. It was the violent nature of Eve's death and the fact that it was so undeserved that Kent couldn't get from his mind. Gradually, he began to think that perhaps God didn't care what happened to His people.

In the weeks following Eve's death, Kent and the children came to church only occasionally. People would approach Kent or one of the chil-dren, asking how they were doing, but they gave either a vague response or no response at all. Sometimes, after the service, Kent remained seated in the pew after the church had emptied. On those occasions, Drew would sit with Kent for a while, saying nothing but just being present with Kent. Drew was afraid, however, that the church was losing Kent and that he was sinking into a deep depression. But Drew was unable to penetrate Kent's mind with anything that made sense to him. And just admitting with Kent that it was impossible to make sense of Eve's death from a hu-man point of view didn't seem to satisfy Kent. Drew also knew that glib answers wouldn't work, nor was he inclined even to offer them.

The rest of the church also continued to grieve for weeks. From out-ward appearances, people were moving on with their lives. But stories cir-culated of people having nightmares that a member of the family was tragically killed. Mothers didn't want their children to play outside unat-tended. People who used the jogging path where Eve was killed no longer went there, but instead used indoor tracks at health clubs. Children were afraid that something would happen to their parents. And fathers admit-ted to worrying about their family's well-being when they were at work or traveling on business. Everyone just seemed to be on edge.

In his sermons, Drew made frequent references to Christian hope and resurrection truth. Reformed in his theology, he emphasized repeatedly the reality of God's grace and presence even in the midst of tragic circum-stances. These comments were not a direct reference to Eve's death, but a general reminder of the character and work of God with His people.

Grief counseling was made available to members of the congregation as needed. The church distributed without charge dozens of copies of a book written by a Christian man whose wife and children had died in a tragic accident.

Drew also arranged a special seminar on self-defense to take place in the church. It was led by the police and focused particularly on defending oneself against assault and rape. People expressed appreciation for it, but Drew also wondered if it kept what had happened to Eve in the forefront. Rather than grieving the loss and moving on, such activities were constant reminders of a violent society, and to many people may have been more unsettling than reassuring. Nonetheless, these activities seemed like the right thing to do.

What people struggled with, probably more than anything, was fear. It wasn't a fear that God wasn't present when evil things happen, but that something bad would happen to them, something that they couldn't prevent. The lack of control over life was unsettling even though people believed that their lives were entirely in God's hands. It was a confusing time, and people were forced to examine their stated beliefs about God's trustworthiness and what they really believed about God and their own well-being.

For Drew, the demands of helping the church process their individual and corporate grief, and the special ministry that Drew extended to Kent, Liz, and Marty, gradually wore him down. Drew was weary to the bone, and he felt himself getting angry with God. When he was honest, he admitted to himself that, at moments he, too, felt betrayed by God. The very thought of that frightened him. It was during this period of struggle within his own soul that his wife was praying fervently for him. Her understanding, patience, and love touched Drew deeply and helped lift him from his own despair.

At one of his low moments, Drew was reading from the gospel of Luke. When he came to Luke 7:20, where John the Baptist sends word from prison asking Jesus, "Are you the one who was to come, or should we expect someone else?" Drew admitted that he'd been asking God a similar question: *Are you the one? Are you really with us in every circumstance? Can we really trust you?*

The answer was in Jesus' reply to John's question:

> Go back and report to John what you have seen and heard: The blind receive sight, the lame walk, those who have leprosy are cured, the deaf hear, the dead are raised, and the good news is

preached to the poor. Blessed is the man who does not fall away on account of me. (Luke 7:22–23)

God used this passage to put things in perspective for Drew. He emerged from his doubts with a firm but humble conviction that God would never abandon His people no matter how bleak things seemed. His theology of the sovereignty of God was renewed, and this gave a peace that was beyond description. At the same time, however, he was aware of, as never before, the reality of evil.

A new need began to emerge in subtle ways from people in the congregation. It was also a need for Kent, Liz, and Marty. And Drew admitted that it was a need for him as well. It was the need to forgive Eve's murderer, even though no one knew who that person was. People admitted that they wanted the murderer to suffer and that, if the person was ever apprehended, the only justice would be the death penalty. Anger and a desire for vengeance were strong on the part of many people. In some ways, the desire for revenge was providing energy for people, but it was also eating away at their souls.

Drew reflected on how to deal with this need for revenge. He knew that Scripture made clear that no one is pure; everyone stands forgiven and justified by God only through the atoning sacrifice of Christ on the cross. Further, Jesus taught His disciples to forgive others as they had been forgiven. And Paul affirmed this teaching to the Colossians:

Bear with each other and forgive whatever grievances you may have against one another. Forgive as the Lord forgave you. And over all these virtues put on love, which binds them all together in perfect unity. (Colossians 3:13–14)

But Drew also realized that knowing the teaching about forgiveness and love was one thing; actually forgiving was quite another.

But the pastoral task that Drew faced was to make this teaching understood and to apply it to his own life and the lives of his people. In some ways, it was a simple act of the will. "Just do it!" as the Nike® ad says. But it wasn't that easy for people, even Drew. It needed, however, to be done.

So Drew began to focus his prayers and thoughts in the direction of forgiveness. Of this one thing he was convinced: People needed to forgive Eve's murderer—even if that person never asked for forgiveness, even if people never knew who that person was. If they didn't forgive, they'd never be able to accept Eve's death and move on in their spiritual lives. How to help people distinguish between justice and forgiveness was the problem. Drew reasoned that both justice and forgiveness needed to be held in balance. Justice without forgiveness can be raw vengeance; forgiveness without justice can be anarchy. Drew pondered how he could present this dilemma to the congregation in a way that would aid their healing and their growth in the faith.

Another thought, too, was always in the forefront of Drew's mind: *What if the perpetrator is caught?* The skin and blood found under Eve's fingernails provided crucial DNA evidence. Police were certain that in due course they would catch the murderer. *What effect will this have on the church and the family?* Drew wondered.

Other questions as well presented themselves to Drew: *If the murderer is apprehended, would the media descend on the church again? How would that be handled? Could the church talk publicly about forgiveness in a way that honored God and His Word and not seem wimpy to the world? And what would the effect be on Kent and the children? What kind of justice should be meted out to the murderer?*

Drew continued to think daily about the family also. By this time, they would have almost nothing to do with the church, and Drew couldn't seem to find a way to reach them. But he never stopped praying for them, nor did others in the church. *Is there more to be done?* he kept asking himself.

Discussion Questions

1. How would you respond to Kent's question, "Is this part of God's plan?"
2. Does a dramatic event such as murder change the way pastoral care should be extended?
3. How can a church leader minister to people when he himself or she herself is struggling with doubt and frustration with God? What effect might sharing these feelings openly have on the congregation?
4. How can pastors help people distinguish between justice and forgiveness?

5. What might be the effect on the family and the church if the murderer is caught?
6. What could the church and pastor do to prevent Kent and his family from leaving the life of the church?
7. What do you think about how the church and pastor handled the media attention resulting from the high-profile murder?

14

ABORTION
We Don't Want to Talk About It

Stuart's thoughts this particular morning centered on forgiveness. He had gotten up early and spent his usual time in Bible reading and prayer. After a modest breakfast of cereal and toast, he sipped his coffee, reflecting on the past several years of his pastoral ministry at Faith Evangelical Church.

Stuart had been the pastor at Faith Evangelical for ten years, and many times he'd witnessed the church's willingness to forgive someone. He'd noted that forgiveness was powerful, setting the offender free from guilt and bondage, the offended free from hatred and vengeance. Too, forgiveness demonstrated to the world that Christians took not only sin but also forgiveness seriously—both forgiveness from God when one is repentant and forgiveness of each other in Christian community.

Stu was particularly touched by the response to a message he'd recently preached from Colossians 3:12–14:

> Therefore, as God's chosen people, holy and dearly loved, clothe yourselves with compassion, kindness, humility, gentleness and patience. Bear with each other and forgive whatever grievances you may have against one another. Forgive as the Lord forgave you. And over all these virtues put on love, which binds them all together in perfect unity.

He'd been preaching through the book of Colossians, and in this particular message he emphasized the necessity for and privilege of

Christians to forgive one another when a wrong has been experienced. Even during the sermon, he sensed that the Spirit of God was working in an unusual way in the hearts of the congregation. So it was no surprise that people afterward commented on how helpful they'd found the sermon, even though they acknowledged that forgiveness was not always easy to extend.

A few days after that sermon, Rose, a woman in the church, phoned to ask if she could talk to Stu. He readily made an appointment and saw her the next day. After exchanging pleasantries, Stu asked Rose what was on her mind. She hesitated and seemed to be on the edge of tears, but after a few seconds she composed herself and began to talk.

"My daughter, Tess . . . " Rose began with difficulty. "She's only fifteen, you know. She . . . had an abortion." What Rose said didn't surprise Stu as much as it saddened him. The family hadn't told anyone about it, and Rose was even uncertain about the propriety of telling her pastor about it now. "But in church last Sunday," she said, "listening to your sermon about forgiveness, I felt forgiven by God for the first time in several weeks." She also wanted the pastor to know the circumstances, although she emphasized that she hoped he'd keep it confidential.

"At this point," Stu assured her, "I see no reason to reveal anything to anyone. But I'd appreciate any details you care to share with me."

Rose and her husband had had no idea that Tess had been sexually active. In family conversations they'd talked about abstinence until marriage, and Tess seemed to agree with this ethic. The family was active in church, and Tess herself gave every appearance of Christian behavior.

Tess was popular, attractive, and never lacked for friends, especially male friends. She was a good student, known for being strong-minded, and was never reluctant to share her opinions. Some people viewed her as a bit stubborn, but chalked it up to youthful enthusiasm. Her grace, charm, wit, and beauty opened many doors for her. But no one ever suspected her of being sexually involved with a boy.

When Tess suspected that she might be pregnant, she bought a self-administered pregnancy test from the drugstore and wasn't surprised when the result was positive. What she didn't count on, however, was her mother's inadvertently discovering the test when she emptied the wastebasket from the bathroom.

After seeing the pregnancy test, Rose confronted Tess and asked what was going on. Readily admitting that she was pregnant, Tess showed no remorse and indicated further that she hadn't intended to tell her mother or father because she knew they'd be upset. In the state where the family lived, girls under the legal age are not required to inform their parents if they get an abortion, nor was the clinic providing the procedure under any obligation to tell the parents. Tess had planned to go visit a friend in another city and get an abortion there.

Rose's finding out about the pregnancy put those plans on hold, at least temporarily. Tess, however, was adamant that she would get an abortion, even though her parents tried to talk her out of it. Their desire was for her to carry the baby to term, then either keep the baby and raise it herself with their help or give up the baby for adoption. Tess would hear none of it; abortion was the only option she'd consider.

Further, Tess stated, "If you try to stop me, I'll run away and have the abortion because I don't need your consent." She said this in a calm and cool manner, but made clear in no uncertain terms that her mind was made up.

When Rose and her husband tried to ascertain the identity of the father, Tess refused to identify him. She did indicate, however, that only one boy was involved, so she knew who the father was. The boy had given her money to pay for the abortion as an indication of his responsibility.

To acquiesce to the pleas of her mother, Tess did agree to see a Christian counselor before she had the abortion. Rose accompanied her daughter to the counselor's office, and Tess was as defiant there as she'd been at home. She would get an abortion. It was as though she couldn't even consider any other option.

The counselor gently asked if he could point out some of the ramifications of her decision. She nodded. He said that she needed to think about some things—guilt that would inevitably come at some point when she would likely question the wisdom of her decision of taking a human life, how her action would affect her self-image later and might adversely affect her walk as a Christian, and the health risks involved in getting an abortion. In addition, from his experience, he observed that when girls had abortions, even if it didn't affect their health, it often affected their sexual experience with their husbands should they later get married.

Further, he emphasized that abortion was taking a life and was therefore a matter of utmost seriousness. He said all of this matter-of-factly without condemnation.

A few seconds of silence followed his comments, the counselor then asked Tess if she'd thought about what would please God in this situation. It was the only time that Tess showed any hint of remorse. Up to this point during the session, she'd looked slightly bored but also a little uneasy. When he asked what would please God, Tess simply commented that she'd already sought God's forgiveness and, on the basis of knowing that she was forgiven, she was determined to get the abortion. She pointed out that her life and future plans were at stake, and that she didn't yet see the "thing" in her as a human being; Even if it was human, she wouldn't consider any other option. Then, before the session was over, she stood and said quietly but firmly, "I want to go now."

Up to that point, Rose had been quiet in the session and had been praying that Tess would listen to the counselor, who was saying many of the things that she and Tess's father had said. *Perhaps Tess will listen to the counselor,* Rose thought. Rose got up quickly when Tess stood, and the counselor put up a hand and said, "One more thing, please."

At this, Tess stopped and looked at the counselor. "I invite you to come see me again after the abortion," he said. "I'd like to help you process any feelings you have in the days and weeks ahead." Tess indicated that she'd do so, but she never did.

As Rose related these details to Stu now, he felt his heart go heavy with the news. He didn't know which grieved him more—that Tess had gotten an abortion or that the family hadn't told him about it before now. He was glad, though, that Rose and Tess had at least gone to see a counselor.

"Rose," Stu asked gently, "why did you wait so long to come talk with me?"

"I didn't know how you'd respond," she replied. She indicated further that she'd never heard Christians talk about abortion except in condemning tones and words. She herself had similar thoughts and feelings about the culture's casual acceptance of abortion, but she never thought that she'd have to deal with an abortion in her own family. "When I had to face it myself," she said, "I didn't know where to turn, so I decided to tell no one."

At this point, only Rose, her husband, Tess, her boyfriend, the counselor—and now Stu—knew anything about the abortion. "It all happened so fast," Rose said. In a matter of days, they'd gone from being a "happy family" to obtaining an abortion. Tess had allowed Rose to accompany her to the clinic where the procedure was performed, and had shown little remorse. Her only physical problems after the abortion was done were a few days of fatigue and minor abdominal cramping.

Rose, however, was having feelings of guilt and remorse. She and her husband had talked incessantly about it, but hadn't shared it with any of their friends. Even the small group to which they belonged in the church was unaware of what had happened. And, even now, neither Tess nor Rose's husband knew that she was talking with Stu.

"I don't know. . . . I just felt like I had to talk to you after last Sunday's sermon," Rose said to Stu. "I've been feeling so guilty and depressed over what happened. But you preached that no matter what someone has done, it's forgivable, and no matter what you've done to someone or they've done to you, it's forgivable. I felt a huge weight lifted from me. God does forgive our sins. I just don't know whether I trust people to do the same."

Stu and Rose talked a bit more about guilt and forgiveness. He suggested that Rose tell her family that she'd talked with him, and that he fully understood their pain and sorrow. When he asked if Rose thought Tess might come to talk with him, she said, "I doubt if Tess will agree. But I'll ask her."

The conversation then shifted to whether the "secret" could be shared with individuals in the church. Stu suggested it could be done on a case-by-case basis, but Rose expressed concern about that possibility. Not only was she was afraid of what people would think about them, but also, more than anything, what it would do to her daughter's well-being. Tess simply didn't want anyone to know about it.

The family was convinced that if anyone found out about it they would be condemned and would likely have to leave the church. Stu gently pointed out that it likely wouldn't remain a secret anyway. In his experience it was inevitable that information about this sort of thing leaked out. "Besides," he said, "I hope the church would handle it in a forgiving and accepting way. And," he added, "I'll do all I can to help to that end." But, at Rose's request, he agreed not to tell anyone. After he prayed for the family, the conversation ended.

Now, some days later, he sat in silence, drinking his coffee and thinking more about how the church might respond to knowing someone amongst them had had an abortion. He knew that the whole subject of abortion was an emotional one. He suspected, though, that many people were unaware of the number of Christian women who'd obtained abortions, or the Christian men who'd impregnated women and were equally responsible for abortions. Other than Tess, Stu was aware of only one other family in the church who, several years ago, experienced an abortion. But he knew from statistics that it was inevitable that such people were sitting in the pews each Sunday, especially in a congregation of two hundred fifty people, many of them middle-aged couples with teenage children. *How many of them have had abortions but haven't told anyone about it?* he wondered.

For a few minutes, his mind wandered over the need to teach sexual ethics in the church—in Christian Formation classes, in youth meetings, and from the pulpit. After following several mental rabbit trails about what could be done, he focused again on the conversation with Rose. He also recalled the earlier abortion involving the other church family, and remembered the details as though it had happened only yesterday.

In some ways, things haven't changed much in the last decade, he thought as his mind wandered back to the earlier situation. It occurred shortly after he'd first come to the church. The situation was similar to that of Tess in that those involved didn't want anyone to know. But there were differences between the two circumstances in how the abortions came about.

In Tess's case, she had insisted on the abortion, concerned about how pregnancy would affect her future. In the earlier case, the parents of a sixteen-year-old girl insisted that their daughter get an abortion because of the physical problems of the fetus.

He'd learned about the earlier situation when Perry and Shirley came to talk with him. They had two teenage children, Tricia, sixteen, and Max, fourteen. When Perry and Shirley made the appointment, Stu sensed something was wrong, but he had no idea what they would reveal.

Through tears, Shirley and Perry talked about what had happened. Shirley had noticed that Tricia was at least several weeks late for her period. When she asked Tricia about it, Tricia said she didn't know why. So Shirley took her to a gynecologist, who informed them that Tricia was pregnant. Both Shirley and Tricia were shocked. The doctor estimated that Tricia was nearing the twelve-week point in her pregnancy.

It was a very quiet ride home from the doctor's office, with Shirley and Tricia lost in their own thoughts. Once home, Tricia went immediately to her room, and Shirley waited for Perry, Tricia's father, to come home from work. When he arrived, Shirley told him immediately about what had been learned at the doctor's office. Perry then went to Tricia's room and talked with her. They both cried, and Perry stressed the availability of God's forgiveness. He prayed with her and then returned to talk with Shirley.

The plan that Perry and Shirley proposed was for Tricia to move to another city, where Shirley's sister lived, deliver the baby there, then give up the infant for adoption. Tricia resisted this idea but at the moment had no alternative to suggest.

Things soon took a different turn, however. During the preceding weeks when Tricia didn't know that she was pregnant, she'd undergone several orthodontic treatments in which she was under anesthesia on three different occasions. She'd also been taking medication for an allergy. Both treatments were known to create problems for a developing fetus. Now, knowing about Tricia's being pregnant, Shirley arranged for a follow-up appointment with the gynecologist. Their worst fears were confirmed; an ultrasound revealed that the fetus indeed had serious birth defects.

The doctor explained the risks of carrying the baby to term, and although he didn't recommend outright that Tricia get an abortion, it was clear from the medical evidence that the infant would have massive deformities and likely would not live long or would require extraordinary treatment to survive. It was also evident that if the baby survived birth, intensive institutional care would be required for however long the baby lived.

Because the pregnancy was in the twelfth week, a decision had to be made soon about whether to terminate the pregnancy. Perry and Shirley spent a concentrated time in prayer for two days, asking the Lord for wisdom and guidance. Afterward, they felt it best to terminate the pregnancy in light of the medical evidence and Tricia's young age. Tricia herself wanted to continue the pregnancy. Under pressure from her parents, however, she acquiesced to their wishes.

The abortion was scheduled immediately because Tricia was at the end of the first trimester. Shirley accompanied Tricia to the clinic where the inducing procedure was performed, and was able to stay with her daughter until the procedure started. Then the clinician asked Shirley to leave the room. So Tricia was alone when the procedure was completed.

After spending one night at the clinic, Tricia returned home to convalesce for a few days. Then it was back to the routine of school. Very little was said between Tricia and her parents, although the atmosphere in the home was tense. A sense of sadness also pervaded the household. Max had been informed of the abortion, although he'd already suspected that Tricia was pregnant. He was aware of her sexual activity with her boyfriend, but said nothing to anyone. He was not surprised to learn that his sister was pregnant.

During the hectic week between learning of the pregnancy and obtaining the abortion, Perry and Shirley confirmed with Tricia that Chad was the father. He was Tricia's boyfriend and had spent much time in their home, studying with her and eating meals with the family. He agreed with the decision to abort the fetus and, at Perry's request, had agreed to pay for the abortion. Perry had talked to Chad "very straight" about Chad's responsibility to treat Tricia with respect, including stopping all sexual activity and covering the costs of the abortion.

After the abortion, Tricia and Chad continued dating, Tricia thinking that eventually they'd get married. But a few weeks later, Chad broke off the relationship, not only surprising Tricia but also crushing her spirit even further. She became more despondent as the days went on but continued to put up a good front with people outside the family. She even continued to achieve good grades in school, where she was an honor student. To the family's knowledge, no one outside the family and the pastor were aware of what had happened.

As Shirley and Perry observed Tricia at home, however, they became increasingly worried about her well-being. They also felt pain and guilt on several levels—for not preventing Tricia's sexual activity in the first place, for forcing her to have the abortion, and now about Tricia's psychological and spiritual downward spiral into despondency. Although they stressed to Tricia how much they loved her and wanted what was best for her in the long run, nothing they said seemed to help. And their prayers for her and themselves didn't seem to bring any relief or change.

One of the results of knowing that Tricia had been sexually active was that Perry and Shirley resolved to build a better relationship with her, one of greater openness and trust. Up to this point, whenever Tricia was un-communicative or distant—as typical teenagers occasionally are—Perry and Shirley would react harshly, which only drove Tricia further from them. Shy by nature, it was easy for Tricia to withdraw from people, including her own family. She enjoyed being by herself, although she was good at relating to people, so much so that many people would never have imagined that she was shy. Her relationship with Chad was one of the few close relationships she had with anyone, which was a factor in her getting sexually involved with him. Being so close to Chad, however, only added to the blow when he broke up with her.

The family was quite active at Faith Evangelical Church, where Perry was an elder and Shirley was a Sunday school teacher. Tricia herself was active in the youth group, as was Max. As far as they knew, no one other than the family was aware of the abortion. Stu certainly never suspected anything and was surprised when Perry and Shirley came to talk with him several weeks after it had been performed.

When Stu asked them why they hadn't come to him sooner, they replied that they knew he was busy, but mostly they were embarrassed and were unsure how Stu would respond. This bothered Stu because he saw himself as open to supporting people who were experiencing crises, and he had a reputation for being a caring pastor. As they talked about it, Perry and Shirley revealed further that one of their basic concerns was how church people would respond to the news.

So, to them, it just seemed best to keep quiet. But over the course of the days and weeks following the abortion, Shirley, especially, found herself feeling sad and very guilty over her part in insisting upon the abortion. Soon thereafter, during the worship service one Sunday when the Lord's Supper was being celebrated, Stu talked about God's forgiveness of sin. During the service, Shirley felt a special presence of God surrounding her and a lifting of the burden that she'd felt in her heart for some days.

After that, she and Perry decided to talk with Stu. As they talked, Shirley said, "The decision to get the abortion was the hardest decision we've ever made. We agonized over it. And then afterward we asked God's forgiveness again and again." With that, gentle tears started flowing again.

After a few seconds of silence, Stu said, "God really does forgive our sins, doesn't He?" Both Shirley and Perry nodded assent. Stu then steered the conversation back to the topic of sharing the experience with other Christians at the church. He was convinced that people in the church would respond in spiritually mature ways, that they'd come alongside Tricia and the family. Their revelation, too, might open opportunities to minister to others who'd faced similar circumstances. But again, Shirley and Perry were reluctant to have anything said publicly. Their primary concern was for Tricia. Stu accepted their wish and assured them that he wouldn't mention anything to anyone. He prayed for them and for Tricia, asking God to bring healing for their pain, and glory to Himself through the experience.

As Perry and Shirley prepared to leave, they talked briefly about whether Tricia and Chad would be willing to talk with Stu. They thought that it would be a good idea, assuming that Tricia and Chad were willing. So Stu phoned Tricia and she agreed.

During the meeting with Tricia and Chad, Stu observed that they were quite nervous. Stu had gone to the house to talk with them, thinking it best to visit in the home rather than have Tricia and Chad come to his office. There, they might be observed by others who would likely wonder what was going on. Perry, Shirley, and Max had left the house so that Stu could talk privately with the two young people.

The conversation was awkward. Usually Stu had no trouble getting people to talk given his easy-going and warm style of pastoral care. But Tricia and Chad said very little, even when Stu phrased questions that required more than a *yes* or *no* response.

So Stu talked about forgiveness and encouraged them to be sexually responsible in the future by observing abstinence in their relationship. He talked about how that would be hard to do but that it could be done with disciplined willpower and help from God. While he talked about this, both Tricia and Chad looked extremely uncomfortable but said nothing. Stu forced the issue a bit by asking if they understood fully what he was saying and if they thought they could abide by it. They nodded but said nothing. Stu felt that he wasn't getting through to them, so he brought his comments to a close, but not before touching briefly upon some of the issues that might come up in the future. He concluded by encouraging them to talk with him if they wanted to discuss anything in the days ahead. At that point, after praying briefly, he left.

Stu didn't know Chad before meeting him on this occasion, but Perry and Shirley had told him that they didn't think Chad was a Christian. Chad, however, seemed to be very fond of Tricia and had listened to her and the family discuss Christian matters a great deal when he was in their home on various occasions. Perry and Shirley had been praying that he would become a Christian, but to their knowledge he hadn't yet made a decision to that effect.

For this reason, during the meeting with Tricia and Chad, Stu talked about the Christian faith, how it was based upon the belief that what Christ had done on the cross brought forgiveness and eternal life. On the basis of this foundation, God, in His grace and mercy, could help Christians live in ways that were God-honoring and were ultimately for our own well-being. As with other things he had said, however, he wasn't sure that anything was getting through to Chad. He left with a heavy heart, but didn't think he could do anything else at that moment.

He knew, however, that God could touch their lives and bring healing in every way. So he prayed often and intensely over the next few days for God to work in Chad's and Tricia's lives. He prayed for the family's well-being, too, and longed to share the story with other mature Christians, asking their prayer support and love to surround the family. He knew, however, that he could say nothing because he'd given his word that he would not disclose anything to anyone.

A day or so later, Shirley called Stu and said that Tricia refused to say anything about her and Chad's conversation with him, nor was Shirley asking for any information from Stu. She just wanted him to know that Tricia seemed more despondent and had requested to see a counselor to talk things over. Stu was thankful that Tricia herself had requested to see a counselor. From his experience, he knew that counseling was most beneficial when the person needing help requested it. He gave Shirley the name of a Christian counselor, whom he highly recommended.

Stu was delighted to learn later that Tricia had seen the counselor regularly for several months, and that the sessions had been helpful in bringing healing to her.

When, however, he first learned that Tricia was more depressed after she and Chad had talked with him, Stu's first thought was that he'd said something or had spoken in a way that contributed to her despondency.

But, in reviewing mentally what he'd said, he was convinced that he was not at fault and shouldn't berate himself for wishing that he'd handled it differently. *I was true to God and His Word,* he thought, *and I was caring and sensitive to their feelings, so if I had it to do all over again, I would say and do the same things.* Being comforted with these thoughts, he prayed again for God to intervene according to His will in the lives of everyone concerned.

Some months later, Tricia shared with Stu little bits of information about what she went through during the time of the abortion and the weeks following. She indicated that she was depressed at that time but had hidden it from everyone as best she could. "I had a reputation to maintain as a Christian girl, so I went along with my parents' decision to get the abortion. I felt trapped, caught," she said to Stu. When she learned that the fetus was deformed, she thought, *Well, that's it. I know what my parents will want me to do now.* But she said little, except to protest mildly when they decided for her to abort the fetus. Thinking about her feelings after the abortion, she said to Stu, "It was surreal, like a bad dream. I felt it was not really happening." She felt that she had greatly disappointed her parents, and this caused her even more inner distress. Then when Chad broke up with her, she wasn't sure she'd survive the pain she was feeling. That's when she requested to see a counselor. Stu was happy to hear that, with the passage of time, she was doing better.

In talking with her about it, Stu asked, "Tricia, what do you wish could have been done differently?" She thought about it for several seconds, and then responded, "I don't think anything could have been different." Stu then asked, "Do you have any thoughts about how the church could have handled the situation if they'd known about it?"

Again, Tricia indicated that she thought it best that the church be left unaware of what happened. She herself wasn't sure she'd ever be able to tell anyone about what she'd done. Fear of condemnation from others and shame for what she had done were paramount in her mind.

* * *

Now, as Stu sipped his coffee, he thought about forgiveness. He thought, too, about the days when he'd met with and counseled the girls and their families. The questions he'd pondered then were still fresh in his mind.

1. Why was such fear involved in confessing abortion?
2. Could the church be trusted to deal with an instance of abortion in a grace-giving manner?
3. Does the church's caregiving to those involved in abortions match its rhetoric about the issues related to abortion? Or do the typical statements of condemnation contribute to the problem?
4. Why do some Christians worry more about their reputations than about doing the right thing?
5. How can a theology of the body of Christ be taught and realized in the life of the church?
6. What is the pastor's responsibility in not only teaching about sexual purity but also in creating a "safe" atmosphere in the church in which people who sin in their sexual lives can find forgiveness and help in dealing with their failures?
7. Is it right for a pastor to agree not to disclose that someone is thinking about abortion or dealing with the effects of it? How should a pastor deal with such requests?

With these questions swirling in his mind, Stu knew that he had to do something, but he wondered where to begin. He knew that continuing to treat abortion as a secret was not an option, but he also wondered if confidentiality could be maintained when needed while somehow also involving the church with people who faced the possibility of abortion?

Discussion Questions

1. How would you answer the questions that the pastor raised at the end of the case?
2. Are you aware of people in your church who've had abortions? How has the church handled this information?
3. In viewing abortion, does it make a difference if deformity is known to exist in the fetus?

4. How can the church minister to both men and women who have been involved in abortions?
5. How do you evaluate the pastor's handling of the two situations in the case study?

Appendix

How to Use Case Studies

C ase studies have been used as a teaching tool for many years. Because issues are often unresolved and questions unanswered at the end of the case, readers or group participants are required to reflect upon the dilemmas portrayed, identify the issues, and determine a resolution. Case studies are thus a method of teaching that engages readers by involving them in the outcome.

Individuals who are not participating in group discussions can read case studies for their own benefit, but discussing a case with others adds the perspectives of other minds. A dynamic is present in group discussion that is not present within an individual. But learning can occur in either context.

There is no one right way to teach using case studies, but your goal as the leader is to involve participants in the group with the issues present in the case. Any method that accomplishes that goal is legitimate.

To teach cases effectively, three essentials must be considered: the case itself, the teacher, and the group.

The Case

Some cases involve a dominant issue but may also involve several subsidiary issues. Other cases may illustrate several issues that relate to the main topic. In this book, each case centers on a particular topic that involves issues related to ministry. When selecting a case for group discussion, keep in mind the dominant issue as well as secondary issues portrayed in the case and how these issues relate to the needs and composition of the group.

When reading a case, then, jot down the dominant issue of the case as well as secondary issues that are worth exploring in discussion. You might decide to introduce the central issue and then list other issues to be explored, or you might ask the group to identify secondary issues they see and want to discuss.

If you ask the group to identify issues in the case they would like to discuss, you must, of course, be not only flexible in approaching potential issues but able to lead and teach in the areas so identified. This ability might be nothing more than skill on your part in facilitating group discussion, but it might also mean you need to have knowledge of particular subjects. Still, the approach has merit, in that it allows group participants to explore issues of interest to them. It also helps the group see that one issue does, indeed, create or impact another, and see how a holistic approach to problem solving can be more effective than isolating one issue from the rest. You may find, too, that expertise in a given area might emerge from a group participant to the benefit of the whole group, in which case you needn't be an expert in every area touched upon in the case.

The Teacher

The role of the teacher is to guide group discussion around the issues in the case. In some instances, a minilecture may be appropriate. Most of the time, however, the teacher's role is to facilitate a productive discussion in which group members are helped to identify the issues illustrated in the case, address those issues, and reach some kind of resolution.

Typical of case studies, the cases in this book do not have an apparent resolution. Thus, there can be no declaration in absolute terms of how an issue is to be resolved or whether a particular outcome can be guaranteed. Such, though, is the benefit of case teaching. The point is not necessarily to resolve the issue to everyone's satisfaction or even to reach unanimity on what did happen or ought to happen; rather, the point is to engage people in thinking for themselves about the issues and about what they can learn from the case to apply in their own roles as leaders.

The Group

Groups have different personalities. Some might be more reflective than others. Others might be more talkative and action-oriented. Some might be more tentative, and approach the case by probing for more information before making a decision. Others might quickly reach dogmatic conclusions. Your task as leader is to help the group function as a group so that both individual and group learning are maximized and not hindered by the discussion process.

Life experience and maturity of age also affect how a group will address a case. A group of experienced ministers may take a different approach discussing a particular issue than a group of seminarians, who will also likely be different from Bible college students. Lay people may also bring a unique perspective to a particular issue. Age, theology, and denominational affiliation are also factors that will affect the mix of ideas expressed. The same case taught by the same teacher to different groups will have different outcomes. That is part of the benefit and learning potential in the case method.

The following are some specific suggestions for effective case teaching.

1. Know the Case Thoroughly

Read the case several times to have adequate knowledge of names and time lines as well as to identify issues. Be aware, too, of the content of particular pages so as to make specific reference to a point of illustration, especially of major issues that you may want to highlight.

Identify significant transition points in the case. In reading through the case, where are you first surprised? What does this tell you about your own involvement in the issue, and how might this affect your approach to the case? If you find some elements intriguing, undoubtedly others will, too, so you might want to focus on these elements with the group.

Thorough knowledge of names, places, sequences, possible cause and effect, and specific details pertinent to the case is essential. You should know more about the details of the case than do the members of the group.

2. Have a Purpose in Mind

When preparing to teach a case, decide upon the purpose you want to accomplish in group discussion. This means that you will want to identify the key issues portrayed in the case and decide how these issues relate to the needs of the group. Which issues do you specifically want the group to address? Why? In the end, what would you like the group to know? What effect might this have on their ministries? Keeping the purpose in mind will guide your thinking, planning, and leading.

3. Plan Your Approach

Think about the outline you will follow in the discussion. Specifically, think about how you will introduce the case, how you will make the transition to the main discussion, how that discussion will be structured, and how you will conclude the case.

The introduction should be brief and can take the form of a statement, a question, picking up a phrase or statement in the case, or providing a summary of the case. Focusing on the time line might be helpful if the sequence of events is important. Asking someone to give a two-minute summary of the case might be a good way to start, focusing the group's collective attention on the details of the case.

In the introduction, identify key issues so the group will know what the focus will be. Key issues can be stated by the teacher or can be solicited from the group.

In long cases, such as those in this book, group members should read the case before coming together for discussion; otherwise, too much group time is spent reading the case. Shorter cases can be read silently at the beginning of the meeting, especially if the leader wants an element of surprise or immediate reaction to the issue at hand. When the case is read ahead of time, an oral summary at the start of discussion is essential.

Plan ahead how to transition from the introduction to the main discussion. One effective transition is to ask group members to recall significant information about the central characters in the case. Jot this information on a chalkboard, newsprint, or overhead projector, and ask if anyone wants to comment on any particular piece of information. These verbal and visual reminders help group members recall names and information about specific people in the case. Use of PowerPoint™ technology is not recommended because it's not easy to change the points of the presentation as the case is being discussed. PowerPoint™ may be used effectively, however, in the introductory presentation or in your conclusion because these elements might have more "fixed" aspects.

After discussing the characters, ask what issues group members noted in their reading. Write this information as well on whatever medium you are using, and state or ask what issues need to be discussed. Let this form the structure for the primary discussion time with the group.

Some case teachers prefer to break a large group into smaller clusters of three to five people to discuss particular aspects of a case. In this method, it is best to have the clusters discuss different issues with some method of reporting their findings back to the whole group. Then the leader should finalize the discussion with everyone reconvened, pulling together any loose strands and summarizing the findings into a coherent whole.

Another approach is to keep the whole group together with you as facilitator, which can be done even in large groups. It allows everyone to hear what others say and keeps the group moving together. Although unanimity might not be achieved—nor is it necessarily the goal—keeping the group together does mean that the group thinks together and may reach deeper understanding of the issues than is possible when the group is broken into smaller clusters.

Another effective method is the use of role-playing. Individuals take on the roles of specific characters in the case and, based upon the information in the case, they talk to each other in that role. This heightens the drama and makes the issues real for the individuals participating in the role play as well as for the observers, but it must be done well to be effective. Some people are uncomfortable role-playing, so either select individuals whom you know will do a good job or let individuals volunteer.

For the conclusion, it is not necessary to have everything neatly wrapped up. People may reach different conclusions on what they think needs to happen in a particular case. The goal, remember, is not to get everyone to agree on a particular issue; rather, the goal is to get individuals to think about specific issues so as to help them in their personal growth and ministry. Often, a member of the group will continue to reflect on the discussion long after the time together, and the result may be further growth and change for the better.

But the discussion does need closure. That can come from a summary of what has been said, a reiteration of the issues and possible resolutions, a challenge to learn from the case in some specific way, speculation on what might have eventually happened in the case, or raising a question upon which participants can reflect individually. Citing biblical references for people to think about or praying for each other in relation to the issues portrayed in the case are further effective ways to conclude the discussion.

4. Guide the Discussion

Your task as leader is to guide the discussion to maximize learning for the group. This should be done without manipulating the group for your own agenda, although you may have a particular point of view that can be expressed for the group to consider. As mentioned earlier, sometimes a minilecture is effective, particularly if it concerns issues relating to a leader's particular area of expertise; but it's sometimes beneficial for the group to address the issues in a discussion format right from the start.

Raise questions and allow people time to think about their responses. Don't ask several questions at once on different aspects of an issue. That hinders the group from focusing on something in depth. Use questions to focus attention on the topic, and avoid going several directions at once.

Sometimes an individual will raise a question or make a comment about an issue that deserves discussion but interrupts the flow of discussion on a particular point. When this happens, jot down the point on the overhead or chalkboard and indicate that the point will be discussed later. Then steer the discussion back to the question at hand.

If someone expresses an opinion that you sense others might not hold, the group should be asked to respond. Or if you know the group members well, a specific individual may be asked to respond. You as leader needn't answer every question; rather, the leader facilitates the group's responses to the issues.

Some members of a group may be quiet and need to be invited to make comments. Often these quieter members have keen insights, and the leader's task is to find appropriate ways to include such people in the discussion without being too obvious or intrusive.

Keep an eye on the clock. Ninety minutes is the maximum time most adults are at their best in thinking and interacting in a group situation. The cases in this book can be discussed effectively in one hour or less. The better your planning, the more effective will be your use of time.

5. Use Visuals When Possible

Case teaching provides a forum that maximizes group interaction. Although a discussion with no use of visuals can be productive, good visuals enhance the outcome and learning. Visuals might involve nothing more than using an overhead projector, newsprint, or white board to jot down major points or to plot a time line. Visuals could also be prepared on transparencies for an overhead projector or in a PowerPoint™ presentation. These are helpful in organizing the major points of a case and facilitate group learning, as long as these materials are prepared in advance and do not control unnecessarily the direction of the discussion, thereby preventing free and open interaction.

Use your imagination. You can introduce something visually in many ways to engage participants and enhance learning.

6. Obtain Feedback for Evaluation

Obtaining information on what worked well and what did not work well in teaching the case will help you evaluate your approach and leadership style in facilitating group discussion. You can solicit such feedback from the group as a whole or request it from selected individuals in a private conversation. Having a colleague join the group to observe your leadership is another good way to obtain helpful information. A tried-and-true, if older, tool used by a colleague is an interaction chart, a graph showing the location of people in the group, who spoke to whom, and how many times an individual spoke.

Focusing on real situations that are not furnished with resolutions forces us to deal with reality, sharpens our thinking, and informs our decision-making on important matters. The more experience you have teaching cases, the more you gain confidence and new ideas in using cases. Everyone involved may discover anew the value of a group discussion to individual learning.

Case teaching is not the only way to learn, of course. Nor does it fit every learning need. But it can be a useful way of helping people address issues in their own lives that might otherwise be ignored. Case stories are often our own stories, or we can, to some extent, identify with specific aspects of a case. Judicious use of cases, either for personal reading and reflection or for group discussion, can be used of God to bring about clarity of thought and facilitate needed change in behavior.

As stated in the introduction, good case teaching will use relevant biblical teaching. The use of cases is not intended merely to exchange human wisdom but more so to wrestle with biblical teaching and how it applies to the dilemmas of real people in real churches.

Colleagues in ministry are a rich resource of support. So, too, are mature Christian people in our churches—people who will love each other, challenge each other, pray for each other, and walk with one another in the various crises that churches face. Nothing, though, substitutes for a thorough knowledge of Scripture, personal zeal for holiness in Christ, and a rigorous application of biblical truth to daily living. Lively and thoughtful discussion generated through teaching cases makes paramount the wisdom of God's teaching.

BIBLIOGRAPHY

GENERAL WORKS ON CRISIS COUNSELING

Berkley, James D. *Called into Crisis: The Nine Greatest Challenges of Pastoral Care.* Dallas: Word, 1989.

Collins, Gary R. *Christian Counseling: A Comprehensive Guide.* Rev. ed. Dallas: Word, 1988.

Crabb, Larry. *Effective Biblical Counseling: A Model for Helping Caring Christians Become Capable Counselors.* Grand Rapids: Zondervan, 1977.

Dillon, David. *Short-Term Counseling.* Dallas: Word, 1992.

Haugk, Kenneth C. *Christian Caregiving: A Way of Life.* Minneapolis: Augsburg, 1984.

———. *When and How to Use Mental Health Resources.* St. Louis: Stephen Ministries, 2000.

Kollar, Charles Allen. *Solution-Focused Pastoral Counseling: An Effective Short-Term Approach for Getting People Back on Track.* Grand Rapids: Zondervan, 1997.

Lampman, Lisa Barnes, ed. *Helping a Neighbor in Crisis.* Wheaton, Ill.: Tyndale, 1999.

McNeill, John T. *A History of the Cure of Souls.* London: SCM, 1952.

Oden, Thomas C. *Classical Pastoral Care.* Grand Rapids: Baker, 1987.

Oglesby, William B., Jr. *Referral in Pastoral Counseling.* Nashville: Abingdon, 1978.

Patton, John. *Pastoral Counseling: A Ministry of the Church.* Nashville: Abingdon, 1983.

Peterson, Eugene. *The Contemplative Pastor.* Carol Stream, Ill.: Word , 1989.

Sanders, Randolph K., ed. *Christian Counseling Ethics: A Handbook for Therapists, Pastors and Counselors.* Downers Grove, Ill.: InterVarsity, 1997.

Shelley, Marshall. *Helping Those Who Don't Want Help.* Waco, Tex.: Word Book, 1986.

Switzer, David K. *Pastoral Care Emergencies.* Minneapolis: Fortress, 2000.

———. *The Minister as Crisis Counselor.* Nashville: Abingdon, 1986.

Welch, Edward T. *Addictions, a Banquet in the Grave: Finding Hope in the Power of the Gospel.* Phillipsburg, N.J.: P & R, 2001.

Welch, Edward T., and Gary Steven Shogren. *Addictive Behavior.* Grand Rapids: Baker, 1995.

Worthington, Everett L., Jr. *Hope-Focused Marriage Counseling: A Guide to Brief Therapy.* Downers Grove, Ill.: InterVarsity, 1999.

Wright, H. Norman. *The New Guide to Crisis and Trauma Counseling: A Practical Guide for Ministers, Counselors and Lay-Counselors.* Ventura, Calif.: Regal, 2003.

———. *Helping Those Who Hurt: How to Be There for Your Friends in Need.* Minneapolis: Bethany, 2003.

ABORTION

Alcorn, Randy. *Pro-Life Answers to Pro-Choice Arguments.* Portland, Ore.: Multnomah, 1992.

Davis, John Jefferson. *Abortion and the Christian: What Every Believer Should Know.* Phillipsburg, N.J.: P & R, 1984.

Fowler, Paul B. *Abortion: Toward an Evangelical Consensus.* Portland, Ore.: Multnomah, 1987.

Koerbel, Pam. *Does Anyone Else Feel Like I Do? And Other Questions Women Ask Following an Abortion.* New York: Doubleday, 1990.

Schlossberg, Terry, and Elizabeth Achtemeier. *Not My Own: Abortion and the Marks of the Church.* Grand Rapids: Eerdmans, 1995.

Stanford-Rue, Susan M. *Will I Cry Tomorrow? Healing Post-Abortion Trauma.* Old Tappan, N.J.: Revell, 1990.

Swindoll, Charles R. *Sanctity of Life: The Inescapable Issue.* Dallas: Word, 1990.

ADULTERY

Ankerberg, John, and John Weldon. *The Myth of Safe Sex.* Chicago: Moody, 1993.

Harvey, Donald R. *Surviving Betrayal.* Grand Rapids: Baker, 1995.

Spring, Janis Abrahms. *After the Affair: Healing the Pain and Rebuilding Trust When a Partner Has Been Unfaithful.* New York: HarperCollins, 1996.

Virkler, Henry A. *Broken Promises.* Waco, Tex.: Word, 1992.

AIDS

A WCC Study Document. *Facing AIDS: The Challenge, the Churches' Response.* Geneva, Switzerland: WCC Publications, 1997.

Hoffman, Patricia L. *AIDS and the Sleeping Church.* Grand Rapids: Eerdmans, 1995.

Hoffman, Wendall W., and Stanley J. Grenz. *AIDS Ministry in the Midst of an Epidemic.* Grand Rapids: Baker, 1990.

Kurth, Ann, ed. *Until the Cure: Caring for Women with HIV.* New Haven, Conn.: Yale University Press, 1993.

Rozar, G. Edward, Jr., and David B. Biebel. *Laughing in the Face of AIDS: A Surgeon's Personal Battle.* Grand Rapids: Baker, 1992.

Russell, Letty M., ed. *The Church with AIDS: Renewal in the Midst of Crisis.* Louisville: Westminster John Knox, 1990.

Shelp, Earl E., and Ronald H. Sunderland. *AIDS and the Church: The Second Decade.* Louisville: Westminster John Knox, 1992.

Weatherford, Ronald J., and Carole B. Weatherford. *Somebody's Knocking at Your Door: AIDS and the African-American Church.* Binghamton, New York: Haworth Pastoral Press, 1999.

Wood, Glenn G., and John E. Dietrich. *The AIDS Epidemic: Balancing Compassion and Justice.* Portland, Ore.: Multnomah, 1990.

CHILD ABUSE

Adams, Carol J., and Marie M. Fortune, eds. *Violence Against Women and Children: A Christian Theological Sourcebook.* New York: Continuum, 1995.

Allender, Dan B. *The Wounded Heart.* Colorado Springs: NavPress, 1990.

Barshinger, Clark E., Lojan E. LaRowe, and Andrés T. Tapia. *Haunted Marriage.* Downer Grove, Ill.: InterVarsity, 1995.

Chu, James A. *Rebuilding Shattered Lives: The Responsible Treatment of Complex Post-Traumatic and Dissociative Disorders.* New York: John Wiley, 1998.

Fortune, Marie M. *Violence in the Family: A Workshop Curriculum for Clergy and Other Helpers.* Cleveland: Pilgrim, 1991.

Garbarino, James, and John Eckenrode. *Understanding Abusive Families.* San Francisco: Jossey-Bass, 1997.

Giardino, Angelo P., and Eileen R. Giardino, eds. *Recognition of Child Abuse for the Mandated Reporter.* St. Louis: G. W. Medical Publishing, 2002.

Huskey, Alice. *Stolen Childhood.* Downers Grove, Ill.: InterVarsity, 1990.

Kearney, R. Timothy. *Caring for Sexually Abused Children: A Handbook for Families and Churches.* Downers Grove, Ill.: InterVarsity, 2001.

DEATH

Bane, J. Donald, Austin H. Kutscher, Robert E. Neale, and Robert B. Reeves Jr. *Death and Ministry: Pastoral Care of the Dying and the Bereaved.* New York: Seabury, 1975.

Bowlby, John. *Loss: Sadness and Depression.* New York: Basic, 1980.

Brabant, Sarah. *Mending the Torn Fabric: For Those Who Grieve and Those Who Want to Help Them.* Amityville, N.Y.: Baywood, 1996.

Brown, Elizabeth B. *Sunrise Tomorrow: Coping with a Child's Death.* Grand Rapids: Baker, 1988.

Bregman, Lucy. *Beyond Silence and Denial: Death and Dying Reconsidered.* Louisville: Westminster John Knox, 1999.

Lampman, Lisa Barnes, ed. *Helping a Neighbor in Crisis.* Wheaton, Ill.: Tyndale, 1997.

DEPRESSION

Anderson, Neil T., and Hal Baumchen. *Finding Hope Again: Overcoming Depression.* Ventura, Calif.: Regal, 1999.

Baker, Don, and Emery Nester. *Depression: Finding Hope and Meaning in Life's Darkest Shadow.* Portland, Ore.: Multnomah, 1983.

Beck, Aaron T. *Depression: Causes and Treatment.* Philadelphia: University of Pennsylvania Press, 1973.

Carson, Herbert M. *Depression in the Christian Family.* Durham, England: Evangelical Press, 1994.

Copeland, Mary Ellen, and Stuart Copens. *The Adolescent Depression Workbook.* Brattleboro, Vt.: Peach Press, 1998.

Hart, Archibald D. *Coping with Depression in the Ministry and Other Helping Professions.* Waco, Tex.: Word, 1984.

Lewis, Thomas Griffith. *Finding God: Praying the Psalms in Times of Depression.* Louisville: Westminster John Knox, 2002.

Minirth, Frank, and Paul Meier. *Happiness Is a Choice: The Symptoms, Causes, and Cures of Depression.* Grand Rapids: Baker, 1994.

Rapee, Ronald M., and David H. Barlow. *Chronic Anxiety: Generalized Anxiety Disorder and Mixed Anxiety-Depression.* New York: Guilford, 1991.

Roesch, Roberta. *The Encyclopedia of Depression.* New York: Facts on File, 2001.

Stone, Howard W. *Depression and Hope: New Insights for Pastoral Counseling.* Minneapolis: Fortress, 1998.

Sutton, Mark, and Bruce Hennigan. *Conquering Depression: A Thirty-Day Plan to Finding Happiness.* Nashville: Broadman and Holman, 2001.

Tan, Siang-Yang, and John Ortberg Jr. *Understanding Depression.* Grand Rapids: Baker, 1995.

White, John. *The Masks of Melancholy: A Christian Physician Looks at Depression and Suicide.* Downers Grove, Ill.: InterVarsity, 1982.

DIVORCE

Houck, Don, and LaDean Houck. *The Ex-Factor: Dealing with Your Former Spouse.* Grand Rapids: Revell, 1997.

House, H. Wayne, ed. *Divorce and Remarriage: Four Christian Views.* Downers Grove, Ill.: InterVarsity, 1990.

Lampman, Lisa Barnes, ed. *Helping A Neighbor in Crisis.* Wheaton, Ill.: Tyndale, 1997.

Miller, David R. *Counseling Families After Divorce.* Dallas: Word, 1994.

Sprague, Gary, comp. *My Parents Got a Divorce.* Elgin, Ill.: David C. Cook, 1992.

Streeter, Carole Sanderson. *Finding Your Place After Divorce.* Wheaton, Ill.: Harold Shaw, 1992.

Wallerstein, Judith S., and Sandra Blakeslee. *Second Chances: Men, Women, and Children a Decade After Divorce.* New York: Ticknor and Fields, 1989.

Whiteman, Thomas. *Innocent Victims: Understanding the Needs and Fears of Your Children.* Nashville: Nelson, 1992.

Whiteman, Thomas, and Debbie Bart. *When Your Son or Daughter Is Going Through a Divorce.* Nashville: Nelson, 1994.

DRUG AND ALCOHOL ABUSE

Cummings, Nicholas A., and Janet L. Cummings. *The First Session with Substance Abusers.* San Francisco: Jossey-Bass, 2000.

Elkin, Michael. *Families Under the Influence: Changing Alcoholic Patterns.* New York: Norton, 1984.

Gold, Mark S. *The Facts About Drugs and Alcohol.* New York: Bantam, 1988.

Lewis, Judith A., Robert Q. Dana, and Gregory A. Blevins. *Substance Abuse Counseling: An Individualized Approach.* 3d ed. Pacific Grove, Calif.: Brooks/Cole, 2002.

McGee, Robert S., Pat Springle, and Susan Joiner. *Rapha's Twelve-Step Program for Overcoming Chemical Dependency.* Houston: Rapha, 1990.

Ross, George R. *Treating Adolescent Substance Abuse: Understanding the Fundamental Elements.* Boston: Allyn and Bacon, 1994.

Todd, Thomas C., and Matthew D. Selekman, eds. *Family Therapy Approaches with Adolescent Substance Abusers.* Boston: Allyn and Bacon, 1991.

Treadway, David C. *Before It's Too Late: Working with Substance Abuse in the Family.* New York: Norton, 1989.

GRIEF

Allender, Dan B. *The Healing Path.* Colorado Springs: WaterBrook, 1999.

Barber, Cyril J. *Through the Valley of Tears.* Santa Ana, Calif.: Promise, 2000.

Davis, Verdell. *Let Me Grieve but Not Forever.* Dallas: Word, 1994.

Lamb, Roger, and Marcia Lamb. *This Doesn't Feel Like Love: Trusting God When Bad Things Happen.* Woburn, Mass.: Discipleship Publications, 1996.

Lampman, Lisa Barnes, ed. *Helping a Neighbor in Crisis.* Wheaton, Ill.: Tyndale, 1997.

Lawrenz, Mel, and Daniel Green. *Overcoming Grief and Trauma.* Grand Rapids: Baker, 1995.

Nygaard, Reuel, and Guy Doud. *Tragedy to Triumph.* Elgin, Ill.: Life Journey, 1994.

Palau, Luis. *Where Is God When Bad Things Happen?* New York: Doubleday, 1999.

Westberg, Granger E. *Good Grief.* Philadelphia: Fortress, 1979.

Wright, H. Norman. *Resilience: Rebounding When Life's Upsets Knock You Down.* Ann Arbor, Mich.: Servant, 1997.

Zonnebelt-Smeenge, Susan J., and Robert C. De Vries. *Getting to the Other Side of Grief: Overcoming the Loss of a Spouse.* Grand Rapids: Baker, 1998.

MENTAL HEALTH

American Psychiatric Association. *Diagnostic and Statistical Manual of Mental Disorders.* 4th ed. Washington, D.C.: American Psychiatric Press, 1994.

Boyd, Jeffrey H. *Affirming the Soul.* Cheshire, Conn.: Soul Research Institute, 1994.

———. *Soul Psychology.* Cheshire, Conn.: Soul Research Institute, 1994.

Ciarrocchi, Joseph W. *A Minister's Handbook of Mental Disorders.* New York: Paulist, 1993.

Johnson, W. Brad, and William L. Johnson. *The Pastor's Guide to Psychological Disorders and Treatments.* New York: Haworth, 2000.

MURDER

Amick-McMullan, A., D. Kilpatrick, L. Veronen, and S. Smith. "Family Survivors of Homicide Victims: Theoretical Perspectives and an Exploratory Study." *Journal of Traumatic Stress* 2 (1989): 21–35.

Bard, Morton, and Dawn Sangrey. *The Crime Victim's Book.* 2d ed. New York: Brunner/Mazel, 1986.

Figley, Charles R. *Trauma and Its Wake: Traumatic Stress Theory, Research, and Intervention.* New York: Brunner/Mazel, 1986.

Lampman, Lisa Barnes, ed. *Helping a Neighbor in Crisis.* Wheaton, Ill.: Tyndale, 1997.

Lord, Janice Harris. *No Time for Goodbyes: Coping with Sorrow, Anger, and Injustice After a Tragic Death.* Ventura, Calif.: Pathfinder, 1987.

Masters, R., L. Friedman, and G. Getzel. "Helping Families of Homicide Victims: A Multidimentional Approach." *Journal of Traumatic Stress* 1 (1988): 109–25.

Ochberg, Frank M., ed. *Post-traumatic Therapy and Victims of Violence.* New York: Brunner/Mazel, 1988.

Rando, Therese A. "Homicide." In *Treatment of Complicated Mourning.* Champaign, Ill.: Research Press, 1993.

———, ed. *Parental Loss of a Child.* Champaign, Ill.: Research Press, 1986.

Van der Kolk, Bessel, ed. *Psychological Trauma.* Washington, D.C.: American Psychiatric Press, 1987.

PORNOGRAPHY

Arterburn, Stephen, and Fred Stoeker. *Every Man's Battle: Winning the War on Sexual Temptation One Victory at a Time.* Colorado Springs: WaterBrook, 2000.

Balswick, Judith, and Jack Balswick. *Authentic Human Sexuality.* Downers Grove, Ill.: InterVarsity, 1999.

Cleveland, Mike. *Pure Freedom: Breaking the Addiction to Pornography.* Bemidji, Minn.: Focus, 2002.

Earle, Ralph H., Jr., and Mark R. Laaser. *The Pornography Trap: Setting Pastors and Laypersons Free from Sexual Addiction.* Kansas City: Beacon Hill, 2002.

Fehlauer, Mike. *Finding Freedom from the Shame of the Past.* Lake Mary, Fla.: Creation House, 1999.

Hall, Laurie. *An Affair of the Mind.* Colorado Springs, Col.: Focus on the Family, 1996.

Laaser, Mark. *Faithful and True: Sexual Integrity in a Fallen World.* Grand Rapids: Zondervan, 1996.

Means, Marsha. *Living with Your Husband's Secret Wars.* Grand Rapids: Baker, 1999.

Means, Patrick A. *Men's Secret Wars.* Grand Rapids: Baker, 1999.

Powlison, David. *Pornography: Slaying the Dragon.* Phillipsburg, N.J.: P & R, 1999.

Roberts, Ted. *Pure Desire.* Ventura, Calif.: Gospel Light, 1999.

Rogers, Henry J. *The Silent War: Ministering to Those Trapped in the Deception of Pornography.* Green Forest, Ark.: New Leaf, 2000.

Wilson, Kathryn, and Paul Wilson. *Stone Cold in a Warm Bed.* Camp Hill, Pa.: Horizon Books, 1998.

SEXUAL ADDICTION

Anderson, Neil T. *A Way of Escape.* Eugene, Ore.: Harvest House, 1994.

Arterburn, Stephen, and Fred Stoeker. *Every Man's Battle: Winning the War on Sexual Temptation One Victory at a Time.* Colorado Springs: WaterBrook, 2000.

Jantz, Gregg. *Too Close to the Flame: Recognizing and Avoiding Sexualized Relationships.* West Monroe, La.: Howard, 1999.

Laaser, Mark. *Faithful and True: Sexual Integrity in a Fallen World.* Grand Rapids: Zondervan, 1992.

Schaumburg, Harry W. *False Intimacy: Understanding the Struggle of Sexual Addiction.* Colorado Springs, Col.: NavPress, 1997.

Sterling, Beth. *The Thorn of Sexual Abuse: The Gripping Story of a Family's Courage and One Man's Struggle.* Grand Rapids: Revell, 1994.

White, John. *Eros Redeemed: Breaking the Stranglehold of Sexual Sin.* Downers Grove, Ill.: InterVarsity, 1993.

SEXUAL HARASSMENT

Conway, Jim, and Sally Conway. *Sexual Harassment No More.* Downers Grove, Ill.: InterVarsity, 1993.

Friedman, Joel, Marcia Mobilia Boumil, and Barbara Ewert Taylor. *Sexual Harassment.* Deerfield Beach, Fla.: Health Communications, 1992.

SPOUSE ABUSE

Adams, Carol J. "Help for the Battered." *Christian Century* 3, no. 20 (29 June–6 July 2004): 628–29.

———. *Woman-Battering.* Minneapolis: Fortress, 1994.

Adams, Carol J., and Marie M. Fortune. *Violence Against Women and Children: A Christian Theological Sourcebook.* New York: Continuum, 1995.

Alsdurf, James, and Phyllis Alsdurf. *Battered into Submission: The Tragedy of Wife Abuse in the Christian Home.* Downers Grove, Ill.: InterVarsity, 1989.

Dixon, Lynn, and Gywnette Orr Robertson. "CBE Speaks Out Against Domestic Abuse." *Daughters of Sarah* 20, no. 3 (summer 1994): 38–39.

Edleson, Jeffrey L., and Richard M. Tolman. *Intervention for Men Who Batter.* Thousand Oaks, Calif.: SAGE Publications, 1992.

Kroeger, Catherine Clark, and Nancy Nason-Clark. *No Place for Abuse.* Downers Grove, Ill.: InterVarsity, 2001.

Lampman, Lisa Barnes, ed. *Helping a Neighbor in Crisis.* Wheaton, Ill.: Tyndale, 1997.

Miles, Al. *Domestic Violence: What Every Pastor Needs to Know.* Minneapolis: Fortress, 2000.

Miller, Melissa A. *Family Violence: The Compassionate Church Responds.* Waterloo, Ontario: Herald, 1994.

Sell, Charles M. *Helping Troubled Families.* Grand Rapids: Baker, 2002.

SUICIDE

Carr, G. Lloyd, and Gwendolyn Carr. *The Fierce Goodbye: Hope in the Wake of Suicide.* Downers Grove, Ill.: InterVarsity, 1990.

Carson, Herbert. *Depression and the Christian Family.* Durham, England: Evangelical Press, 1994.

Clemons, James T., ed. *Perspectives on Suicide.* Louisville: Westminster John Knox Press, 1990.

Demy, Timothy J., and Gary P. Stewart, eds. *Suicide: A Christian Response.* Grand Rapids: Kregel, 1998.

Hewett, John H. *After Suicide.* Philadelphia: Westminster, 1980.

Hicks, Barbara Barrett. *Youth Suicide: A Comprehensive Manual for Prevention and Intervention.* Bloomington, Ind.: National Educational Service, 1990.

Hsu, Albert Y. *Grieving a Suicide.* Downers Grove, Ill.: InterVarsity, 2002.

Lampman, Lisa Barnes, ed. *Helping a Neighbor in Crisis.* Wheaton, Ill.: Tyndale, 1997.

Rando, Therese A. "Suicide." In *Treatment of Complicated Mourning.* Champaign,
    Ill.: Research Press, 1993.
Shamoo, Tonia K., and Philip G. Patros. *Helping Your Child Cope with Depression
    and Suicidal Thoughts.* San Francisco: Jossey-Bass, 1997.
Tada, Joni Eareckson. *When Is It Right to Die?* Grand Rapids: Zondervan, 1992.
Tadman-Robins, Christopher. *Suicide–The Last Taboo: A Professional Handbook
    in Search of Understanding.* Bristol, Ind.: Wyndham Hall Press, 2001.